lovers
of
philosophy

how the intimate lives of seven philosophers shaped modern thought

Warren Ward

Ockham
Publishing

Published in 2022 by Ockham Publishing in the United Kingdom

ISBN 978-1-83919-152-7

Cover illustrations Bella Tobin

www.ockham-publishing.com

To Ross Smith, for philosophy
To Zoe Walsh, for love

About the Author

Warren Ward is Associate Professor of Psychiatry at the University of Queensland. His writing has appeared in numerous publications, including *Aeon*, *New Philosopher*, *Prairie Fire*, and *Overland*. He won the New Philosopher Writers' Award in 2016 and 2019. In 2020 he was awarded a Denis Diderot Artist-in-Residence Grant at the Chateau Orquevaux.

Acknowledgements

The idea for this book came to me in a flash in Ev's consulting room and I am forever grateful to her for that. After rushing home and scribbling out the first few pages, Zoe-Anne Walsh encouraged me to continue. None of this would have happened, however, without the many preceding years of patient tutelage in continental philosophy from Ross Smith.

I might have given up if it weren't for the steady and skilful support of Krissy Kneen. And Fiona Reilly, who helped me nurse this baby from its youngest days to its final manifestation as a fully-grown book.

I am indebted to Martin Beckmann for introducing me to the Heidegger family, and to Hermann, Jutta, and Arnulf Heidegger, for so graciously inviting me into their home in Freiburg. Thanks to Lydia Rusch for translating this interview into English.

Many people encouraged me throughout this project's long gestation and/or provided feedback on earlier drafts: Ruth Gough, Derek Baines, Chris Neild, Barbara Buderus, Meg Vann, Sophie Hamley, Vanessa Radnidge, Peter Watson, Alexandra Payne, Rose Michael, Henry Rosenbloom, Fiona Stager, Edwina Shaw, Rachel Crawford, Matt Condon, Kári Gíslason, Nigel Featherstone, Nadine Davidoff, Martin Shaw, Damon Young, Mary Cunnane, and all the wonderful members of my writing critique group, Dead Darlings Society.

Thanks to Zan Boag and the team at New Philosopher for encouraging my early development as a writer with awards and commissioned pieces.

The following organisations have provided invaluable feedback and/or support throughout the life of this project: Queensland Writers Centre, Avid Reader, Hazel Rowley Literary Fellowship, Australian

Association of Group Psychotherapy, RANZCP Special Interest Group in Philosophy, Katharine Susannah Prichard Writers' Centre, Château d'Orquevaux, Varuna, Australian Society of Authors, Disquiet International Literary Program, Yale Writers' Conference, Vermont Studio Center, Arteles, and Can Serrat.

I'd especially like to thank the organisers and participants of the QWC/Hachette Manuscript Development Program, as well as the ACT Writers Centre HARDCOPY Program funded by the Australia Council.

Thanks to my fellow lovers of philosophy, Ann Webster-Wright and Rossven Naidoo, for all the inspiring discussions.

My eternal gratitude to Zoe, and to Alexandra and Dominique Ward, who put up with years of me beavering away in *that* office, only to be greeted by faraway and quizzical looks whenever they asked me anything about the real world.

I'd also like to express my appreciation to Robert Johnson and Sarah Hembrow of Ockham Publishing, who believed in this book from the beginning, and for their gracious and thoughtful editorial oversight. Also, a big thank you to Bella Tobin for the cover design illustrations, and to Matt Tobin for his expert input.

Finally, I'd like to thank the philosophers whose work and lives provided the material for this book, especially Simone de Beauvoir who first opened my eyes to the idea of philosopher as lover.

Contents

Introduction

Although long interested in philosophy, I have often felt daunted by its classic texts. *Being and Time. Being and Nothingness. Critique of Pure Reason. Thus Spake Zarathustra.* Each title has stood like a frowning marble bust, staring me down, mocking my efforts to understand the genius within. I know I am not alone in finding some of these works difficult to decipher, a barrier rather than a gateway into the vast, bewildering world of philosophical discourse.

Fortunately for me, I came across an easier entry point early in my reading: the novels of Sartre and Beauvoir. Sartre's first novel, *Nausea,* showed me rather than told me what existentialism was. I experienced, through its protagonist Roquentin, what it was like to live in a world without meaning, to be confronted by the cold, hard indifference of existence. Later, in Sartre's *Roads to Freedom* trilogy, I was exposed to the ways that different characters try to tackle the conundrum of freedom in a godless world that doesn't care.

But it was Beauvoir's first novel, *She Came to Stay*, that turned philosophy from an intellectual curiosity into a burning passion for me. I was mesmerized by Beauvoir's account of the ménage à trois between her, Sartre, and their nineteen-year-old student Olga Kosakiewicz. Sartre's slow but inevitable seduction of this young woman challenged Beauvoir's efforts to stay true to her existentialist ideal of free love, agreed to in a pact with Sartre a few years earlier.

By describing Sartre with all his flaws and foibles laid bare, Beauvoir opened my eyes to the fact he was, above all else, a man. *She Came to Stay* brought the philosopher down from the pedestal on which I had placed him to a position where I could see him as a lover. An imperfect human being. Just like me.

After that, the world of philosophy didn't seem so daunting.

For several years, inspired by the examples of Sartre's and Beauvoir's novels, I have tried to find out as much as I can about the romantic lives of other philosophers. The lasting partnership of Sartre and Beauvoir led me to explore other crucial couplings in philosophy – Heidegger and Arendt, Nietzsche and Salomé, Kant and Keyserlingk, Hegel and Burkhardt, Derrida and Agacinski, Foucault and Defert.

In my efforts to uncover the intimate secrets of the continent's greatest thinkers, I have travelled to Europe several times. I have patronised cafés these thinkers pondered in, peered into the houses in which they lived, and visited the cemeteries where they were laid to rest. I have trawled through mountains of letters, interviews, and other biographical material. My explorations led me to some unexpected places, such as the living room of Martin Heidegger's ninety-three-year-old son in Freiburg, where I asked him about his parents' infidelities, his memories of family life, and the vexed question of his father's association with Nazism.

During these explorations, I have done what comes naturally to me in my daily work as a psychiatrist and psychotherapist. I have looked for connections between these philosophers' experiences of intimacy and the way they came to see the world. The overall structure of the book, exploring the lives and ideas of seven philosophers in chronological order, also provides the reader with an easy-to-follow overview of the progression of ideas in continental philosophy.

The following pages present, for the first time, the psychoanalytic and philosophical significance of Kant's infatuations, Hegel's premarital liaisons, Nietzsche's heartbreak, Heidegger's hypocrisy, Sartre's experiments in promiscuous polyamory, Foucault's exploration of gay liberation, and Derrida's dalliances in extramarital desire.

Chapter 1

Kant and the Countess

The Graduate *very old*

On a clear, blue-skied summer's day in 1753, a twenty-eight-year-old unemployed philosophy graduate called Immanuel Kant arrived by horse and buggy at the grounds of the famous Keyserlingk Palace. He was there to apply for a position as family tutor for the Keyserlingks' two young children. Kant's potential new employer had arranged for a driver to collect him at his modest cottage in the centre of Königsberg and bring him to the palace, a few miles outside the city.

This was Kant's first time outside the city gates; he had not previously met the twenty-five-year-old Countess Caroline von Keyserlingk who was about to interview him. But he had, like others in the town, heard the descriptions of her as 'beautiful, intellectually agile and artistically creative'.[1] He was also aware of rumours that she had a passionate interest in philosophy.

Kant was in desperate need of employment at this time. His beloved father, a harness-maker, had died a few years earlier, leaving the family destitute. As the oldest male, it had been Kant's duty to bury his father in the Königsberg cemetery, alongside his mother who had died nine years earlier.

Kant's circumstances had, since then, become increasingly dire as he looked for work to support himself and his siblings. Positions for philosophy graduates were hard to come by, so he sought a job as a *Hofmeister*, a private family tutor. Such employment did not carry a very high social standing or many prospects for career advancement, but it could at least bring some much-needed income. After a couple of short-lived and unsatisfactory appointments, Kant jumped at this opportunity to work for Königsberg's leading noble family.

As his buggy pulled into the driveway, Kant was greeted by a large green garden in the French style, backgrounded by a sprawling baroque palace. This son of a humble artisan, only recently graduated from university, felt immediately out of place in this sumptuously decorated setting.

But Kant was not only offered the position, he soon became a close confidante of the Countess. Classically educated, Caroline von Keyserlingk had a good working knowledge of both classical and contemporary philosophy. At the time Kant met her, she was translating a work by the German philosopher Johann Gottsched into French.

Keyserlingk had been married since the age of fifteen to the Count, thirty years her senior. At sixteen, she gave birth to her first son. Her second came a year later. Her two children were now at the age, eight and nine, where they could benefit from a family tutor. But the Countess insisted, on offering the handsome new tutor the position, that he regularly put time aside to engage with her in philosophical debate.

The Countess

The Countess had long-standing interests in not only philosophy, but in literature, music, and the arts. She was a proficient lutenist, and arranged for her sons to have singing lessons from a very young age. She was enamoured of all things French; she spoke the language fluently, and the palace's furnishings and decorations reflected the latest styles from Paris, as did her wardrobe. Unfortunately for the Countess, her cultural and intellectual interests were not shared by her husband, nor, for that matter, by anyone else in the court. She was delighted, therefore, when the learned young Kant joined her court, and arranged for him to attend the palace as often as possible.

We do not know if the Count had any concerns about the new tutor's repeated visits upon his wife. Gossip had, however, already begun to circulate in the palace corridors. As one observer of the Countess noted:

> The young beauty was passionately interested in philosophy; rumour had it that she was no less interested in the visiting philosopher.[2]

A Harness-Maker's Son

The Countess soon learned that her new employee had an upbringing vastly different to hers.

Born in 1724, Kant had spent his whole life in Königsberg, a small, windswept city on Prussia's Baltic coast. Königsberg was not a centre of political or academic importance like Berlin or Halle, but it was close enough to these cities to keep in touch with the ideas of the day. And its location on the Baltic navigation routes meant its citizens were regularly exposed to the goods and services, but also the ideas, of the English and Dutch.

Kant's father, Johann, whose descendants had emigrated from Scotland several generations earlier, was a bridle-maker of modest means, but highly respected within his community. He and his wife, Anna Regina, had nine children, with four dying before reaching maturity. Immanuel was the fourth-born child, and the oldest surviving son.

Kant's early world was one of horses, carriages, and harness-making. He spent his childhood in a part of the city the Countess had never set foot in, where the city's master craftsmen all lived and worked. His childhood neighbourhood bustled day and night with the sounds and smells of saddlers, harness-makers, tanners, and blacksmiths.

While the Countess's early years were populated with servants, tutors, music, and manicured gardens, Kant's were suffused with the smells of hay, manure, and leather. In Königsberg's wet, cold, and windy winters these ever-present aromas blended with the homely scents of woodfire, ash, and rainwater. Every morning, the young Kant woke to the sounds of neighing horses, cracking whips, and craftsmen hard at work.

On Sundays the Kant family, like everyone else in their community, proceeded to church, the main event of the day. The Kants belonged to the Pietist faith, and their churches, like those of their Lutheran forebears, were spare, stark, and simple, free of the iconography of the Roman Catholic houses of worship they distinguished themselves from. These were the only mornings that Königsberg's streets were empty, apart from worshipping women in bonnets and long dresses and men in hats, wigs, stockings, and tunics, all making their way to the Sunday service as church bells rang out.

Although Kant's parents weren't overly strict in their religious beliefs, they did pass on to their son, mainly through their own example, the Pietist values of humility, thrift, hard work, and self-sacrifice. Such an upbringing instilled in Kant a discipline and dedication that would stand him in good stead when he later embarked on tackling the thorniest philosophical problems of his day.

Kant's parents had been forward-thinking enough to send their son, who had shown academic promise from a young age, to a Pietist school from the age of eight, where he received a schooling in the classics until his mid-teens.

Kant's mother, however, would not live to see the results of her foresight. When Kant was only thirteen years old, she died in tragic circumstances.

Having already endured the loss of four children of her own, Anna Kant became very distressed on learning that her dearest friend was at risk of dying from scarlet fever. Taking it upon herself to nurse her friend, she encouraged her to take her medicine by sipping some herself. Immediately afterwards, she realised with horror she had exposed herself to the deadly fever. Her friend died after many tortured hours of painful delirium, followed a few days later by Anna herself.

Despite the trauma of being left alone at age thirteen with his father and siblings, Kant managed, with his father's generous help, to enrol at the age of sixteen at Königsberg University, where he would graduate with a degree in philosophy six years later.

Magister

After being hired by Countess Keyserlingk, Kant accustomed himself surprisingly quickly to palace life. He worked hard to familiarise himself with the ways of society, an effort that would not only bring him closer to the Countess, but also accelerate his trajectory to becoming a respected and renowned man of letters.

In 1754 the twenty-nine-year-old Kant started spending days he wasn't required at the palace at his old alma mater, Königsberg University. Perhaps his return to formal study was inspired by the philosophical interests of his beguiling new employer. In any case, he spent an increasing amount of time in the institution's libraries immersing himself in texts on philosophy and a wide range of other subjects. As a contemporary observed, 'he collected in his miscellanies from all the parts of human knowledge, all that somehow seemed useful to him'.[3]

He also started writing, and published a couple of minor papers in a local journal.

In 1755 Kant completed his master's thesis and was awarded the title of *Magister*. At this point he stopped working for the Keyserlingks, but continued, at the Countess's insistence, to regularly visit her at the palace.

Portrait

When Kant turned thirty, the Countess asked if she could draw his portrait.

The Countess had, by this time, become an artist of considerable repute. Her watercolour paintings and pencil drawings, mainly historical scenes and portraits, were already held in high regard throughout Prussia. (In later years, her artistic achievements would be acknowledged with an honorary membership of the Royal Prussian Academy of the Arts.)

Although the Countess sketched and painted many dignitaries and other persons of import who visited the palace, her portrait of Kant is the only work that survives to this day. Her rendering of Kant provides us with a glimpse of her feelings towards the young philosopher at this time.

She represents him, in fact, in a most flattering light with fine, handsome features, elegantly dressed in cape and wig. The Kant she sees has gentle eyes, a high noble forehead, and soft, youthful face.

What this head-and-shoulders drawing of Kant doesn't show is how short the young scholar was. At five-foot-two, he would have struggled to stand face to face with the elegant, dark-haired

8

noblewoman who was sketching him. Kant was quite self-conscious about his height, as he was about another imperfection – a caved-in chest that he believed made him prone to the many respiratory allergies he suffered from. (He was known to sneeze every time he came into contact with newsprint.) The fastidious philosopher was, in fact, plagued by numerous hypochondriacal concerns throughout his life. In later years, he would regularly embarrass his friends by repeatedly expressing concerns about the regularity of his bowel.

Despite these temperamental peculiarities, Kant became highly successful during these years in refashioning himself as an elegant Magister who could comfortably mix in society's highest circles. He started to dress in the Rococo style, a look imported from Paris, much to the delight of his Francophile Countess. His gold-trimmed coats and ceremonial swords provided a refreshing contrast to the sombre blacks and greys worn by most dignitaries at the palace.

With his slight stature, Kant had to rely heavily on his intelligence and natural charisma to engage and entertain the Countess. As a visitor to the palace observed, he certainly possessed notable gifts in this regard:

> In societal conversation he could at times clothe even the most abstract ideas in lovely dress, and he analysed clearly every view that he put forward. Beautiful wit was at his command, and sometimes his speech was spiced with a light satire, which he always expressed with the driest demeanour.[4]

Although the Countess's drawing suggests she was somewhat enamoured with the young Magister's blonde hair, fair complexion, and searching eyes, she wasn't the only one to be captivated by Kant's physiognomy. Another contemporary noted that although 'the colour of his face [was] fresh, and his cheeks showed…a healthy blush', it was the philosopher's eyes, the window to his clear-sighted mind, that struck one the most:

> Where do I take the words to describe to you his eye! Kant's eye was as if it had been formed of heavenly ether from which the deep look of his mind, whose fiery beam was occluded by a light cloud, visibly shone forth.[5]

The Countess's beauty and class, however, far outshone Kant's, and he would have felt most honoured that she had deigned to draw his portrait. A drawing of the Count and Countess at around this time reveals her as a dark-haired woman of natural beauty, wearing an open-necked dress with simple adornments. The soft youthfulness of her intelligent, pretty, open face provides an unsettling and somewhat incongruous contrast, in this picture, to the wizened and distant visage of her much older husband standing by her side.

Upwardly mobile

In the years following the drawing of this portrait, Kant's reputation as a brilliant and engaging lecturer at Königsberg University grew rapidly. This was despite the fact he had only secured an appointment as a *Privatdozent*, an unsalaried lecturer with private fee-paying students his only source of income. During these years, Kant continued to be a regular guest at Keyserlingk Palace.

The Countess hosted musical recitals in which she sang and accompanied herself on the lute. Kant was always high on the guest list of these celebrated occasions.

In 1758 this pleasant state of affairs – with Kant rising through the ranks both at university and in Königsberg society – appeared as though it might be disrupted. Prussia was invaded by the Russians, who immediately took control of all Königsberg's institutions.

The Russian occupation turned out, however, to have a benign, and even beneficial, effect on the city. The Russians brought with them an outlook that was considerably more cosmopolitan and cultured than that of the parochial and inward-looking locals. The invaders were interested in all things French. Their officers spoke the language fluently and were connoisseurs of caviar, champagne, and the latest Paris fashions. As a result, they soon became positively disposed to Countess Keyserlingk and her court, including the upwardly mobile Kant.

When the Keyserlingks first heard that an invasion was imminent, they moved to one of their country residences further out from the city. This precaution, however, proved unnecessary. The coup turned out to be bloodless and uneventful, with the Russian military leaders more interested in attending the Countess's galas and complimenting her on her beauty, taste, and knowledge, than in carrying out any acts of aggression.

The occupation changed Königsberg society in many positive ways, enlivening it and softening the difference between the classes. There was also a dramatic increase in the number of garden parties and other events, many of these hosted by the Countess.

Kant's philosophical teachings were in great demand with the Russian officers; they swelled the numbers attending his already popular lectures, and paid handsomely for private tutorials with the up-and-coming philosopher.

In 1761, with the Russians still in Prussia, the Count died suddenly at the age of sixty-two, leaving Caroline Keyserlingk a widow at the age of thirty-three. By this time, Kant had started describing the Countess to his friends as the 'ideal' of a woman, the sort of woman he would like to marry.[6] Whatever thoughts he entertained in this regard, however, he knew that such a possibility was unthinkable, given the yawning chasm in class between him and his beloved. While he watched from afar, a long list of respectable suitors presented themselves, including the commanding general of the Russian army.

Arrangements were soon made for the Countess to be remarried to the Count's nephew, a man with whom she would endure another long and loveless marriage.

Soon after this wedding, in 1762, the Russian occupation ended.

The Countess's second marriage did not stop Kant from continuing to visit her. At the lavish balls and garden parties she continued to host, the Countess unfailingly had Kant seated, as her favourite guest, in a place of honour to her right. The Countess insisted on this arrangement to ensure that when the conversation became dull, as it often did at such palace events, she had her learned friend at her side to talk about philosophy and other topics dear to both their hearts.

Midlife Crisis

Despite being brought up with a strong work ethic, and now socially connected well beyond his expectations, Kant's career came to an impasse in his late thirties. He had written nothing since achieving his Magister's degree, and although he still had a good reputation as a teacher, he was only receiving a sporadic income.

His previously well-disciplined life began to unravel as he found himself whiling away more and more time in billiard halls, card-playing dens, and other places of dubious repute.

It wasn't just Kant's career that was getting nowhere. As a result of his patchy academic achievements and lack of secure income, his marriage prospects were becoming increasingly slim.

During these years, encouraged by friends and associates, he did make a few half-hearted attempts at finding a wife. But the opportunities that presented themselves to him all paled in comparison to the 'ideal' of a woman he admired from afar.[7]

The few prospects that did come Kant's way all presented themselves when he was in his late thirties and early forties.

According to one of Kant's biographers, there was 'a well brought up and beautiful widow' who regularly came to Königsberg 'and visited relatives'.[8] From all reports she was quite beautiful, and Kant was interested in her, but the fastidious philosopher procrastinated, 'calculat[ing] income and expenses and delayed the decision from one day to the next'.[9] She eventually married someone else.

Kant was also interested in a young girl from Westphalia who visited Königsberg in the company of a noblewoman. Kant was 'pleased to be with her in society, and he let this be known often'.[10] He seriously considered an offer of marriage, but she left and returned to Westphalia before he could come to a definite decision.

There is no doubt that Kant had the ability to touch a woman's heart, as evidenced by the letters he exchanged with another woman called Charlotte Amalie of Klingspor. In 1772 she wrote to Kant, remembering him long after they had met back in the 1750s. Charlotte had to move town soon after meeting him, but continued to write for several years, saying in her letters how she felt certain he was still her friend 'just as [he was] then'.[11] In one piece of correspondence, rendered in long beautiful ink-strokes, she assured Kant she had benefitted from his 'benevolent instruction' that 'in philosophy truth is everything and that a philosopher has pure faith'.[12] She thanked him for sending her a poem years earlier, and for educating her as a young woman with his pleasant conversation.

Towards the end of this period, there was also a woman called Maria Charlotta Jacobi who tried her utmost to seduce him. In the early 1760s this confident and extraordinarily beautiful twenty-two-year-old was the most revered socialite in all of Königsberg. She made it unmistakably clear to Kant that she was interested in him, inviting him to join her in a box at the theatre, and other society events, on many occasions.

As a member of the *bourgeoisie*, Maria Charlotta was much closer than the Countess to Kant's station in life, and therefore a realistic marriage prospect. She was also well-endowed financially. There was only one problem – she was already married. This was not an obstacle as far as she was concerned, but the sense of decency and propriety that had been part of Kant's make-up ever since his early Pietist upbringing meant there was little chance of him responding to her advances.

Maria Charlotta was married at fifteen to a man twenty-two years her senior as part of an arrangement between both parents to secure a business contract. There had never been much love or affection in the marriage, and for years Maria Charlotta, known as 'the queen of balls and parties in Königsberg', had made no secret of the fact she was interested in other men.[13] The strength of her attachment to Kant is underlined in a letter she sent him when recovering from an eye operation in Berlin, in which she scolds him for failing to come and collect her.

Earlier in her efforts to win Kant's heart, just after she first met him, the young socialite wrote him a teasing letter:

Dear friend: Aren't you surprised that I am undertaking to write to you as a great philosopher? I believed to find you yesterday in my garden, but since…I sneaked through all the avenues and could not find you…, I busied myself with making you a band for a sword, which is dedicated to you.[14]

In the same correspondence she brazenly suggests a rendezvous with the Königsberg bachelor:

> I lay claim to your society tomorrow afternoon. "Yes, yes, I will be there," I hear you say. Good then, I will expect you, and then my clock will be wound as well…I send to you a kiss by sympathy.[15]

There seems little doubt from these letters that the ravishing young Maria, at the time fifteen years younger than Kant, was his if he so desired her.

Maria was not a patient woman, however. She soon tired of waiting for the scrupulous philosopher to make up his mind, and within a short period of time left town with the master of the Königsberg mint, Johann Gröschen, creating a furor that set the tongues of Königsberg wagging for years.

Perhaps as a result of these dramatic and difficult events, Kant soon afterwards made it clear to those around him he had decided marriage was not for him, and asked his friends to refrain from any further efforts at matchmaking. He would, in later years, cause considerable mirth amongst friends and associates with his explanation that:

> When I could have benefited from marriage I couldn't afford it, and when I could afford it, I could no longer benefit from it.[16]

An English Merchant

Although Kant would never marry, it was a new relationship that would eventually pull him out of his midlife torpor and propel him into fulfilling his extraordinary intellectual potential. This was the close and intimate friendship he formed with the English merchant Joseph Green.

15

Kant was forty years old when he first met Green in 1764. At first glance their worlds seemed miles apart. Green was an English merchant of abstemious habits who prided himself on his punctuality and self-discipline. Kant, at the time he met Green, was a drifting and directionless philosophy graduate whiling away much of his days in card and billiard halls.

Despite these differences, the two men immediately became very close, spending nearly every afternoon together in long discussions on a subject dear to both their hearts – philosophy. This common passion helped to ignite a lasting friendship between the two men that would endure for the rest of their days. Green became Kant's best friend.

A bachelor like Kant, Green was the most esteemed of a handful of English merchants who lived in Königsberg. He regularly sailed the Baltic Sea route to and from London, trading in grain, herring, coal, and manufactured goods. But at heart, as a contemporary observed, he was 'more a scholar then a merchant'.[17] He loved to read, and was well-acquainted with the works of the British philosophers of his homeland, in particular David Hume, whose work would turn out to be critical to the development of Kant's future thought.

Green also shared Kant's passion for the French philosopher Jean-Jacques Rousseau, whose ideas inspired the revolution in France that would soon arrive and change Europe's political landscape forever. At the time that Kant and Green met, Rousseau's name regularly featured in the newspapers, as the French authorities had just expelled him from his home country, forcing him to take shelter in England.

Kant and Green were especially interested in a philosophical debate that had been raging for some time between the rationalists, who believed all knowledge came from the mind, and the empiricists, who believed that knowledge could only come from what we experience through the senses.

Kant and Green enjoyed exploring this debate in all its complexities and details in their daily discussions on the porch of Green's house. The merchant's house was situated, along with other houses in Königsberg's English colony, in a location well-suited to long hours of philosophical speculation, on the water's edge of the port looking out across the Baltic Sea.

Green's friendship would prove to be life-changing for Kant. He not only restored Kant's passion for philosophy, as the Countess had done years earlier, he inspired Kant, through his own example, to become more disciplined and focussed. Green had a highly organised, almost obsessive approach to life, and it started to rub off on Kant. As one observer explained, Green had 'a decisive influence on his [Kant's] heart and character'.[18] Soon after befriending Green, the forty-year-old philosopher stopped frequenting gaming rooms and re-established for himself a rigorous schedule of study, reading, and writing that would eventually bear fruit in a way that neither Kant nor Green could ever imagine.

In 1766 Kant's new habits resulted in him getting his first ever paid academic position as Second Librarian of the Royal Library of Königsberg. Although a fairly minor appointment, it would prove to be the start of a new and promising phase in Kant's career. Soon afterwards, he submitted a dissertation, *On the Form and Principles of the Sensible and Intelligible World*, that received much acclaim from his university colleagues. This, along with the fact that he had resumed lecturing with a new vigour, led to him being appointed Professor of Logic and Metaphysics at Königsberg University.

For some time now, Kant had been telling his friends about an odd conviction that had inexplicably planted itself in his mind. His strange, unbidden idea was that a man doesn't choose his destiny until the age of forty. This notion might have seemed a highly dubious

17

proposition to Kant's associates, given the average life expectancy at the time was not much higher than thirty.

Kant, however, would live for many years to come, only working seriously on his philosophical ideas at the age of forty-six. Thus began the start of a period of intense contemplation that would become known as his 'silent decade'.

The Silent Decade

Kant worked alone, hidden away in his study, for eleven years, meticulously creating the work that would become his masterpiece. For eleven Königsberg winters, as the cold northern Baltic winds came in over the town, he worked on his eight-hundred-page analysis of the nature of reality and mind. For eleven Königsberg summers he hardly ventured outside, determined to solve the problem he had set himself to solve. Apart from his continuing visits to the Countess and Green, he completely shut himself off from the outside world.

What was this problem that occupied Kant for a whole decade? And what drove him to spend so many years on one philosophical question?

Kant's intellectual journey was inspired by the work of two philosophers who preceded him: Isaac Newton and David Hume.

The first he admired; the second he was determined to prove wrong.

Not many today would think of Newton as a philosopher. They would be more likely to label the man who discovered gravity, the laws of optics, and other fundamental physical laws of the universe as a scientist, physicist, or mathematician. But at the time Newton and Kant lived, science had not yet developed an identity separate to philosophy. Philosophy at that time included all abstract thinking – fields as diverse as theology, psychology, political theory, and what we would today call science. The branch of philosophy that Newton's work belonged to, that was concerned with understanding the physical universe, was known as *natural philosophy.*

As a young man, Kant had been fascinated by the work of the natural philosopher Newton, who appeared to be discovering the mathematical laws inherent in the universe, literally unlocking its mysteries. Newton's advances revealed a universe governed by elegant laws waiting to be uncovered by a human mind brilliant and bold enough to seek them. In this regard the seventeenth century, when Newton's theories came to the fore, was a time of breathtaking discovery and potential.

Prior to Newton (and his forerunners Galileo, Kepler, and Copernicus), the Church had decreed – effectively *decided* – what the truth was. Church positions such as those that the earth was stationary with the sun moving around it in a circle, were dogma that could not be questioned without life becoming very uncomfortable for the questioner. Whereas Galileo and others started what we call science by doing experiments in the real world and measuring what happened, Newton's genius lay in not just conducting experiments, but in discovering mathematical formulae and physical laws that could be used to predict the behaviour of anything in the universe, from everyday objects to heavenly bodies such as planets and stars. Whereas the Church claimed that all knowledge came from God, and Galileo said knowledge could come from investigation of the facts, Newton was able to demonstrate that understanding the universe could come from combining both careful observation and the powers of reason.

In recent times, however, Kant had become increasingly concerned that Newton's great work in discovering the laws of the universe was coming under threat from the sophisticated and convincing arguments of the up-and-coming British philosopher David Hume.

A pioneer of the empiricist school of philosophy, Hume believed that all knowledge comes from what is experienced through the five senses. Hume asserted that all we can ever know is what we have seen, heard, and touched. He believed events that regularly occurred together, such as the sun rising in the east every morning, led to a habitual association in the mind that gives us an illusory sense of cause and effect. According to Hume, Newton's laws of physics were not real – they had been created by the human mind's need to believe in universal patterns of predictability. This disturbed Kant, who wanted to provide a solid philosophical foundation for Newton's theories.

Kant famously confessed that 'it was the remembrance of David Hume which, many years ago, first interrupted my dogmatic slumber and gave my investigations in the field of speculative philosophy a completely different direction'.[19]

Kant aimed with his work to resolve the impasse between the rationalist tradition, promulgated by Descartes, Leibniz, and Spinoza, who saw reason as the source of all knowledge, and the newer wave of British empiricists – Hume, Locke, and Berkeley – who saw knowledge as deriving solely from experience.

During the decade of intellectual hibernation in which Kant worked away on buttressing Newton's work against the assaults of Hume's dogmatic empiricism, he let his friends and associates know he would be unavailable for an extended period of time. In 1778 he responded to one of many well-intentioned offers, on this occasion from a former student, to bring him out of isolation:

My great thanks…to my well-wishers and friends, who think so kindly of me as to undertake my welfare, but at the same time a most humble request to protect me in my present situation from any disturbance.[20]

Kant was not, however, totally an island unto himself during this decade. As mentioned, he still stayed in contact with the two most important people in his life, Caroline Keyserlingk and Joseph Green.

The Countess remained a steadfast admirer throughout this period of not only Kant himself, but of the promise of his work. Although quite knowledgeable in philosophical matters, she never alienated Kant by challenging his ideas, unlike many of his academic colleagues who made the mistake of doing so, never to be spoken to again. When it came to criticism of his own work, Kant, the future champion of critical thought, was surprisingly thin-skinned. When others disagreed with his ideas, his usual response was to become highly indignant and cut off all communication with them. The Countess and Green were amongst the few to survive Kant's extreme sensitivity to critique and enjoy a longstanding friendship with him.

A visitor to the Keyserlingk Palace in 1778, the astronomer and geographer Johann Bernoulli, reports seeing Kant there with the Countess during one of his rare social outings during this period:

> I ate at lunch at the count of Keyserlingk with a scholar, whom the University of Königsberg honors as one of its greatest members, professor Kant…Herr Kant had not published philosophical writings for a long time, but he promised that he would soon bring out a little volume.[21]

This 'little volume' would not come out for another three years, and would turn out to be anything but little.

Kant's ongoing visits to the Countess during this time show how important she remained to him. One cannot help but wonder how much of Kant's dogged persistence during these long and lonely years came from a desire to write something worthy of the woman he admired more than any other. It was almost as if the master of abstract thought preferred a perfect and ideal love, even if it was unattainable,

21

to one that was sullied by the tawdry realities of physical consumma-
tion.

The only person that Kant visited more than the Countess during
this decade of self-imposed confinement was Green. Kant, in fact, en-
trusted his best friend with the important task of reviewing his monumental philosophical work, page by page, as it progressed. No one else
was given this privilege. As a mutual friend of the two men noted at
the time, Kant 'did not write down a single sentence in the *Critique of
Pure Reason* unless he had presented it to Green and had his unpreju-
diced judgment'.[22]

Critique of Pure Reason

On an autumn mid-morning in 1781, Kant wrote the last sentence of
the work he had decided to call *Critique of Pure Reason*.

The fifty-seven-year-old now had eight hundred pages of manuscript that he believed would address and resolve the most pressing
philosophical question of his time. He was convinced that he had
found a way through the age-old conundrum of mind versus matter,
or more exactly, the endlessly see-sawing debate as to whether reason
or experience provided us with our truest knowledge of the world.
Kant, who would never marry himself, had found a way to marry the
seemingly irreconcilable positions of rationalism and empiricism. He
had exposed the limitations of pure reason, demonstrating with a
lengthy and highly complex series of arguments that drawing solely on
the mind without reference to the outside world led only to paradox
and confusion.

But he had also exposed the problems associated with the empiricist position that the mind is merely a blank slate receiving knowledge
through the senses. Kant claimed, with this work, to have convincingly
demonstrated something that Hume had asserted did not exist – *a*

22

priori knowledge; that is, knowledge held by the mind independent of any experience. Such knowledge, Kant contended, included the mind's inherent grasp of space, time, substance, and cause and effect, which it uses to structure and shape any sensory information that it receives from the outside world.

Kant's main finding in *Critique of Pure Reason* was that the mind transforms and alters all sensory data that comes into it. He concluded, consequently, that all we can ever truly know is *the world as shaped by our mind*. This led him to a second, rather surprising conclusion, that we can never know the world as it actually is. Despite all the breakthroughs in science since, this irreducible philosophical finding of Kant's has never been convincingly refuted or disproven.

Kant had demonstrated that the rationalists and empiricists were both right. And that they were both wrong. True knowledge could only be arrived at through a combination of reason and experience. We need, as it turns out, both sense and sensibility.

Although it is, perhaps, drawing a long bow, it is interesting to speculate as to how much Kant's relationship with Countess Keyserlingk – a woman who engaged both his intellect and his senses – contributed to this conclusion.

Three Critiques

Following the publication of *Critique of Pure Reason*, Kant began to enjoy considerable acclaim as philosophers and other intellectuals throughout Europe came to understand the significance of his landmark work.

He was, therefore, assured of a large and interested audience a few years later when he published his second major work *Critique of Practical Reason*. Here, Kant shifted his focus from what we can know to how we should live. Kant's second *Critique* was the first text on ethics

23

since ancient Greek and Roman times to propose a moral system that didn't require a belief in God. Kant explored how what was right and or wrong could be determined through reason, rather than religion. His famous *categorical imperative* urged that we should always act according to moral precepts that we would be happy to have as universal laws. Accordingly, he argued that some acts, such as killing another human being, are always wrong, because they breach a deep sense of inner duty we all innately possess. At the time, his declaration that society could develop a system of ethics based on reason rather than God was rather radical, though in keeping with the ideas of the Enlightenment capturing the minds and hearts of many at the time. His ideas would also be congruent with the guiding principles of the French Revolution that was soon to come.

Kant's third major work, *Critique of Judgment*, published in 1790, was concerned with aesthetics, in particular the nature of beauty. Again, Kant drew on reason to try to explain why the human mind found some things more aesthetically pleasing than others. (Again, one wonders how much Kant's idealisation of the Countess's beauty, in her case complemented by a perspicacious intellect, contributed to Kant's thoughts around this subject.)

Most philosophers are known for their contribution to one area of philosophy. But Kant, with his three *Critiques,* written over a span of just a few years, had now made lasting and revolutionary contributions to three branches of philosophy: epistemology, ethics, and aesthetics. He set the agenda for subsequent philosophical discussion for a long time to come with his tripartite exploration of truth, goodness, and beauty.

By the time Kant reached his late sixties, he had become the most influential, celebrated, and renowned philosopher in all of Europe. The bulk of philosophy written over the next hundred years in

German-speaking lands, and to a large extent throughout Europe, would be in response to his new so-called *critical philosophy*. Kant's breakthrough, putting the human mind (rather than God, or alternatively the external world) at the centre of how we know things, was somewhat immodestly described by Kant himself, in the preface to his second edition of *Critique of Pure Reason*, as a revolution akin to the one made by Copernicus in astronomy.

Kant's new-found renown made him an even more celebrated guest at Keyserlingk Palace, where he now had a standing invitation. According to Lady von Recke, a regular visitor to the Keyserlingk court, the philosopher could be seen visiting the Countess almost daily in the years immediately following the publication of *Critique of Pure Reason*.

And so, as the eighteenth century came to a close, Kant found himself not only well regarded and successful, but also extraordinarily happy. He was now spending a significant proportion of his time with the woman of his dreams, basking in – and sharing with her – the hard-earned fruits of his grueling decade of philosophical labour.

Four Deaths

Not everything went rosily, however, for Kant during this time. His celebration at the success of his first *Critique* was considerably dampened by concerns about the worsening health of Joseph Green.

In October 1781, six months after *Critique of Pure Reason* was published, Green suffered a severe bout of gout in his abdomen and intestines. According to one observer, he was only able to chase 'it into his feet with [the help of] heated wine'.[23] Over the next few years, Green suffered progressively worsening relapses of this painful and immobilising affliction. In 1786 his condition deteriorated to a point where he was incapable of leaving his bed. According to one observer:

Kant was very worried about his old friend Green, with whom he is every day punctually until 7 p.m. and on Saturdays until 9 p.m. He is as much as accounted for; and he is incapable of leaving his bed, where alone he finds life bearable.[24]

On 27 June 1786 Kant's closest companion passed away, leaving the philosopher inconsolable. Having never enjoyed the intimacy of a marriage or family of his own, Kant suffered greatly at the loss of the friend he had visited almost every day for the past twenty years.

After Green died, apart from his weekly visits to the Countess, Kant never accepted another dinner invitation for the rest of his life. As one of his contemporaries explained:

> It appeared as if he wished to spend the time of day that was previously devoted to the most intimate friendship as a sacrifice to his close friend quietly alone until the end of his life.[25]

Two years after Green's death, Kant was notified of another passing, that of Count Keyserlingk. At sixty-one, the Countess found herself widowed for a second time.

Then, a year after completing his third great *Critique*, Kant heard news he had been dreading for some time. The woman who exemplified for him, more than any other, the philosophical ideals of truth, goodness, and beauty, passed away at the age of sixty-four. He would be meeting with his 'magnificent royal' Countess, 'highly gifted and open to all things beautiful', no more.[26] Soon afterwards, Kant published one of his final works, a meditation on anthropology. He dedicated it the Countess, referring to her in the book's first page as an 'adornment to her sex'[27].

At Caroline Keyserlingk's funeral, the presiding pastor Georg Heinrich Leo echoed the feeling of many, not least the bereft philosopher, when he bid her farewell with these words:

You were the joy of those who knew you, who enjoyed the reward
of the good deeds by which your whole life was garnished.[28]

Within months of the Countess's death, Kant's concentration started
to slip away. He became increasingly enfeebled, and confined himself
to 'a much more withdrawn life'.[29] In 1797, a year after he retired 'because of age and indisposition', a visitor to Kant's house found the
venerable philosopher's once-brilliant mind 'so much declined that it
was unreasonable to expect [him] to contribute anything new and
original to…philosophical debate'.[30]

The last few years of Kant's life were a long, undignified, and
drawn-out affair. He wrote, and expressed to those closest to him, a
wish to die much sooner than he did. The great analytical thinker lost,
at first, his short-term memory, then his long-term memory, then his
sense of reason altogether.

In his final days, Kant's younger sister and closest friends took
turns nursing him. One of these friends, former student Andreas
Wasianski, was there when the venerable thinker breathed his last
breath. Kant's last words, as he received a mixture of wine and water
from Wasianski, were:

Es ist gut (It is good).[31]

Kant was buried in the Königsberg cathedral, where his tomb can still
be visited to this day (although his home city has since changed its
name to Kalingrad, and is now part of Russia).

On Kant's tombstone there is a quote from the last pages of *Critique of Practical Reason* that reflects his never-ceasing wonder for the
natural and human world, a wonder that took him from his humble
beginnings as a harness-maker's son to his esteemed position as the
greatest philosopher of the Prussian Enlightenment:

Two things fill the mind with ever new and increasing admiration and reverence more often and more steadily one reflects on them: the starry heavens above me and the moral law within me. I do not need to search for them and merely conjecture them as though they were veiled in obscurity or in the transcendent region beyond my horizon; I see them before me and connect them immediately with the consciousness of my existence.[32]

Chapter 2

Hegel: Domestic Dialectic

The Birth of German Idealism

Kant's ideas dominated European philosophical thought for many decades following his death. But his ideas also came to inspire a new movement that Kant would have been highly unlikely to endorse. The German Idealists took Kant's central idea and extrapolated it to what they saw as its only logical conclusion.

Although Kant believed that the 'external' world existed, he had convincingly demonstrated it could never be known. He had shown that all we could ever know is the world as perceived and shaped by our minds. The German Idealists believed Kant had demonstrated, despite himself, that *the mind* is the only thing we can be certain of as existing. For them, mind, spirit, or consciousness – what they referred to as *Geist* – was the primary and, in fact, only reality. This belief fit in with another movement emerging in Europe at that time, the Romantic movement. Championed by writers such as Lord Byron and composers like Beethoven, the romantics celebrated feeling, spirit, and intuition as a reaction against the focus on intellect and reason that had pervaded the Enlightenment.

Into this mix of Enlightenment, Romantic, and Idealist influences was born a man who would go on to become the greatest of the German Idealist philosophers. The creator of the grandest intellectual

29

vision to sweep Europe in the nineteenth century had a suitably grand name – Georg Wilhelm Friedrich Hegel.

G.W.F. Hegel, as he came to be known, is not a name recognised by many amongst the general public today. His ideas, however, have possibly helped to shape the world we live in today more than any other modern European philosopher, in that they laid the groundwork for the ideas of another thinker many *have* heard of – Karl Marx.

Hegel was the first philosopher to place the study of history firmly within the province of philosophy. He conceptualised the world as a seething maelstrom of giant, powerful, and opposing forces that have come together to produce the changes seen in society throughout history. As we shall hear, the opposing historical forces that Hegel wrote about mirrored the turmoil he experienced in his love life, where he was caught up in an endless cycle of opposing urges and obligations that he could never fully reconcile.

Early Years

Hegel was born in Stuttgart in 1770, just as the thousand-year-old Holy Roman Empire was coming to an end. Within twenty years of Hegel's birth, the barricades and muskets of French revolutionaries would turn the tide of history, sweeping aside a millennium of medieval feudalism, and ushering in the foundations of democratic society that endure to this day. These dramatic historical events would leave a lasting impression on the young Hegel, and greatly influence his later philosophy.

Hegel's upbringing was, in some ways, similar to that of his predecessor Kant. He had five siblings, with three not surviving to adulthood. And when he was eleven years old, his much-loved mother died of 'bilious fever'.[1] Immediately after his mother's death, Hegel developed a speech impediment that would stay with him for the rest of his life. Hegel's father, whom he greatly admired, was a minor official in the Holy Roman Empire but he died, too, just before Hegel's twenty-ninth birthday.

Hegel's parents sent him to a German school when he was three, and to a Latin school when he turned five. He showed academic promise from a young age, and was sent to Stuttgart's *Gymnasium Illustre* at the age of fourteen. There, he was schooled in the classics, ancient and modern languages, physics, and mathematics.

In accordance with his father's wishes, he enrolled in a seminary in Tübingen at the age of eighteen. In this small town thirty miles south of Stuttgart, he commenced the lengthy training required to become a pastor. Many of Hegel's uncles were pastors, a common and respectable profession in those times, and Hegel's father hoped he would follow their lead.

Tübingen

Today Tübingen, with its narrow, winding cobblestone streets and close proximity to the beautiful Black Forest, is a popular university town, but in Hegel's day it was a cultural and educational backwater with little to offer the intelligent and inquiring student. Hegel found the pedestrian teaching at the seminary unbearably tedious. He did, however, make two new friends who shared his restless idealism and provided him with the camaraderie and stimulation he so desperately craved.

The first was Friedrich Schelling, who would go on to become a renowned figure in the German Idealist movement. His star would shine much earlier than Hegel's (though in the end Hegel's would shine brighter).

Hegel's second companion was the brilliant but sensitive Friedrich Hölderlin, who would become one of Germany's most revered Romantic poets, a celebrated leader of the *Sturm und Drang* movement.

Although Hegel and his newfound friends found the seminary's theology lessons dull and wearisome, they managed to feed each other's hunger for knowledge by delving into the works of philosophers, both ancient and modern, outside the classroom. Together, they explored the works of the ancient Greeks, and Schelling and Hölderlin introduced Hegel to the work of Immanuel Kant.

But what excited this trio most of all, however, was the sensational news of the French Revolution in the west. Hegel was only nineteen years old when he and his comrades heard the news from Paris that France's ruling aristocracy had fallen to the will of the people. After that, all he and his friends wanted to hear about were details of the revolution and its aftermath. They were exhilarated that the ideas of their philosophical heroes – Kant, Voltaire, and Rousseau – were inspiring and guiding the French nation into a radically new type of society. For the first time since Ancient Rome, a government would be based on the ideas of men of reason, and the ideals of equality and liberty for all. Hegel and his friends hoped the revolution would come east and rescue them from the drudgery of their backward, almost medieval existence in Tübingen.

Hegel and his classmates often went out drinking in Tübingen's local taverns and wine bars. Hegel's favourite establishment was a wine bar in which a young woman called Auguste Hegelmaier served behind the counter.

Hegel was twenty-one when he met Auguste, the first girl he had ever spoken to. He became instantly smitten. We know about Hegel's romantic interest in Auguste from the Tübingen seminary's yearbook of 1791, in which Hegel wrote:

Last summer was beautiful;
this one more beautiful!
The motto of the former was: Wine;
Of this one, Love!
V.A.!!! [Vive Auguste][2]

The wine bar Auguste worked in was a bakery by day. She and her mother lived upstairs in the baker's residence. Auguste's father, a renowned professor of theology, had died when she was very young. In the year that Hegel met Auguste, she had just been named queen of a local ball, indicating that Hegel was not the only one who appreciated this young woman's beauty.

Hegel and his classmates became very fond of the wine bar in which Auguste worked, preferring to drink, flirt, joke, sing, and play there than spend time at the seminary. One imagines that Auguste, serving behind the bar, would have got to know this crowd of idealistic, ambitious, and boisterous young men quite well, hearing of their boredom with the seminary's routine, their excitement about the revolution in the west, and their hopes that it would spread to their sleepy and staid corner of the world.

By this time Hegel had attracted the nickname 'old man' amongst his classmates, earned as a result of his serious and studious manner.[3] Perhaps Auguste noticed the quiet respect he received from his peers.

One imagines that in private conversations, snatched amidst the Tübingen wine bar's noisy din, Auguste might have learnt about Hegel's love for the writers who inspired him: the ancient Greeks and Romans, the architects of the French Revolution – Voltaire, Rousseau, Jacobi, and Montesquieu – and the poetry of Friedrich Schiller. And one expects she would have become acquainted with the 'old man's'

33

closest friends, the bold, confident Schelling and the quiet and thoughtful Hölderlin.

Perhaps she even joined in with Hegel and his friends at the bar as they shouted the motto of the revolution – *Liberte, Egalite, Fraternite* – and bellowed out the refrain of *La Marseillaise*. We can imagine the excitement felt by Hegel and his comrades, and Auguste, as they thrilled at the prospect of eastward-marching revolutionaries coming their way, liberating everything in their path, including their modest little bakery and wine bar.

Hegel's feelings for Auguste, however, would remain unrequited. When he graduated from the Tübingen seminary at the age of twenty-three, he was still a virgin, inexperienced in the ways of love.

Berne

When Hegel completed his five-year course at Tübingen, the French Revolution had still not made its way to Hegel's homeland, much to his and his friends' disappointment. It was now time for he and his fellow graduates to decide what to do next. Hegel's father hoped that Hegel would, like the majority of his Tübingen classmates, take up one of the many available positions in regional towns for new pastors, and settle down to a respectable life. But Hegel was desperate to avoid such an intellectually suffocating fate. As much as he loved and re-spected his father, and wanted to make him proud, he had been irrev-ocably inspired by the ideas of the Enlightenment thinkers and their application in revolutionary France. Hegel had decided that he, too, wanted to make his mark on the world of ideas.

But he had little to offer the world at this point, with only a theol-ogy degree from a little-known seminary to his name. Career oppor-tunities outside of pastoring were scarce. Like his predecessor Kant, however, he managed to secure a modestly paid position as a private tutor. His first appointment was with a wealthy family in Berne. Bidding farewell to Schelling and Hölderlin, he left Tübingen and headed south to take up his first ever paid employment there.

Hegel's time with this family was a most unpleasant experience in many ways. The children were dull and reluctant students, and they treated their new tutor with a sullen disdain. The parents hardly bothered to interact with their new employee, who, as far as they were concerned, was just another house-servant. But the other servants envied what they saw as Hegel's privileged position and shunned him too. Hegel suddenly found himself feeling terribly alone and at a loss at how to occupy himself in this new environment.

Fortunately, however, Hegel's wealthy employer boasted one of the most extensive private libraries in the land. Hegel hungrily devoured its collection of classic and contemporary texts. It was here that Hegel came across the book that kicked off his fascination with history, *The History of the Decline and Fall of the Roman Empire*, written only four years earlier by the British historian Edward Gibbon. Gibbon's text was the first in modern times to document the changes in a civilisation over a course of hundreds of years. (In Hegel's time history was an embryonic, almost nonexistent discipline.)

Gibbon's detailed and comprehensive account of the rise and fall of Europe's greatest empire made a deep impression on the young theology graduate, and would later become a major source of inspiration for his philosophical work.

Flirtation before Frankfurt

In 1797 the twenty-seven-year-old Hegel returned from Berne to Stuttgart to spend some time in the family home with his father and younger sister Christiane. The visit was especially enjoyable for Hegel, thanks to the presence of a friend of his sister staying with the family.

Her name was Nanette Endel, a twenty-one-year-old trainee milliner. For the second time in his life, Hegel found himself feeling attracted to a young woman, this time in his own home. Nanette was Catholic, leaving a considerable social gulf between her and Hegel, who had just spent five years studying theology at a Protestant seminary. Despite this, and the fact she was from a lower class, Hegel and Nanette soon became quite enamoured of each other, flirting as much as decorum would allow in a late eighteenth-century Stuttgart middle-class residence.

Hegel explained to Nanette that he saw himself as someone destined to translate the classics and explain their importance to the general populace. He explained that he wanted to lift up the uneducated masses and infuse them with *Bildung* ('cultivation'). Nanette joked that he should consider converting to Catholicism, and not take himself so seriously. She helped Hegel to lighten up and laugh at himself, something she could see the serious young man sorely needed. She took to calling him 'Magister'.[4] He seemed to appreciate this friendly teasing, and returned a bit her way.

After three weeks under the same roof, Hegel, much to his sister's horror, made a pass at Nanette. Nanette immediately blamed herself for this awkward development, and, convinced that she must have somehow initiated it, promptly took herself off to church to confess her sin and seek forgiveness. On Hegel's last day in Stuttgart before he left for another position as a family tutor, this time in Frankfurt, he went to kiss Nanette farewell, but she extended both arms to prevent him, her self-imposed 'penance'.[5]

Hegel and Nanette corresponded for at least a year afterwards. In a letter from Frankfurt, he wrote:

I have every reason to assume that longer association with you would have liberated me more and granted me a greater capacity for merrymaking.[6]

They continued to correspond with a mutual promise to meet if they were ever within a day's ride of each other, but such an opportunity failed to eventuate, and they never saw each other again.

Jena

In January 1801 Hegel's old Tübingen classmate Friedrich Schelling encouraged him to move to the central German university town of Jena. Schelling had established a name for himself there in the newly emerging philosophical school of German Idealism. Although a move to Jena didn't offer exactly what Hegel was looking for – an academic position in which he could be paid for teaching and writing philosophy – it at least had a forward-looking university brimming with new ideas. Overseen by Johann Wolfgang von Goethe, the University of Jena had in recent years become renowned as a centre of post-Kantian philosophy, Weimar Classicism, and the Romantic and Idealist movements.

Soon after arriving, Hegel managed to find some rental accommodation close to the university. Although his lodgings were modest, comprising a cramped single-roomed bedsit, he was pleased to be close to the university and have access to its library. He soon settled into a routine of helping Schelling edit the *Critical Journal of Philosophy* by day, and reading and writing by candlelight in his quarters late into each night.

During this time, he studied two texts in depth that would, in conjunction with *Decline and Fall of the Roman Empire*, go on to influence his first major philosophical work. The first was the work of the ancient Greek philosopher Heraclitus, whose notion of the *dialectic* –

37

where opposing forces within the universe were seen as the cause of its constant changes – immediately captured Hegel's imagination. The second text, or rather group of texts, that Hegel examined closely during this period were those of the German Idealist philosophers, including his friend Schelling.

Pulling these ideas and influences together, as well as his recent observations of the French Revolution, Hegel sketched out a theory he called *dialectical idealism*, which contended that the evolution of society throughout history is shaped by huge contradictory forces within the universe's collective consciousness. He found a publisher who was interested in his bold new ideas, and promised to forward them a manuscript by the following year. But as it turned out, Hegel struggled to clearly articulate his new philosophical system on paper. It would eventually take him several laborious re-drafts, and many years, before he could present the publishers, located in the nearby town of Bamberg, with a completed work he was satisfied with.

But it wasn't just the challenge of pulling together the strands of his highly abstract new theory that delayed Hegel's progress. Halfway through drafting his first major work, the budding philosopher found himself caught up in a distraction of a much more personal nature.

Johanna Burkhardt

Hegel's landlady was a woman in her late twenties called Johanna Burkhardt. She was also his housekeeper, and every day she would come to clean his bedsit, attached to the small house in which she lived with her husband and four young children. She had married in her teens, and the happy days of her marriage, if they ever existed, had long since gone. It is unclear whether her husband had gainful employment, but we do know that Burkhardt's situation was desperate, both financially and emotionally, when Hegel moved in.

Burkhardt's new tenant must have seemed a strange beast to her, deeply immersed in his books whenever she called in to clean his room, collect his washing, or enquire about his need for a meal. If he did take a rest from his labours to engage in small talk with his landlady, one imagines such conversations would have been a welcome break for both of them from the drudgery of their daily routines.

It seems that Burkhardt took pity on her tenant sitting alone in his cold room, and, on one fateful day, invited him back to her house to share in the warmth of her kitchen stove. At the time Hegel would not have known anyone else in the city apart from Schelling, and may well have been feeling rather lonely and dejected. While Schelling was enjoying considerable recognition and success for his philosophical writings, Hegel's career was going nowhere. He had been working on his first book for several years now, and its completion still seemed as far away as ever.

Perhaps, in the warmth of her kitchen, Burkhardt opened up to her guest about the desperate circumstances of her marriage: the alcohol, the gambling, and the cruel abuse she suffered at the hands of her husband. Perhaps she confided, in hushed tones, how she had to steal small amounts of money from her husband's purse to provide for herself and her children's most basic needs.

Burkhardt had no previous acquaintance with philosophy, nor anything else remotely academic or scholarly. One wonders if she enquired about her tenant's writing, and whether he tried to explain the mysterious and complex concepts he was writing about. If he did, perhaps she sensed in his unfamiliar words another world – beyond anything she had ever known – that could help her forget her miserable life situation.

We are wildly speculating here, but perhaps Johanna's naïve interest in Hegel's ideas pampered his fragile pride, which had, after all, been severely tested in recent times. Whatever transpired, it seems that Hegel and his landlady took to having longer and longer conversations in her tiny kitchen while her husband was out, because at the age of thirty-six, the great philosopher-to-be Georg Hegel tasted for the first time, in Burkhardt's bed, the pleasures of illicit sex.

Taking Hegel as a lover would have provided, for Burkhardt, some welcome moments of respite from the ceaseless demands of house-work, children, and an abusive husband. One can imagine her enjoy-ing these moments of pleasurable peace behind a locked bedroom door, as her children took the opportunity to run wild throughout the house.

It is likely Hegel spent the daylight hours with Burkhardt, while her husband was out, returning each night to his room to work on his book. There is, in fact, evidence that his sexual awakening with Burkhardt influenced some of the thinking that went into his first philosophical work. As he speculated about the invisible gigantic forces shaping human history, he also became interested in the smaller, per-sonal, but no less important forces he had encountered in his liaison with Johanna Burkhardt, the mysterious pull of sexual attraction be-tween a man and a woman.

He wrote notes at around this time on how a sexual relationship could be seen as a perfect analogy for how consciousness arises from matter. In an early draft of *Phenomenology of Spirit,* his first major phil-osophical work, he observed that in an encounter between the sexes:

> Impulse comes to an intuition of itself...becomes knowledge of what it is.[7]

In the margins of these notes he wrote, for his own personal refer-ence:

The man has desires, impulse; the feminine impulse is rather to be only the object of impulse; to *entice*, to awaken impulse and to allow it to satisfy itself in it.[8]   ⟶ *seductiver*

Although Hegel and Burkhardt had the next few months to bask in that seemingly never-ending glow of pleasure that only first-time lovers can know, each is likely to have sensed that their reverie would soon be broken. Burkhardt would have been in constant fear of her drunken and unpredictable husband returning home and discovering her in bed with her secret lover. Hegel, too, would have been apprehensive about this, but another matter was also likely to be playing on his mind. Along with everyone else in Jena, he would have heard reports that Napoleon's troops were rapidly progressing eastwards, and might soon descend upon the city he had only just started to feel at home in.

As it turned out, Johanna and Hegel didn't have to worry long about her husband. He abandoned her soon after she and Hegel started their affair.

Then, several months later, in the autumn of 1806, Burkhardt told Hegel some news that caused him to forget, at least for a moment, all his other concerns. She told him that she was pregnant with his child. *Oop...*

Napoleon

Hegel didn't have much time to process the news about Johanna's pregnancy, as in the following weeks he was faced with two other pressing issues – his increasingly impatient publisher issuing him with an ultimatum, and the imminent arrival of Napoleon's troops.

Hegel's publishers made it clear they would not wait any longer for the manuscript he had been promising for years. They gave him one final deadline, 18 October, a little more than a week away.

Meanwhile, news arrived that Napoleon's armies were only days away from the city.

On 13 October 1806, the residents of Jena beheld a sight they had long been dreading. Napoleon's forces could be seen gathering on the horizon, on the high plateau that overlooked the city. A terrified silence enveloped the city, punctuated only by the distant and ominous thunder of cannon fire. Businesses closed their doors, and the streets suddenly emptied as residents awaited their fate.

The day before Napoleon's armies entered the city, Hegel completed the manuscript for his first philosophical work, a work he had been labouring at for five years. Within its pages, he had written what now seemed to be a chilling and timely prophecy. He stated that the French Revolution was akin to a long novel, and although it had begun with French politics, its last chapter would be written by German philosophers.

With Napoleon's troops only hours away, Hegel was as anxious about his manuscript as he was about his own personal safety. He hurriedly sent the bulk of it off to his publisher, and stuffed the last few unedited pages in his pockets before moving to the other side of town to stay in more secure lodgings offered to him by the well-placed parents of one of his students. Burkhardt and her children were not invited to join him.

Hegel would have presented a bizarre spectacle to any residents watching from their windows – a hunched, solitary figure scurrying to safety on the city's deserted streets, his pockets overflowing with crumpled pages of manuscript.

On his way to this temporary shelter, Hegel caught a glimpse of the man who was bringing the revolution to his homeland. He saw Napoleon, whom he had idolised from afar for the past decade, leading his troops into the city. Hegel later wrote to a friend about his sighting of the man who, for him, embodied the future of Europe, the world-changing Spirit he was writing about in his first philosophical work:

> The Emperor – this world soul – I saw him riding through the city to review his troops; it is indeed a wonderful feeling to see such an individual who, here concentrated, into a single point, sitting on a horse, reaches out over the world and masters it…This extraordinary man, whom it is impossible not to admire.[9]

As Hegel hid out in relative safety with his hosts, Napoleon's troops unleashed their full fury on the city. The deafening sounds of battle enveloped the streets – the fire of cannons, the stampede of hooves, the screams of the injured, and the crackle of buildings catching fire. Nearly all the houses in Jena's main street, the Johannisgasse, were set aflame.

After several hours, the sounds of battle ceased. The Prussian forces had been no match for the French master of military strategy and tactics. Jena was now part of France. Hegel's dream, since his teenage years, that the French Revolution would spread to German-speaking lands, had, at last, come to pass.

Hegel hadn't imagined, however, the cost that such a dream would entail. As he grimly reported to a friend soon afterwards:

> Nobody has imagined war as we have seen it.[10]

On returning to his old lodgings, Hegel was no doubt relieved to find Johanna and her children unharmed. His bedsit, however, had been ransacked and almost totally destroyed by invading troops. Describing the scene in his room to a friend, he wrote:

> The knaves have, to be sure, messed up my papers like lottery tickets.[11]

Although they had survived Napoleon's invasion of their city, Hegel and Johanna were now faced with another challenge – they no

43

longer had any source of income. The private fee-paying students who, up until now, had been providing Hegel with enough to get by, had disappeared. After the arrival of Napoleon's troops, the university had closed, and all of its academics, including his friend Schelling, had fled to other cities. It was now more important than ever for Hegel to get his book published, so that he could bring in some money for his newly adopted family, especially the extra hungry mouth just about to arrive.

A Child is Born

It is unclear how Hegel and Johanna made it through the next few months, but we know that by 5 February 1807, when Johanna gave birth to a baby boy, they were almost destitute.

Two weeks before the baby was born, Hegel sent the publisher a preface for his book, and for this they favoured him with a small advance. Hegel also managed to secure a small loan from his friend Friedrich Niethammer, classmate from his Tübingen days.

Hegel and Burkhardt's son was christened Georg Ludwig Friedrich, but thereafter known simply as Ludwig. A few weeks after Ludwig's birth, Niethammer found Hegel employment as a newspaper editor in Bamberg, the same city in which his book was being published. Although 120 miles and several days' ride south of Jena, Hegel felt he had no choice but to accept the position.

As Hegel prepared to leave for Bamberg, news arrived that Johanna's estranged husband, the father of her other children, had died.

Hegel desperately wanted to stay with his new and now grieving family, but their dire financial situation required that he leave immediately.

As he bid farewell to his newly widowed lover and her five children, he promised he would send money as soon as he was able. He also promised Johanna, as she stood there with their crying babe in her arms, that he would return to marry her in the spring.

Phenomenology of Spirit

Although Hegel's new job in Bamberg was still a far cry from the academic position he would have liked, it was at least a position that carried some responsibility, and, of course, it provided a much-needed income. The image of Johanna waving goodbye with young Ludwig in her arms would have still been fresh in Hegel's mind when he posted a long letter and his first pay cheque. In the weeks that followed, he continued to send money, but after a while the letters became shorter and more infrequent.

Hegel's first philosophical work, *Die Phänomenologie des Geistes* (*The Phenomenology of Spirit*), was published in Bamberg in April 1807, only a few weeks after he moved there.

Readers of Hegel's work had never encountered writing such as this before – a mishmash of philosophy, politics, world history, and romantic mysticism. In this grandiose and sweeping overview of the universe as he saw it, Hegel had ambitiously tried to explain the history and evolution of human consciousness. *Die Phänomenologie* portrayed a world constantly pulled in opposite directions by contradictory, invisible historical forces. According to Hegel's account, society was always on the verge of being torn apart.

What Hegel couldn't see was that this description of the world mirrored, and had partly arisen out of, his own personal unconscious conflicts, the disturbing dilemmas that were stirring in his heart. Although part of him knew he should return to his landlady-lover and marry her as promised, another part of him insisted he was destined for greater things, for the fame, success, and adulation he had seen his friend and rival Schelling enjoy. And the more he imagined these things, the

45

harder he found it to fit Johanna and her five children into that picture.

Hegel had been developing the ideas in *Phenomenology of Spirit* since his Tübingen days. It arose, as we have heard, out of several different sources of inspiration – Kant's conclusion that the external world could never be truly known, his study of history, his observations of the French Revolution, and, more recently, his first experiences of the ecstasies of physical love.

In this work, Hegel described history, rather mystically, as the process of human consciousness coming to know itself. He traced how, over the ages, western societies have become more sophisticated, each one getting successively closer to what he saw as the ultimate state of self-knowledge. Hegel predicted that the historical process would eventually culminate in society and consciousness becoming perfectly self-aware, reaching a state he called *Absolute Spirit*. For Hegel, the true nature of reality was consciousness – mind, not matter – and the history (and destiny) of the world was a history of humanity coming to realise this.

Hegel saw the French Revolution and events unfolding in its wake as providing support for his theory about the evolution of society. According to his theory, each phase in history is driven by a central tendency he called its *thesis*, as well as a tendency within it that is its opposite, its *antithesis*. Hegel believed that tension between thesis and antithesis would, after much upheaval, always give way to what he called a *synthesis*, a higher and more advanced form of society. In the case of the French Revolution, Hegel saw the people's push for freedom as the *thesis*, the violent and chaotic Reign of Terror that followed as the *antithesis*, and the subsequent development of a constitution that enshrined citizens' rights as the *synthesis*.

As already mentioned, Hegel's notes and marginalia in earlier drafts of this work suggest his own recent experience of sexual desire reinforced his conviction that the world and its history were shaped by mysterious, invisible contradictory forces more powerful than the will of any one individual.

The Phenomenology of Spirit would go on to become recognised as one of the most influential works of the nineteenth century. But its description of history as inevitably progressing, unfolding, and evolving in the face of unstoppable hidden forces would have an even greater impact on the twentieth century, directly inspiring the revolutionary, world-changing political philosophies of Marxism and Communism.

When it was first published, however, *Phenomenology of Spirit* stimulated only a modest response in philosophical circles and the wider reading public. This was no doubt partly due to the fact that it was written in an extremely turgid and difficult-to-read style, a style that would come to characterise all of Hegel's work. In the months following its publication, however, as readers untangled and deciphered the philosopher's awkward prose, and better grasped his groundbreaking ideas, appreciation of the work grew, as did his reputation and standing in the academic and wider community. Eventually, Hegel started to gain the respect he had craved for so long. As he moved in more reputable circles, he felt even less beholden to his earlier vows to Johanna and their illegitimate child back in Jena.

Hegel also seemed to quickly forget how much his newfound fame was due to the patronage and generosity of his friend Friedrich Schelling, who, despite his own early successes, had always reached out to help Hegel during his times of need. In what can only be understood as an act of spiteful envy, Hegel introduced *Phenomenology of Spirit* with a preface that scathingly dismissed Schelling's work, describing his philosophical ideas as fundamentally flawed and inadequate.

Schelling was understandably taken aback at this unprovoked attack on his work, and responded with a letter to Hegel in which, although his tone was restrained, his displeasure was abundantly evident:

> Insofar as you yourself mention the polemical part of the Preface, given my own justly measured opinion of myself I would have to think too little of myself to apply this polemic to my own person.[12]

At the end of this response, written in August 1807, Schelling did, however, leave open an opportunity for reconciliation with the man who, ever since their days together in Tübingen, he had considered his closest friend:

> All the best; write me again soon and keep me in your mind as your true friend, Schelling.[13]

Hegel, much to his discredit, did not even acknowledge Schelling's letter.

Hegel is unlikely to have appreciated the fact that when *Phenomenology of Spirit* was published, some reviewers described it as a piece of Schellingean philosophy. Schelling, however, heartily agreed with these assessments, telling all who would listen that Hegel was becoming famous on the back of his ideas.

Years later, Schelling would still maintain that Hegel had copied his ideas without acknowledging them. In a letter to a friend, Schelling complained that Hegel was like 'a creeping insect [that] believes that by appropriating the leaf of a plant, it has wrapped itself in its own weaving'.[14]

In the same letter, Schelling scathingly described Hegel's philosophical accomplishments, now well-recognised throughout

Germany, as no more impressive than 'transposing a violin concerto for piano'.[15]

After the publication of *Phenomenology of Spirit*, Hegel and Schelling would not speak to each other for another twenty years.

Nuremberg

After a year in Bamberg, Hegel was offered a position in nearby Nuremberg as rector of a prestigious high school, providing him with an opportunity to increase his social ranking even further. On taking up the position, Hegel applied himself with great diligence to the reform of the school. He soon made a name for himself in Nuremberg society with his bold speeches at school events and gatherings, in which he extolled the values of cultivation, knowledge, education, and reason. He was consequently invited to join one of Nuremberg's leading gentleman's clubs, *The Museum*, described by one observer as a 'meeting point for members of the cultivated estates…to conduct gentlemanly and learned debates about modern literature'.[16] *The Museum* contained men from some of the highest levels of Nuremberg society.

A letter Hegel wrote to his good friend Karl Frommann more than a year after he had left Jena, shows that he was feeling at least some pangs of conscience about his failure to return and marry Burkhardt as he had promised:

> I continue to regret painfully that so far I have not been fully able to extricate from her present situation the woman who is the mother of my child, and who has a right to call upon me to perform obligations of all sorts. I am very obliged to you for facilitating for me what relief I am able to provide in the matter.[17]

Over the subsequent years, Hegel would repeatedly ask From-mann, whom he had appointed as Ludwig's godfather, for loans to help support his illegitimate son.

Another letter Hegel wrote at this time makes it clear that although he felt some ongoing responsibilities to Burkhardt he no longer had any intentions of marrying her. In this letter, to his friend Nietham-mer, Hegel announces his desire to find a marriage prospect more in keeping with his recent acceptance into the higher echelons of Nurem-berg society:

> I would like to take up and successfully conclude another business, namely, to take up a wife, or rather to find one![18]

Niethammer wasn't the only one privy to Hegel's plans. Another friend, the theologian Heinrich Paulus, joked to Hegel that his wife was making enquiries about a 'faithful, slow Nuremberg woman' for him.[19]

Marie von Tucher

It didn't take Hegel long to find a suitable marriage prospect in the higher circles in which he now moved. Her name was Marie von Tu-cher, a simple-hearted and pious young woman from a well-known Nuremberg family. Hegel met nineteen-year-old Marie through her father, Jobst Wilhelm Karl von Tucher, a founder of *The Museum* and highly regarded member of Nuremberg society. The von Tuchers be-longed to the nobility long before Napoleon's reforms had, with only partial success, removed such class distinctions. As a commentator on German society noted at the time, despite Napoleon's best efforts to bring equality to all, the Germans could still 'be roughly divided into two classes, the von's and the non-von's'. For Hegel, who was not of aristocratic background, the prospect of such an engagement was a big step up from the life he could expect if he had fulfilled his promise to Johanna.

A rather dry note in Jobst von Tucher's diary documents Hegel's approach for his daughter's hand:

> At the beginning of April (1811), rector Hegel let his wishes be known…to marry my daughter and to request an opportunity to speak with the latter.[20]

Baron von Tucher made it clear to his daughter he would be guided by her wishes in the matter.

Marie's first impression of Hegel, who, at forty, was twice her age, was of an odd, somewhat bumbling man with a speech impediment. Although somewhat eccentric, Marie did find her suitor personable and attentive. She and her father were impressed by how quickly he had made a name for himself in Nuremberg society in his new role as school rector. And although he was from a lower class than she hoped to marry, he was clearly a man of intelligence, diligence, and ambition.

After seeking counsel from her parents – and several weeks of deliberation – she consented to the marriage.

Correspondence between Hegel and von Tucher during their yearlong engagement revealed a considerable amount of tension in the early days of their relationship. Von Tucher was not afraid to express her own opinions, even if they conflicted with those of her older and much more well-read husband-to-be. Hegel, on the other hand, showed no sign of tempering his longstanding tendency to criticise those whose views differed from his, even if the person disagreeing with him was his young fiancée. He often infuriated von Tucher by telling her that her arguments demonstrated the female preponderance of emotion over reason. Hegel, it seems, found it very difficult to take a woman's thoughts seriously. (There would be evidence in later correspondence, however, of a softening of Hegel's stance in this regard, with him displaying much more humility, tenderness, and respect in letters to his wife.)

Hegel and Marie's different outlooks on the world also resulted in some significant disagreements early in their relationship. Marie became quite upset on reading a letter Hegel wrote to his sister Christiane about his upcoming marriage, in which he stated he expected to be happy, 'insofar as happiness belongs to my life's destiny'.[21] Marie was troubled that Hegel would even think to cast any doubt on his expectations of marital happiness. In Marie's uncomplicated view of the world, one shouldn't question such things as one's faith in God or one's prospects for a happy marriage. She didn't appreciate Hegel's need, perhaps not surprising for a philosopher, to question and analyse everything. In his efforts to reconcile with Marie after she became upset with this letter, Hegel reminded her that he had previously discussed his views, not inconsistent with his dialectic philosophy, that in 'non-superficial natures every sensation of happiness is connected with sensation of melancholy'.[22] It is hard to imagine this intellectual and rather awkward response having the effect that Hegel was hoping for.

While Marie was a pragmatic young woman of faith who trusted her feelings without any need to reflect or doubt them, Hegel was analytical, uncomfortable with emotion, and at times pedantic to the point of obtuseness. He himself admitted as much in a pacifying letter he wrote her after a similar squabble:

> Oh, how much more I could still write – about my perhaps hypochondriacal pedantry, which led me to insist so greatly on the distinction between "being satisfied" and happiness, a distinction which is once again so useless.[23]

A Woman Scorned

These ups and downs in Hegel and Marie's early courtship were minor, however, compared to what followed when Burkhardt, hearing of Hegel's plans to marry, arrived in Nuremberg demanding justice.

Hegel had been dreading such a situation for some time now, knowing that any revelation of his past indiscretions could rapidly undo his plans for a new life of comfortable respectability. He had been doing everything he could to ensure Burkhardt didn't hear about his upcoming wedding.

In fact, he had thought he was safe when he heard from his friend Frommann that Johanna was no longer able to care for Ludwig, and had handed him over to the care of Frommann's sister-in-law, who had just opened up an orphanage for boys. On hearing this news, Hegel had assumed that Johanna's situation was so dire he wouldn't hear from her again. Just to be sure, however, he wrote Frommann's sister-in-law a letter:

> I ask you still to keep this circumstance [of the upcoming marriage] a secret, since otherwise it might incite even more the impudence of that Burkhardt woman, should she find out about it before everything is completely settled with her.[24]

In this letter, Hegel even flagged plans to engage legal advice should Johanna try to impede his upcoming marriage.

In the end, however, all these precautions failed to prevent the showdown that Hegel was trying to avoid.

We don't have many details about Burkhardt's visit to Nuremberg in the lead-up to Hegel and von Tucher's wedding, but we do know that this was how von Tucher first heard about Hegel's bastard son.

One wonders how the near-destitute Burkhardt even managed to make the hundred-mile journey from Jena to Nuremberg. And when she arrived, we don't know if the jilted mother of Hegel's first-born son stated her claim quietly and with dignity, or whether she created a terrible fracas. Either way, Hegel was left in a position where he had some difficult explaining to do, to Burkhardt, to von Tucher, and to von Tucher's family.

It seems that Hegel eventually convinced Burkhardt to leave him and his fiancée alone. Whether he used monetary compensation, legal action, or further false promises to achieve this is unknown. Whatever transpired, we know this is the last time he ever saw her.

The unexpected arrival of Burkhardt demanding restitution for her and her baby became, not surprisingly, the talk of the town for some time. It also left Marie's father seething, and for a while it wasn't clear whether the marriage would proceed.

Marie and her father, remarkably, did not break off the engagement. In fact, throughout this whole unpleasant affair, there is no record of Marie expressing any criticism or judgement of her husband-to-be. It seems she conducted herself, as she would throughout their long and fruitful marriage, with admirable grace, dignity, and restraint.

A Wedding

Like most scandals, the one involving Hegel's past misadventures eventually died down as the townsfolk lost interest and moved on to other, newer sources of gossip and outrage. Overcoming the challenges that had plagued their engagement, Hegel and von Tucher were married on 15 September 1811, in the city's main cathedral before a crowd of some of the most esteemed members of Nuremberg society. In keeping with the traditions of the time, Marie, surrounded by young flower girls, wore a black wedding dress decorated with ribbon. As they left the cathedral, the newlyweds, in keeping with another tradition of the day, threw coins to scores of children from the town who had gathered outside.

The day after their nuptial celebrations, Hegel wrote a letter to his friend Niethammer, in which he could barely contain his feelings of joy:

> I have now reached my earthly goal. For what more does one want in this world than an official post and a dear wife?…What is left over no longer makes up chapters in themselves but perhaps only paragraphs or remarks.[25]

Although Hegel couldn't be happier, for Marie the first half-year of their marriage wasn't quite the joyous time she had been hoping for. She often found herself alone and ignored as her husband absorbed himself, night after night, in writing his second highly acclaimed philosophical work. *The Science of Logic*, published in three volumes over four years, helped Hegel to achieve a long-awaited goal – being appointed to a professorship of philosophy.

Even with that appointment yet to come, the forty-one-year-old Hegel found himself happy and fulfilled. He was respectably married to the beautiful young daughter of a highly regarded patrician, and welcomed without question now as a member of society. He had one major work published, and another on the way. His long-awaited academic career was just about to take off. Everything he had dreamed of, and more, was coming true.

With all this outward success, one wonders if Hegel ever found himself lying awake at night, troubled in particular by two images from his past – the first, Burkhardt with babe in arms waving him goodbye in Jena; the second, Burkhardt's crestfallen face before the wedding in Nuremberg, when he sent her away with her hopes crushed.

In Hegel's philosophical works he had described a universe in which each action triggers an equal and opposite reaction, and in Hegel's life from this time on, it was almost as if his broken promise to Johanna had unleashed the anger of a conscious universe. For despite his upward climb into fame and success, a succession of misfortune and disasters hounded the ambitious philosopher until his dying day.

The first of these would strike even before Hegel and his new wife could celebrate their first wedding anniversary.

Demons Knocking at the Door

In the summer of 1812, the Hegels lost their first-born child. Susanna Maria Louisa Wilhelmine had brought great joy to her mother when she was born on 27 June 1812, but she died only two months later. Marie was inconsolable. Coming from a fortunate and well-to-do family, the twenty-year-old was totally unprepared for this terrible trauma, but in the months that followed there would be worse to come.

Later that year, Marie and Hegel each lost a brother in Napoleon's ill-fated Russian campaign. Their brothers were amongst many from across Europe who had answered the call to fight for the French, their revolutionary cause having now garnered the support of the majority of people in German-speaking countries. Both brothers died on the Russian front less than a year after attending Hegel and Marie's wedding. Hegel's brother Georg was thirty-six years old when he perished on Russia's frozen steppes; Marie's brother was in his early twenties. The brilliant world-conqueror Napoleon, whom Hegel so admired, had made a fatal miscalculation in his attempt to invade Russia. Like aggressors before and since, Napoleon's armies wilted against the combined forces of the Russian army and equally deadly Russian winter. Napoleon's army, the largest ever assembled in Europe, lost more than three hundred thousand men on the Russia front to a combination of battle injuries, cold, and starvation. In the wake of Napoleon's defeat, his enemies throughout Europe moved quickly to take advantage of his weakened state, bringing his once-glorious empire to an end.

Shortly after these losses, however, Marie and Hegel were blessed with the birth of a healthy baby boy, Karl Friedrich, in 1813. But joy turned to grief again when, a week after Karl's birth, Marie's much-beloved father passed away. Almost a year to the day after losing her baby daughter, the loyal, dutiful, and dignified Marie laid her father to rest.

The only portrait of Marie that still survives today was sketched just after she experienced this terrible series of bereavements. It shows a dark-haired woman looking much older than her years. Her hollow, sad eyes stare out at the viewer, shielding a quiet and muted pain. Her dress and lace bonnet, though fashionable for the time, are sombre and conservative in their dark shades; a chemise made of heavy material modestly covers her shoulders, arms, and throat. One can't help but get the impression from this portrait that its subject is struggling to contain her grief behind an expressionless and tight-lipped face.

Madness

Marie's resilience was tested even further the following year when, just after her second son, Immanuel, was born, Hegel invited his sister Christiane to come and stay with them. Hegel felt moved to make the invitation after hearing that Christiane had lost her job as a governess after falling ill. What Hegel didn't realise at the time was the nature of his sister's illness. She was, in fact, in the early stages of a severe psychotic breakdown.

Oblivious to the seriousness of his sister's condition, Hegel wrote to Christiane on 9 April 1814:

[W]e invite you to move in with us permanently, to live with us, and receive the care you need…My wife will be delivering this fall, and if you could lend her a hand your presence would be doubly advantageous.[26]

Hegel thought that Marie would appreciate the help of another woman in the house, given that he was often away at work for long periods of time. But it became evident soon after her arrival that Christiane was not her usual self. Indeed, she had almost completely lost touch with reality. Marie found herself bearing the full brunt of Christiane's descent into psychosis. Disastrous scenes ensued as Marie and her two young children tried to stave off Hegel's now completely deranged sister. According to family friend Ludwig Friedrich Göriz, who visited the Hegel household during this period, Christiane was 'beside herself all the day, wailing and crying on the sofa', venting a 'deep hatred' of Marie, and a 'thorough dissatisfaction with her brother'.[27]

After a particularly vicious outburst in which she abused, threatened, and totally disowned her brother and sister-in-law, Christiane was committed to a sanitarium.

This last incident caused a rift so deep that Hegel and his sister would never speak to each other again.

Hegel's sister wasn't the only person he would lose to the scourge of mental illness. Soon afterwards, the clear and beautiful mind of his poet-friend Friedrich Hölderlin succumbed to a similar schizophrenic illness. Hölderlin's tragic collapse came just after his rapid but short-lived rise to literary stardom, during which he produced some of the finest poetry ever written in the German language.

Meanwhile, Marie's woes were far from over. After Christiane's departure, she went on to have a series of traumatic miscarriages. In one of these, she almost died from the ensuing haemorrhage and infection. These highly debilitating events, along with the grief of losing her baby girl, her brother, and her father in quick succession, took a terrible toll on the young Marie. It was certainly not the life she had imagined for herself as a new wife and mother. The fortitude and forbearance she exhibited in the face of these trials awakened, however, new feelings of admiration and respect from Hegel, feelings that would only increase in the years to come.

Ludwig moves in

Five years into their marriage, Hegel asked his wife if they could take Ludwig, then aged nine, into their home.

Marie was initially reluctant, given the disastrous experience with Hegel's sister, and her own still-fragile health. She was also concerned at the effect another disruption to the household might have on her two young sons, now aged three and two. In the end, out of pity for Ludwig and respect for her husband, she consented. On 16 July 1816, Hegel wrote to tell Frommann, whose sister-in-law was still caring for little Ludwig in her orphanage:

My wife and I are resolved to take Ludwig into our home.[28]

In Frommann's reply to Hegel, he informed him of some shocking news. Ludwig's mother, Johanna Burkhardt, was dead. Little was known about the circumstances of her passing, other than the fact that, at only thirty-eight years of age, she had died destitute, miserable, and alone.

A few days after taking Ludwig into his home, Hegel told him the news about his mother. Hegel later told Frommann that Johanna's death 'seemed to have affected him [Ludwig] more than me...my heart had long ago finished with her'.[29]

One of the reasons Hegel could take Ludwig in was that he could now afford it, having just been offered a professorship of philosophy at the University of Heidelberg.

A few months after Ludwig arrived in the family home, Hegel set off on a three-day journey to Heidelberg to commence his new position. At the time Marie was recovering from yet another miscarriage, and was too unwell to travel. The plan was that she and the children would join Hegel a few months later.

Although Marie wasn't well enough to join her husband immediately, she was quite excited about her new role as wife of a university professor. In a letter Hegel sent Niethammer about his upcoming new appointment, Marie wrote in the margin, 'Yes! Yes!' adding, 'We often talk together about it.'[30]

During the three months Marie stayed back in Nuremberg, her younger sister 'Fritz' moved in with her and the three boys. Marie wrote frequently to Hegel during this time, as did Hegel's mother-in-law, who often sent him parcels of his favourite food and drink. Hegel had moved quite comfortably into the role of family patriarch since Marie's father had died.

In late 1816 the extended family of Hegel, Marie, Fritz, Ludwig, Karl, and Immanuel settled into their new home in Heidelberg. Although it was an exciting time for the family, it soon became clear that Ludwig would have difficulty fitting into the bourgeois and staid Hegel household. Years in the orphanage had taken their toll, and the morose and moody Ludwig regularly clashed with his younger, more cultivated half-brothers. His adjustment wasn't helped by the fact that Hegel and Marie treated him very differently to their own two children. They made a point of sending Ludwig to a less expensive school that provided much less in the way of educational and other opportunities. Marie's letters to family and friends during this time often mentioned Karl and Immanuel, but never Ludwig.

As it turned out, Hegel's ever-growing family didn't stay in Heidelberg for very long, as after two years Hegel was offered an even more prestigious position, Professor of Philosophy at the University of Berlin.

Arrival in Berlin

Hegel and his family arrived in the grand old city of Berlin on 5 October 1818. At the time Berlin was the fourth largest city in Europe, and a thriving centre for music and the arts. Hegel and Marie immediately fell in love with the city's wide tree-lined streets and stately architecture, including the newly built Berlin University where Hegel would take up his position. Berlin society, in turn, welcomed the famed philosopher and his elegant young wife with open arms. At forty-eight, Hegel had reached a peak in his career. The recent publication of his three-volume *Science of Logic*, which had further expounded on his central idea in *Phenomenology of Spirit* – that reality is not only shaped by the mind, but properly understood *is* the mind – had cemented his reputation as one of Germany's most bold and original thinkers since the Kantian revolution.

The university dominated the Prussian capital's skyline at that time, occupying a central position in its main boulevard. Diagonally across from the university stood an older and even grander building, the *Opernhaus*, built in 1742.

Hegel started lecturing at the university five times a week. Each day, late in the afternoon, he presented two regular lectures – the *Encyclopaedia of Philosophy* and *Natural Right and Political Science*. These lectures were well attended and much talked about. His obscure manner of speech, ridiculed by some in the past, was now seen as part of the larger-than-life philosopher's charm and intrigue.

A common sight in those years was Hegel's distinctive silhouette, head bowed, hurriedly leaving the university in the early evening to catch the latest performance at the *Openrhaus*.

At Hegel's inaugural lecture, delivered on 22 October, he exhorted his audience, using his characteristically tortured prose, to embrace cultivation and learning, in particular the study of philosophy:

> The cultivation (*Bildung*) and flowering of the sciences is here one of the essential moments itself in the life of the state; at this university, the university of the focal point, philosophy, the focal point of all cultivation of spirit, of all science and truth, must find its principal furtherance.[31]

Hegel was impressed with the sophistication of Berlin's residents. As he relayed in a letter in 1819:

> [Not only are youth] receptive to and interested in philosophy. One even finds majors, colonels, and privy councillors attending one's lectures.[32]

Professor and Frau Hegel received many invitations to galas, parties, and concerts in their new home town. Marie grew to relish her role as wife of Berlin's most acclaimed academic. In a letter Hegel wrote to Niethammer at around this time, she added, in her own handwriting:

> I see my Hegel content in his profession, cheerful with me and the children, and *recognized* – and that is what matters to an honourable, upright woman above all else.[33]

Coming from a family of significant repute, Marie was thrilled to see Hegel achieving recognition in his own right. She worked hard to keep the house and family in order whilst he lectured and wrote.

Hegel and Marie led a comfortable and cultivated existence in the new home they set up in Berlin. Their house was decorated in the *Biedermeier* style, very popular at the time amongst the refined middle class. Those embracing this style prided themselves on their simplicity and practicality, distinguishing themselves in this post-revolutionary period from the ostentatiousness of the old aristocracy. The Hegels' home had a *Wohnzimmer* (living room) with a sofa, a desk, simple practical furniture, and portraits of family members adorning its walls.

In addition to an oval wooden dining table, various worktables, a sewing table, and a piano, the house featured the other obligatory furnishings of the day – an upright clock, a hanging wood-framed mirror, and two occasional chairs. Hegel also had his own study with a desk, chair, and bookshelves.

In keeping with the fashion of the day, the Hegel residence also boasted several birdcages and exotic plants. The first sight to greet any visitors to their home was a flowering cactus proudly displayed in the entrance, along with two mating doves and a canary in a large wrought-iron cage.

Many of the rituals of the Hegel household wouldn't be too unfamiliar to middle-class households today. Hegel loved his morning coffee and newspaper, and in the evening he liked to sample from his extensive wine collection. He saw himself as a connoisseur, buying wine by the barrel as well as the bottle. One of his favourite drops was a Haut-Saterne from France. He was also a great snuff aficionado. The Hegels regularly invited guests to their house for musical parties, a popular activity in the city at that time. Marie and the three boys all took lessons on a baby grand piano she had purchased, and Ludwig, who, to his father's surprise had shown considerable promise as a vocalist, had even been allowed to take singing lessons so that he could better entertain their guests.

Hegel was on a generous salary of two thousand thalers a year, supplemented by honoraria for lectures and examinations that amounted to about another five hundred. He arranged for the honoraria to go directly to Marie, which she used to oversee the running of the household. She hired and paid the various artisans and jobbers needed to keep their comfortable middle-class residence running. Hegel paid for the rent, the maids, and the wine. He also regularly splurged on tickets in the state lottery, hoping for a win to make up for his habit of always spending just beyond his means.

The Philosophy of Right

In Berlin, Hegel saw his role as one in keeping with the vision of his youth, to help create a culture and society where learning and appreciation of the classics were fostered, and free thinking was valued. He dreamt of universities as places where critical thinking could flourish, rather than just being institutions where one learnt the knowledge and skills needed for a particular profession. He continued to hope for a progressive republic based on the principles of the French Revolution, despite the setbacks to such a cause after Napoleon had been defeated and right-wing monarchists had regained control of Prussia's political apparatus. It would be drawing a long bow to say he supported democracy, but he certainly wanted a more progressive politics than was present in his time.

In 1821, at the age of fifty-one, Hegel published his third major work, the *Philosophy of Right*, which described his thoughts in the area of political philosophy. Much to Hegel's disappointment, this publication, in which Hegel argued that the law was the cornerstone of the modern state, was widely seen as demonstrating his sympathies with the right-wing Prussian monarchy.

This unexpected reaction to his work left Hegel feeling plagued by two conflicting anxieties. On the one hand, he had a longstanding fear that the monarchist government might censor or punish him for promoting free thought, as had happened to several of his students and colleagues. On the other hand, he resented the fact that he was seen by many liberal critics as being 'in bed with' the ruling government. Once again, Hegel found his life mirroring the dialectic tensions he wrote about in his philosophy.

Hegel was also getting caught up in a seemingly irreconcilable dialectic on the domestic front. Here he felt torn between a sense of obligation towards his long-suffering illegitimate son and his desire to keep the peace in his marriage.

On entering his teenage years, Ludwig – who had done very well at school despite the limited educational opportunities made available to him – expressed a wish to study medicine. Although Ludwig had been successful enough in his studies to qualify for such a career, Hegel made it very clear he should abandon any such intentions. Hegel and Marie had agreed years earlier when they took Ludwig into their home that they would not be providing any financial support above and beyond that required for his basic needs. Hegel therefore duly informed his son that, in contrast with his younger brothers, he would not be supported to attend university, and should seek to learn a trade as soon as he came of age.

This harsh approach to Ludwig's aspirations led to increasing tensions between father and son that would soon culminate in an unimaginably tragic sequence of events.

Batavia

During his teenage years, Ludwig ran away from home several times. His feelings of inferiority and unworthiness, progressively reinforced by the less favourable treatment he had received in the Hegel household, reached a point where he eventually felt completely unloved and unwanted. The final straw in the tenuous relationship between Ludwig and his father came when he was caught stealing from the family money box. Ludwig had taken eight groschen, a trifling amount, but the punishment meted out was far from trifling. At the age of eighteen he was banished, cast out of the family household, and barred from using the Hegel name. From that time on he called himself Ludwig Fischer, taking on the surname of his mother's husband. In an anguished letter to a friend at the time, he complained:

Hegel will not let me take all my clothes, let alone a book.[34]

Desperately needing paid employment to survive, Ludwig moved to Amsterdam where he signed up to work in a part of the European economy booming at the time – mercenary soldiering in the colonies. Holland's maritime expansion was in full swing, and young men were needed to hold and advance the colonial frontiers. After signing up for a six-year contract, Ludwig wrote a letter to his friend Ebert that showed he was well aware of the dangers that lay ahead:

I will finish June 24, 1831…but who knows in the endless war over there, …through battle after battle, [I] may be exposed to enemy bullets, or infectious disease.[35]

Although they were still estranged, Hegel did hear through various sources that his son had joined the Dutch army. In 1827 Hegel visited his friend Peter van Ghert in Holland and told him he was concerned about Ludwig's welfare. Van Ghert, who held a senior post in the Dutch government, later wrote to Hegel asking which regiment Ludwig belonged to, assuring him that if he was able to provide any assistance in his official capacity, he would.

But Hegel's efforts were all in vain. After surviving a gruelling six-month voyage from Belgium to Batavia, Ludwig fought in the Java War, one of the Netherlands' largest and most costly colonial wars. The Dutch forces suffered heavy losses against the Indonesian Prince Diponegoro and his guerrilla forces. In the rainy season, malaria and dysentery also struck the Dutch troops, causing many fatalities. One of those was Ludwig Fischer, the eldest forsaken son of European philosopher Georg Hegel.

Ludwig's death was documented in the Records Department of the Dutch East Indies, Death Register, Folio 44. The certificate read:

> Fischer, Lodewijk, aged 24 years, was born in the province of Jena […], last worked as a helmsman in subdivision 2 Infantry, died on August 28 1831 in Batavia, due to inflammatory fever.[36]

But Hegel would never get to hear about his first-born's death, as at around the same time he was caught up in a terrifying, life-threatening ordeal of his own. Along with everyone else in Prussia, Hegel and his family were becoming increasingly concerned by news reports about a worldwide cholera epidemic, which had already claimed hundreds of thousands of lives around the globe and was just about to strike Berlin.

Epidemic

This worldwide cholera epidemic had begun in India in 1817, swept through Asia and the Middle East in the 1820s, and more recently, in the autumn of 1830, broken out in Russia, killing hordes of people in Odessa, Crimea, and Moscow.

In May 1831, the first cases of cholera were reported inside Prussia, in the border town of Danzig. Authorities acted quickly, sealing the country's eastern borders and putting under quarantine all travellers from the affected regions, and any others without proper papers.

Although these measures were put in place, no one really understood at the time what caused the spread of cholera. Theories abounded, but most experts believed it was transmitted by dirty or unhealthy air. Others saw it as a plague coming out of the 'barbarian' East to engulf the 'civilised' West.

One commentator who had observed first-hand the havoc wreaked by this mysterious disease described it as follows:

> No barriers are sufficient to obstruct its progress. It crosses mountains, deserts, and oceans. Opposing winds do not check it. All classes of persons, male and female, young and old, the robust and the feeble, are exposed to its assault; and even those whom it has once visited are not always subsequently exempt; yet as a general rule it selects its victims preferably from among those already pressed down by the various miseries of life and leaves the rich and prosperous to their sunshine and their fears.[37]

As the people of Berlin braced themselves for the worst, the city was divided up into medically supervised regions, and pamphlets were distributed about the early signs of the disease. But these were not really needed; rumours about the disease's modus operandi had already spread through the city like wildfire. Those fleeing from nearby affected towns relayed in gruesome detail to Berlin's terrified citizens what they had seen – how people who started their day in good health had within hours become violently ill. These wild-eyed survivors of the advancing plague described how their loved ones had turned a ghastly tint of blue before collapsing and dying in a pool of their own dysentery.

The first case of cholera hit Berlin in the August of 1831. Immediately afterwards, all slaughterhouses, schools, and other public buildings were closed until further notice. In another precaution, royal orders were given for all coins and mail to be fumigated with smoke or sulphur. As more cases were reported, the King issued a decree that all affected houses were to be quarantined. As an increasing number of bodies turned up at the city morgue, an ordinance was issued that all affected corpses must be soaked in calcium chloride and buried at night, with only immediate family in attendance.

In the midst of these frantic attempts to contain the spread, the real cause of this terrifying disease's lightning-fast transmission, Berlin's open sewers, continued to flow through the city as they had for years, unnoticed and unsuspected by the city's medical and civic authorities.

As the city succumbed, Hegel was beside himself with worry, whispering to his wife on more than one occasion:

With my weak stomach it wouldn't take much to contract cholera.[38]

The family decided to leave the city. After frantically packing their belongings, they left their comfortable home and joined a crush of other residents streaming for the city gates. Fortunately, they knew a family living in Kreuzberg, just outside Berlin, who allowed them to rent out the top floor of their house.

The epidemic raged for months in Berlin as Hegel and his family waited it out in Kreuzberg. Although Hegel remained extremely concerned about the cholera spreading to their new location, these months were a time of quiet and precious respite for the family. Marie did her best to make light of their predicament, referring to their temporary top-floor living space as the *Schlösschen* – their little palace. Hegel whiled away the days in the house's back garden playing chess with his sons, reading the newspaper, and writing philosophy, but he dared not venture on to the streets outside.

After the epidemic was officially declared over, Hegel's family moved back to their home in Berlin. They were shocked at the sights that greeted them – ghostly and sullen survivors, appearing dazed and confused, wandered aimlessly through the city's near-empty streets. The town's whole atmosphere felt heavy with devastation and grief. Hegel didn't feel at all comfortable despite assurances from authorities that the epidemic was over. He complained bitterly to Marie about the dirty Berlin air, telling her he felt 'like a fish that had been taken out of a fresh spring and thrown into a sewer'.[39]

As it turned out, the philosopher's gloomy premonitions were not misplaced. At 11 a.m. on Sunday, 12 November, only a few days after he had arrived back in Berlin, Hegel was struck with an attack of pain so severe it doubled him over and he was hardly able to breathe. A doctor was summoned and arrived at 2 p.m., by which time his abdominal pains had eased considerably. The doctor diagnosed a simple stomach irritation and prescribed a mustard plaster to be applied to Hegel's abdomen. A few hours after the doctor left, however, the ailing philosopher began vomiting up copious amounts of bile and fluid. Hegel took to bed early, but had a long and restless night, in which he was plagued by severe cramping abdominal pains. Marie kept a vigil at her husband's bedside throughout the night, reassuring him, wiping his sweaty brow, and repeatedly applying mustard plasters and leeches to his belly as advised by the doctor. In the early hours of the next morning, an exhausted Hegel fell asleep, followed immediately afterwards by Marie at his side.

The next morning, when Hegel opened his eyes, Marie couldn't help notice that although he was alert and conscious, he was as white as a ghost. He insisted, despite the protestations of his family, on getting out of bed. On his way to the living room, however, he collapsed, and was then too weak to get up. Marie's sons brought a bed into the living room and lay him in that, whereupon he quickly fell asleep. The doctor was called again, and applied another mustard plaster before leaving in what seemed an unseemly haste.

As the day progressed, Hegel's condition deteriorated. He was no longer able to urinate, and started wildly hiccoughing. He then awoke in the middle of the afternoon to a sight that filled him with pure terror. Standing at his bedside were not only his wife and sons, but two doctors in earnest consultation. Hegel immediately knew what this meant: Prussian law required the summoning of a second doctor in cases of suspected cholera. He was too weak to voice his panicked thoughts, so he lay in helpless and terrified silence as the two physicians applied mustard plasters over his feverish body and soaked him in chamomile. He slipped in and out of consciousness as his family prayed at his bedside.

A few hours after the two doctors left, at around 3 p.m., Hegel woke with a start, complaining of tightness in his chest and of not being able to get enough air. His sons turned him on his side and propped his head up with pillows, until he eventually fell asleep again. Soon afterwards, however, his breathing became laboured and erratic, and then much weaker until it stopped and his face turned a stony grey. Hegel's eldest son, Karl, placed his hand on his father's face. It was ice-cold. The doctor was called again. He arrived almost immediately, again with a second physician by his side, and together they pronounced the death of the city's latest cholera victim.

The River

Christiane Hegel did not cope well with the news of her brother's death. Almost immediately, she relapsed into a dark and deep depression. Although she had been discharged from the asylum some years earlier, the physician who looked after her there, Dr Karl Schelling, still saw her regularly. Concerned about her welfare, he insisted that her maid take her to Bad Teinach, a spa town in the nearby Black Forest. He suggested that its healing waters might help lift her out of her melancholic stupor.

A few days before leaving for the spa town, Christiane broke the long silence between her and Marie Hegel. She wrote her a letter which included many pleasant memories of her and her brother's childhood.

Christiane stayed at Bad Teinach throughout the winter, but its health-giving waters weren't enough to assuage the grief and torment she felt at losing her brother. In late January, whilst still at the resort town, she wrote out her will, asking that her possessions be divided equally amongst Hegel's three sons. (At this point she, like everyone else in Hegel's family, was still unaware of Ludwig's fate.)

Three days later, on 2 February 1832, she walked down to the Nagold River and ended her torment by throwing herself into its icy, fast-flowing waters.

Chapter 3

Nietzsche: Human, All Too Human

Hegel, Marx, Nietzsche

At the height of his fame and in the immediate wake of his death, Hegel was seen as the thinker of his age, the spokesman par excellence for post-revolutionary, post-Napoleonic Europe. After his death, Hegel's students hurried to transcribe his lectures, believing he was one of the few who grasped the changes sweeping Europe as the church and aristocracy gave way to Napoleon's vision of a more egalitarian society.

Even after his death, the ebb and flow of Hegel's influence resembled the moving tides of history he had described in his philosophy. His followers split into two opposing camps: the Left Hegelians who believed further revolutionary changes were needed, and the Right Hegelians who ardently defended the Prussian monarchist state.

Within only a few decades of his passing, however, Hegel went from being one of the most admired thinkers in Europe to being all but forgotten. Although his philosophy had convincingly explained the changes in Europe following the French Revolution, the arrival of the Industrial Revolution called for a different perspective.

That different perspective would be provided by a young Left Hegelian called Karl Marx. Twenty years after Hegel's death, Marx developed a philosophical framework that made sense of the Industrial

Revolution, in particular the oppression and exploitation of the newly formed working class.

Marx would transform the next century's political landscape with his radical ideas on how Europe should respond to the challenges and inequities posed by the rise of capitalism and mass industrialization. Although today we refer to these ideas as 'Marxism' or 'Communism', Marx called his theory *dialectical materialism*, in acknowledgement of the fact it was inspired by Hegel's *dialectical idealism*. Marx's main point of difference with Hegel was that he saw historical change determined not by the opposing forces of a universal Spirit or Mind, but by the contrasting *material* relations between the owning and working classes.

Although Hegel's rather mystical philosophy is out of keeping with the scientific, materialistic worldview that dominates contemporary thinking, his interest in understanding history has had a persisting influence, not just in continental philosophy, but more broadly in both academic and popular thought.

By incorporating history into philosophy, Hegel laid the groundwork not only for Marxism, but for the explosive ideas of another continental philosopher. Friedrich Nietzsche would take the lead from Hegel's examination of history to focus on the collapse of Christianity. This *enfant terrible* of nineteenth-century thought would declare, infamously, that 'God is Dead', and warn Europe that a new type of man, a Superman, was needed to face the challenges of this new Godless society.

But simmering beneath Nietzsche's grim pronouncements about the state of Europe lay an even grimmer personal reality. Nietzsche was a complex and sensitive man whose outlook was at least partly coloured by his experiences of being repeatedly rejected in love.

Early life

Nietzsche was born in 1844 in Röcken, a small and otherwise unremarkable village in rural Saxony. His early childhood was marked by a series of devastating traumas. When he was only two years old, he watched his father, a pastor, die from rapidly progressing brain disease. Two years later, his baby brother died, leaving him the only male in a family comprising his mother, his sister, his grandmother, and two elderly aunts.

Despite living in a household full of women, the young Nietzsche didn't receive much in the way of maternal affection. His mother, Franziska, a devout, strict, and stoic Christian lady, was distracted by grief through most of his childhood, and his grandmother and aunts were – like many provincial German women of the time – practical, resourceful, and community-minded, but not generally given to displays of emotion.

Nietzsche was, however, adored by his younger sister, Elisabeth. Filling a void left by his deceased father and emotionally unavailable mother, Elisabeth gave the brittle young Nietzsche a sense he was special – that he was loved. *aww...*

The Scholar

Nietzsche started elementary school at the age of six. There was nothing notable about his academic performance at this time, but he did show an early interest in music and the arts. After sitting through a performance of Handel's *Messiah* at the age of nine, he 'immediately made the decision...to compose something similar'.[1] Staying true to his vow, he wrote at least one piece of music every year from that time until his early twenties. *Musician too*

75

The shy and short-sighted Nietzsche did not, however, mix well with the boys from the 'lower orders', and his mother soon moved him to a private *gymnasium*.[2] In this new environment, he worked 'extremely hard, often until eleven or twelve at night'.[3] At the age of eleven, he developed a passion for Goethe, wrote more than forty of his own poems, and progressed in the piano to a point where he could play Beethoven with ease. Nietzsche's grandfather described him as brighter than 'his own six sons put together'.[4]

By fourteen, Nietzsche had become a serious young aesthete who preferred solitude and the company of books to people. As he would later explain:

> I had, in my young life, already seen a great deal of tragedy and sadness, and was therefore not as wild and jolly as children usually are. My schoolfellows used to tease me on account of my seriousness.[5]

In 1858 Nietzsche received a scholarship to Germany's 'best and most famous secondary school', the *Schulpforta*, where he further immersed himself in music, and made his first forays into ancient history and the classics.[6] At sixteen he was leading his class in both Greek and Latin.

After high school, Nietzsche went on to Bonn University to study theology – an unconscious attempt, perhaps, to please his long-gone father – but he couldn't accept what he saw as the platitudes of religion, and turned to philosophy instead. He also took up philology – the study of ancient texts – an area in which he would prove most gifted.

At Bonn University Nietzsche joined a fraternity, reasoning that it might help him overcome his natural shyness. At first, he felt quite positive about his newfound associates, writing to his mother 'we are all philologists, at the same time all music lovers...I like the older

76

people a lot'.[7] But his feelings about the group soon changed. He left after only seven months, complaining that 'the expression of conviviality on nightly drinking socials…made me highly uneasy…I knew some individuals whose beer materialism I could hardly stand'.[8]

Nietzsche concluded after this brief venture into the wider social world that his temperament was more suited to 'intimate relations with one or two friends', a maxim that would guide his social life from that time onwards.[9]

Nietzsche switched his major to philology, attracted by the excellent reputation of the department's two renowned teachers, Otto Jahn and Friedrich Ritschl. Soon afterwards, however, intellectual differences between Jahn and Ritschl erupted into a fully blown feud, and Ritschl left Bonn to take up a position in Leipzig. Nietzsche decided to relocate as well, as he explained in a letter to his mother and sister in late May 1865:

> I have made up my mind about the choice of university for next year…I intend to go to Leipzig…I don't know if you have heard that our Ritschl will be going to Leipzig; that's the chief reason.[10]

Ritschl, a gentle and supportive teacher, would be the first, but not the last, man to play the role of father-figure in Nietzsche's tumultuous adult life.

In December 1865 Ritschl invited the twenty-one-year-old Nietzsche to tea at his house, where, along with several other students, he was encouraged to form a philological society. Within months, the society, which met every Thursday, had swelled to more than ten members.

On 24 February 1866 Ritschl summoned Nietzsche to his office to discuss a paper on Theognis that Nietzsche had recently presented to the group. Ritschl was astounded that a student in his third semester could produce a work of such high calibre, and suggested he give serious consideration to turning his essay into a book. Ritschl also invited Nietzsche to join his inner circle of professors who met regularly to discuss each other's essays.

But Nietzsche had not abandoned his earlier interest in philosophy. Indeed, he was known to remark to others that he wasn't interested in philology for its own sake, he was primarily interested in it as a means to explore philosophical problems from a different perspective. This attitude would later cause much grief for him and his philological colleagues.

It was around this time, while browsing in a second-hand bookshop in Leipzig, that Nietzsche discovered an 1818 copy of Schopenhauer's *Die Welt als Wille and Vorstellung*. He immediately began 'a close, intense reading', becoming totally 'enthralled by the work'.[11] Schopenhauer's philosophy, somewhat overlooked until then, painted a pessimistic picture of the world that the increasingly misanthropic Nietzsche could readily identify with. In particular, Schopenhauer's description of a 'will to survive' driving all creatures forward through life appealed to Nietzsche, and would greatly influence his own ideas in the years to come.

Nietzsche's interest in Schopenhauer lay dormant, however, while he focussed on his philological studies. He penned papers on Roman history, Greek poetry, and his favourite topic, Greek tragedy. He wrote an essay on Diogenes Laertius, which won a prize and was published in the journal *Rheinisches Museum*. One of his teachers observed that his papers had the ability to 'astonish through their juvenile freshness and penetrating view'.[12]

Nietzsche meets Wagner

Nietzsche first met Richard Wagner at a small party in Leipzig on 8 November 1868. The party was arranged by Ritschl's wife, a close friend of Wagner's sister. Nietzsche had been a fervent admirer of Wagner's work since his late teens – the mythic themes of Wagner's *Tristan and Isolde* had even inspired a few of his own private efforts at composition, and although he had by now developed a firm aversion to social gatherings, Nietzsche had no intention of missing this opportunity to meet his musical idol.

As Nietzsche later relayed in a letter to Erwin Rohde, Wagner was the life of the party. He delighted partygoers by playing excerpts from his latest work, *Die Meistersinger,* and reading humorous passages from his recently published autobiography. Wagner surprised Nietzsche by spending a large part of the evening speaking with him. The two men discovered they shared an interest in the works of Schopenhauer. At the end of the night, Wagner shook Nietzsche's hand, and insisted, 'with great friendliness', that he visit him 'to make music and talk philosophy'.[13]

Although Ritschl had provided Nietzsche with paternal guidance sorely lacking in his younger years, Wagner promised, as a mentor, possibilities well beyond anything Nietzsche had ever imagined. Nietzsche was instantly captivated by the composer's fierce and seemingly limitless ambition.

Ritschl was, however, able to help Nietzsche with the next big step in his career. He secured him a position as full professor at the University of Basel at the unheard of age of only twenty-four. Fortuitously for Nietzsche, the new position was located a few miles from the village in which Wagner lived.

Ritschl, when asked by the outgoing professor at Basel about a suitable successor, spoke of Nietzsche's limitless talents, observing that he had never seen anyone like him in forty years.

The usually reticent Ritschl continued, in this unsolicited reference:

If – God grant – he lives long enough, I prophesy that [Nietzsche] will one day stand in the front rank of German philology. He is now twenty-four years old: strong, vigorous, healthy, courageous physically and morally, so constituted as to impress those of a similar nature...He is the idol and, without wishing it, the leader of the whole younger generation of philologists here in Liepzig who – and they are rather numerous – cannot wait to hear him as a lecturer.[14]

Basel's administrators were so impressed by Ritschl's recommendation they offered Nietzsche the position forthwith, despite the fact he had not even completed his doctorate. His appointment remains, to this day, one of the youngest professorial appointments in history.

Cosima

Wagner lived in Tribschen, a picturesque town on the edge of Lake Lucerne, in a villa he rented for a trifle from his royal patron, King Ludwig of Bavaria.

When Nietzsche arrived at the magnificent lakeside home in the spring of 1869, he found Wagner openly cohabitating with his mistress Cosima von Bülow, the thirty-one-year-old daughter of Hungarian composer Franz Liszt. Cosima had been living there for several years, despite being married to Hans von Bülow, one of Wagner's most esteemed conductors.

Cosima's romantic life at this time was incredibly complicated. In the space of seven years, she had given birth to four daughters, two to von Bülow in 1860 and 1863, and two to Wagner in 1865 and 1867. Von Bülow had raised Wagner's first daughter, Isolde, as his own, resisting repeated requests from Wagner and Cosima for a divorce. During this tumultuous period, Hans von Bülow had continued to conduct for Wagner, presiding over two of his most successful premieres – *Tristan and Isolde* in 1865 and *Die Meistersinger* in 1868.

On 17 May 1869, when Wagner, Cosima, and Nietzsche had their first of many luncheons together on the grounds of Wagner's residence, Nietzsche felt immediately drawn to the sensual and self-assured Cosima. She was pregnant with her third child to Wagner, and her heavily protruding belly, draped in a soft, flowing dress, seemed to accentuate her expectant state rather than hide it (as women in Nietzsche's home town would have done). This flagrant display of fertility provoked a range of new feelings in the young visitor. Nietzsche's exposure to the opposite sex until that time had been limited to the five small-town women he had been raised with. Cosima von Bülow couldn't have come from a more different world. The illegitimate daughter of a short-lived affair between Liszt and a Parisian socialite, she had attended the French capital's best boarding schools, and been raised by expensive governesses who taught her how to conduct herself in society. Her clothes, her hair, her speech (she was fluent in both French and German), the manner in which she carried herself, were all novel for Nietzsche in ways he found both confronting and scintillating.

The first thing to strike Cosima about Nietzsche, on the other hand, was his unfortunate appearance, his large square head bisected by a preposterously oversized moustache. This initial impression of her lover's strange acquaintance soon gave way, however, to feelings of sympathy, even during their first encounter. She became intrigued by this man who, though clearly gifted with a precocious intelligence, seemed to be afflicted by intense emotions and strong opinions about almost everything.

We can catch a glimpse, perhaps, of the charged atmosphere of their early interactions from a letter Nietzsche wrote his sister at this time. In it he asks:

> Do we after all seek rest, peace, and pleasure in our inquiries? No, only truth – even if it be most abhorrent and ugly.[15]

A Cosy Triangle

Nietzsche, Wagner, and Cosima soon became hopelessly enamoured of each other's company. Nietzsche worshipped Wagner, seeing the grandiloquent composer, as Wagner saw himself, as a true hero of the German people, an embodiment of a lineage many Germans believed they had inherited from the ancient Greeks. Wagner was most comfortable when surrounded by admirers, and in Cosima and Nietzsche he now had two in his thrall. Nietzsche and Cosima also became close during this time, frequently exchanging letters whenever Nietzsche was away from what soon became, for him, a second home.

It is easy to understand why Nietzsche felt so drawn to Tribschen: here he had found not only a majestic father figure he could idolise, but the warm maternal presence he had longed for since he was a boy.

In the summer, when Wagner had to leave Tribschen for extended periods to pay visits on patrons and prepare recitals, Nietzsche kept Cosima company. They spent many hours together playing piano, reading poetry, and discussing the parlous state of German politics.

Nietzsche presented Cosima with numerous gifts during this period. He dedicated two lectures to her: his inaugural lecture at Basel University, *Homer and Classical Philology*, and a later presentation called *Socrates and Tragedy*. Cosima confided in her diary that she found the Socrates lecture 'very stimulating'.[16] Whether Nietzsche was trying to impress, educate, or seduce Cosima is unclear, but it seems that from the beginning he considered her an intellectual equal, lending or giving her books on an impressively wide range of topics, from Shakespeare and Schopenhauer to Handel and Renaissance Art. On 19 August 1869, Cosima described how, while she was 'working with the children, a package arrives from Professor Nietzsche: Semper's lectures on architectural styles'.[17]

A few months later, she received 'a little treatise by Prof. Czermak on Schopenhauer's color theory'.[18]

Nietzsche and Cosima spent much time discussing their thoughts on these varied works, with Wagner joining in whenever he was at home.

Cosima revelled in these high-minded discussions with her new friend, but she also appreciated the news and gossip he brought back from Basel. In November 1869, she wrote:

> In the afternoon a visit from Professor Nietzsche, who tells me it is quite incredible what lies are circulating in the world, both written and spoken, about R. (how, for instance, he stands before a mirror in an effort to equate himself with Goethe and Schiller – then about his luxury, his *harem*, his intimacy with the King of Bavaria, whom he incites to all his follies, etc.). We wonder what picture of him will go down in posterity.[19]

The Franco-Prussian War

In 1870 the Franco–Prussian war broke out, and Nietzsche took leave from his position at Basel University to volunteer as a medical orderly. Nietzsche's experiences in this conflict would contribute to his later disdain for Prussian militarism and nationalist politics.

But Nietzsche was soon evacuated from the front after falling seriously ill with diphtheria and dysentery. He recovered quickly, but then developed a new constellation of symptoms – searing headaches and burning pains in his arms and legs. These all-consuming ailments, which would torment him for the rest of his life, were, unbeknownst to Nietzsche, the early signs of syphilis. who was he fucking?!?

Although we don't know exactly how Nietzsche contracted syphilis, one theory is that he visited one of the makeshift brothels that had sprung up behind the front lines soon after the Franco–Prussian conflict began. Others believe it more likely that he caught the illness from a prostitute during his student days. One of Nietzsche's classmates from Bonn, Paul Duessen, recounts a story of the young philologist walking into a brothel whilst on a visit to Cologne, but walking straight out again when he realised what sort of premises he had entered. Thomas Mann would later recount Duessen's story, word for word, in his novel *Doktor Faustus*. In Mann's fictionalised – and much more compelling – account of Nietzsche's misadventure, he returns to the brothel soon afterwards to search for the woman who brushed her arm against his cheek just before he managed to flee.

Christmas Day, 1870

After Nietzsche returned to Basel to convalesce, Wagner and Cosima invited him to stay with them over Christmas.

It just so happened that 25 December 1870 was also the date of Cosima's thirty-third birthday. Early that morning, she received an extraordinary gift from her new husband, Wagner. Along with the rest of the household, she was startled awake by the fanfare of glorious music. It would be the first performance of Wagner's symphonic poem *The Siegfried Idyll*, named after their recently born son.

Nietzsche also presented Cosima with a gift that he had been labouring over for some time – the draft manuscript for his first book, *The Birth of Tragedy.* whou!

The Birth of Tragedy

Although it is today regarded as a seminal work of philosophy, *The Birth of Tragedy* is more a work of textual archeology. Nietzsche uncovered material from ancient Greek texts that he believed had profound implications for our understanding of the origins of Western society.

Nietzsche posited that Ancient Greece had comprised two major societal groups, each with valuable, but opposing, ways of thinking about the world. According to Nietzsche's investigations, the insights of one group had been lost at the dawn of history after its domination and suppression by the other.

These two groups were mystery cults, each with its own Gods and sacred rituals.

The cult that prevailed worshipped Apollo – the God of reason, logic, and light. The Apollonians were ascetic, self-disciplined, and abstemious; they excelled in mathematics, geometry, philosophy, and other science-like disciplines of the mind. Nietzsche claimed that the whole Western philosophical tradition, and the subsequent movements of Christianity, science, and democracy that grew out of it, were a continuation of this Apollonian way of thinking. According to Nietzsche, the works of Socrates, Plato, and Aristotle, which reflect this tradition, represent only one side of the West's ancient Greek birthright.

In *The Birth of Tragedy*, Nietzsche also described a rival cult – defeated, suppressed, and all but forgotten – that had worshipped the God Dionysius. The followers of this cult embraced music, dance, and sexuality. Whereas the Apollonians valued thinking and reasoning, the Dionysians celebrated the realms of feeling and the senses. Nietzsche shocked many readers with details he unearthed of Dionysian cult members honoring their gods of pleasure with orgiastic feasts, at which ritual chanting and feverish ecstatic dancing would culminate in an unbridled release of instinctual passions.

Nietzsche claimed that although our Dionysian history was almost totally suppressed, remnants of it still survive. He believed that the theatre, in particular the ancient theatrical form of the *tragedy*, had its origins in the rites of the Dionysians. *Fact*

In *The Birth of Tragedy*, Nietzsche provided a vivid account of what patrons in Ancient Greece might have experienced at a performance of one of these early tragedies. A chorus of singers chanted the story, using repetition to draw the audience into an ecstatic trance. The storyline always featured a central character who possessed great strengths, but also a flaw (most commonly hubris) that would, inevitably, lead to his downfall. Fate would also play an important role in the hero's demise.

Nietzsche believed that the tragedy in theatre, and a few other musical and dance forms, were the only remaining vestiges of our suppressed Dionysian heritage. He saw music, particularly the music that accompanied these early tragic performances, as one of the most precious gifts bequeathed by the Dionysians. He devoted a whole section of *The Birth of Tragedy* to his thoughts about what music in his time best reflected this important but forgotten aspect of cultural history. He concluded that the contemporary composer who best captured the gravitas of this glorious heritage was Richard Wagner.

Although Nietzsche's first work was clearly influenced by his adulation of Wagner, its central premise – that Western civilization had lost something precious by having its sensual side suppressed – was almost certainly also inspired by his close association with Cosima von Bülow. He started work on *The Birth of Tragedy* immediately after meeting Cosima, and it was to her that he presented his first draft.

Nietzsche's feelings for Cosima, a woman much freer – sexually and intellectually – than any he had previously encountered, would later be revealed in the most dramatic of circumstances, but for now they could only be expressed in a disguised form in his first work of philosophy.

A few months before Nietzsche gave Cosima the *Birth of Tragedy*, he had lent her a book called *The Philosophy of the Unconscious* by Eduard von Hartmann. Perhaps, with this gift, he was trying to hint at the feelings he had for her, but was unable to disclose, even to himself. Cosima returned the book largely unread, however, complaining that its ideas only aroused in her feelings of great repugnance.[20]

One can also see how Nietzsche's emotionally deprived childhood might have contributed to the themes he explored in his first work. Surely this awkward and conflicted pastor's son was, at least in part, referring to himself when he 'discovered' – in the ancient texts he read – evidence of the tragic suppression of human sensuality.

Reception

Soon after *The Birth of Tragedy* was published in 1872, several articles and pamphlets appeared denouncing the work, including one by leading philologist Ulrich von Wilamowitz, who wrote that Nietzsche's 'imaginary genius and impudence in the presentation of his claims stand in direct relation to his ignorance and lack of love of the truth'.[21]

With his controversial work, Nietzsche had committed several unforgivable sins in the eyes of his fellow philologists.

First, he had given free rein to his imagination, an unacceptable transgression in a discipline that was, at the time, trying to establish itself as a serious science.

Nietzsche's greater sin, however, may have been to suggest that the ancient Greeks were not the pure and undivided paragon of virtue that most philologists held them to be. For many, ancient Greece was the aspirational model on which a new united German state could be built, guided by the highest principles of reason and aesthetic purity. Nietzsche had dared to challenge this idealised representation.

Nietzsche's colleagues were also irritated by the fact that *The Birth of Tragedy* was not a pure work of philology, but rather a confusing mishmash of philology, psychology, philosophy, and Wagnerian hagiography. Even Friedrich Ritschl felt unable to defend his former protégé's strange new work, dismissing it as 'geistreiche Schwiemelei' [ingenious inebriation].[22]

Nietzsche's peers turned against him with a brutal vehemence, fanned, perhaps, by a feeling that one of their most promising young stars had betrayed them. Academics throughout the country advised their students to stay away from his lectures.

A couple of lone voices did speak up in Nietzsche's defence. Edwin Rohde wrote a piece in the *Norddeutsche Allgemeine Zeitung* praising Nietzsche's debut work, and Wagner wrote an open letter supporting his young friend. This letter, however, opened Nietzsche up to accusations he was an intellectual lackey for the controversial composer, accusations he would find difficult to dispel in the coming years.

The efforts of Nietzsche's friends were, however, not enough to salvage his reputation. In an acknowledgement that his career in philology was over, Nietzsche requested a transfer to the philosophy department, but was refused. Although the university continued to employ him for several more years, his presence was tolerated, no longer celebrated as it had been before.

Although *The Birth of Tragedy* spelled the end of Nietzsche's academic career, it only increased his standing in Tribschen. Wagner and Cosima immediately warmed to its themes of a lost sensuality that urgently needed to be reclaimed. On 3 January 1872 Cosima described the atmosphere in her home on the day the first published copy appeared:

> Arrival of Professor Nietzsche's book *The Birth of Tragedy*. [Richard says] he is happy to have lived to have read it. He calls me his priestess of Apollo – he says I am the Apollonian element, he is the Dionysian...[23]

Two days later, Cosima and Richard read the book together 'with solemn feelings and ever-increasing pleasure'. On finishing the book, Wagner told Cosima:

> This is the book I have been longing for.[24]

Although *The Birth of Tragedy* sold few copies when it was originally published, its central message – that society had become unbalanced with its idolisation of the mind at the expense of the body – would resonate greatly with future generations.

As Nietzsche saw it, society had set itself on a perilous course by disregarding the world of emotion, feeling, and sensuality. With his rediscovery of this important aspect of ourselves, Nietzsche anticipated the ideas of Sigmund Freud, the father of psychoanalysis. Echoing Nietzsche's observations, Freud would soon speak of a seething id of unconscious instinctual urges haunting every human heart.

Falling Out

In the wake of Nietzsche's controversial first work, the feelings of mutual admiration between him, Wagner, and Cosima only increased, helped along by a sense they were all under siege from a world that didn't understand. As Cosima observed:

We are literally being outlawed; yesterday the dean told us that one of the precepts of the Catholic party is that its members must speak against Wagner…I told R. I believed that we had now entered a particularly bad phase as far as the outside world is concerned. He laughs and says, "Oh, it is always bad."[25]

Even during their happiest days together, however, there were signs this idyllic situation would not last. On 19 September 1969, Cosima described an argument between Wagner and Nietzsche about, of all things, vegetarianism:

Coffee with Prof. Nietzsche; unfortunately he vexes R. very much with an oath he has sworn not to eat meat, but only vegetables. R. considers this nonsense, arrogance as well, and when the Prof. says it is morally important not to eat animals, etc., R. replies that our whole existence is a compromise, which we can only expiate by producing some good…Since the Prof. admits that Richard is right, yet nevertheless sticks to his abstinence, R. becomes angry.[26]

Over time, Nietzsche's relationship with Wagner shifted from one in which he acted largely as Wagner's mouthpiece to one in which he felt increasingly emboldened to voice his own opinions.

On 3 August 1871 Cosima noted, somewhat ominously:

Lunch [with]…Nietzsche…The latter is certainly the most gifted of our young friends, but a not quite natural reserve makes his be-havior in many respects most displeasing. It is as if he were trying to resist the overwhelming effect of Wagner's personality.[27]

Wagner and Nietzsche's diverging views about Germany became a frequent source of conflict. During one of their discussions, Nietzsche declared that using the German language no longer gave him any pleasure, and he would rather speak Latin. For Wagner, who had an unwavering belief that the new German state was destined for great-ness, this statement bordered on the sacrilegious.

More fuel was thrown on this fire in the autumn of 1876, when Nietzsche invited two friends to lunch, the writer Malwida von Meysenbug and scholar Paul Rée. Nietzsche had first met Rée in 1873, when the latter was working on a dissertation exploring psychological approaches to the problems of philosophy. Rée's ideas had recently been published in his first book, *Psychologiste Beobachtungen* (Psychological Observations), and Nietzsche was looking forward to discussing its contents.

But the luncheon did not go well.

Nietzsche immediately noticed that it lacked the *joie de vivre* usually associated with gatherings at the Wagner household. The whole afternoon, in fact, was punctuated by long and uncomfortable silences; Wagner and Cosima hardly contributed to the conversation at all. Meysenbug would later record how Nietzsche tried to compensate for this unpleasant atmosphere by putting on 'a certain forced naturalness and cheerfulness, that was otherwise quite foreign to him'.[28]

The next day, Nietzsche found out the reason for his hosts' unusual behaviour. During a long walk with Nietzsche, Wagner explained the reasons for his 'insuperable aversion' to Rée, the most prominent being the fact that he was Jewish.[29] Wagner ended the conversation by advising Nietzsche how helpful the Christian sacraments could be in warding off malign influences such as that posed by his new associate.

Wagner was fully supported in his prejudices by Cosima, who wrote in her diary on the day of the luncheon:

Dr. Rée['s] cold and precise character does not appeal to us; on closer inspection we come to the conclusion that he must be an Israelite.[30]

Later, Cosima would provide, in a letter to a friend, her perspective on how Rée had caused her and her husband's friendship with Nietzsche to unravel:

Israel came...in the form of Dr. Rée, very smooth, very cool, at the same time captivated and subjugated by Nietzsche, in truth however duped by him [Rée], a microcosm of the relationship between Judea and Germany.[31]

Cosima went on to explain that as a result of Rée's influence, Nietzsche had 'broken faith with Schopenhauer and Wagner'. She concluded, rather dramatically, that 'evil has triumphed here'.[32]

Wagner's snubbing of Nietzsche's Jewish friend brought tensions that had been building between the two men to a boiling point. The final rupture in their increasingly fraught relationship came, however, when Nietzsche published a piece called *Richard Wagner in Bayreuth*. Nietzsche wrote this piece, more or less at Wagner's bidding, to help launch a new centre for the arts that Wagner was setting up in Bayreuth. By the time Nietzsche had completed the final draft of this essay, his increasing resentment of Wagner couldn't help but find its way into the text. While the essay rather grudgingly acknowledged Wagner's genius, it also alluded to his many shortcomings; at one point it referred to him as a seductive destroyer of all who came within his power. Wagner responded to these accusations by cutting off all communications with Nietzsche, telling all who would listen that Nietzsche's misguided views were the result of him falling under the influence of degenerate Jewish friends.

From that time on, open warfare broke out between the two men. They took turns publishing increasingly acrimonious articles about each other, but never spoke to each other ever again.

Cosima would later destroy all her correspondence with Nietzsche. Whether she did this out of loyalty to her husband, or to keep something hidden about the nature of her friendship with Nietzsche, we will never know.

Proposal in Geneva

Leaving the rancour of his falling out with Wagner behind, Nietzsche decided to take a trip to Geneva. He hoped that such a trip might improve his health. In recent months, his eyes had had become extremely sensitive to light, and, as he complained in a letter to Rohde: *C*

> It still goes badly with my head, I can't read or write, and [I have] now...given up all lecturing. A pretty piece of animal torture![33]

Whilst in Geneva, Nietzsche visited Hugo von Senger, Director of the Geneva Orchestra, whom he had met through Wagner a few years earlier. Von Senger insisted on introducing him to his piano students Mathilde and Anna Trampedach, two sisters who had arrived from Riga with their parents two years earlier and were staying in a boarding house not far from von Senger's residence.

When the women first encountered Nietzsche on their sunlit verandah, they didn't know whether to laugh or take pity on him. As Mathilde recalled:

> Unfortunately we couldn't see [him] since...he held a thickly-lined green sun-shade over his head, undoubtedly on account of his weak eyes.[34]

When Nietzsche's vision had improved enough for him to venture outside, he joined von Senger and the Trampedach sisters for a stroll along the shore of Lake Geneva. On this occasion, Nietzsche made a more favourable impression on twenty-one-year-old Mathilde and eighteen-year-old Anna, charming them with his extensive knowledge of the great poets. During this discussion, Nietzsche remarked in passing that he had never read Longfellow's *Excelsior*. Mathilde, who as propriety dictated had let the gentlemen dominate the conversation until then, mentioned she would be happy to write out a German translation. Nietzsche was immediately impressed by his new acquaintance's gracious manner and advanced literary tastes.

Von Senger arranged a carriage to take the four of them on a tour of the city's sights, including the villa in which Lord Byron once lived. During this outing the men spoke approvingly of Byron's concern for liberating the oppressed people of the world. Mathilde remarked that she found it quite strange that men were so interested in removing oppression in society, when clearly they were all so oppressed themselves. After this provocation, Mathilde would later recall looking up and catching 'Nietzsche's intense eyes fixed on me'.[35]

Nietzsche, it seems, did not sleep well that night, for he was on Mathilde's doorstep at an early hour the next morning, unannounced and in a state of agitation. When Mathilde answered the door, she was greeted by a spectacle even more bizarre than the first day she had met Nietzsche:

> He came to say goodbye and was led into the reception hall where he greeted us with a solemn bow. Then he turned to the piano and began to play with increasing waves of stormy feeling until these subsided into solemn harmonies, finally disappearing into a *pianissimo*. Shortly after, he parted without a word.[36]

Nietzsche left Geneva that day, but before departing he handed von Senger a letter to give to Mathilde. It read:

> Gather together all the courage of your heart, and be not frightened by the question I hereby address to you: are you willing to become my wife? I love you and for me it is as though you already belonged to me. Not a word [to anyone] about the suddenness of my inclination! At least there is no blame in the matter, nothing therefore needs to be excused. But what I would like to know is if you feel as I do – that we have not been strangers to each other, not for an instant.[37]

Unfortunately for Nietzsche, however, Mathilde was already involved in a secret affair with von Senger and would become his wife within a year. Although Mathilde couldn't accept Nietzsche's proposal, she was flattered enough to put the letter away for safekeeping, holding on to it for the rest of her life. She also wrote a kindly worded response, leaving its recipient in no doubt as to her positive feelings towards him.

In Nietzsche's subsequent reply, he was clearly in a more thoughtful state of mind than at the time of his impetuous proposal:

> You are sufficiently magnanimous to forgive me, I sense it in the gentleness of your letter, which I honestly did not deserve. I have suffered so much from reflecting on my terrible, violent manner of behaving that I cannot be grateful enough for this gentleness.[38]

As he approached his thirty-third year, Nietzsche was, once again, alone.

He had only ever been interested in two women, but both had been bound by stronger loyalties elsewhere.

Cosima and Mathilde both displayed a quality that would always appeal to Nietzsche – independence of spirit. In the wake of these rejections, however, Nietzsche was coming to the view it was safer to embrace his own independence than seek it in another. As he confided in a letter to his colleague von Gersdorff at around this time:

> I won't marry; in the end, I hate restrictions and being enmeshed in the whole "civilised" order of things.

In any case, he added:

> Hardly any woman will be free-spirited enough to follow me.[39]

Nietzsche's 'Middle Period'

In 1882 Nietzsche travelled further south to Italy, driven by what had become a never-ending quest for warm weather to relieve his worsening health problems. He was now suffering almost constant pains in his limbs as the syphilis progressed inexorably throughout his nervous system.

Nietzsche had resigned his post at Basel University three years earlier, and more recently had renounced his German citizenship, disgusted by what he saw as the militarism and mindless conformity of German people during and after the Franco-Prussian war. He had applied for Swiss citizenship, but his application was refused, leaving him stateless. He consulted two physicians during this period, including Dr Otto Eiser, who noted that his patient had 'considerable damage to the retina in both eyes, which is with virtual certainty the cause of his headaches, and to which must be added a general predisposition to irritability'.[40] The doctor failed, however, to detect the venereal cause of Nietzsche's symptoms, nor was he able to offer any effective treatments.

Despite his suffering, or perhaps as a result of it, Nietzsche had managed to write three major works since *The Birth of Tragedy*. In *Human, All Too Human*; *The Gay Science*; and *The Dawn*, Nietzsche left behind any ideal of German superiority, and with it, his idolization of Wagner. In *Human, All Too Human*, published in 1878, he expressed his ideas in short provocative aphorisms more in the style and tradition of French literature. (The most famous of Nietzsche's aphorisms, 'Whatever does not kill me, makes me stronger', is still heavily quoted today.) $\quad \mathrel{\rightarrow}$ Kelly Clarkson

In *The Dawn* (1881), Nietzsche controversially declared himself an 'immoralist' opposed to all ethical systems, whether they be Christian, Kantian, or Utilitarianist. With this work, Nietzsche started in earnest what he would eventually become best known for – railing against the reason and reasonableness of polite, self-satisfied Enlightenment and Christian thinking.

Although these works of Nietzsche's so-called 'middle period' lacked a systematic focus, they contained seeds of ideas he would later examine in great detail, including his notion that 'the will to power' lies at the heart of all human behaviour. He also explored, in depth, the role of the artist and free thinker (*Freigeist*) in society. He challenged the belief that great art comes from divine inspiration and genius, arguing, instead, that it mostly comes from hard work.

Not many people, however, were noticing Nietzsche's hard work at this time. Of a thousand copies of *Human, All Too Human* he had printed in 1878, only a hundred and twenty were sold.

Invitation

Although his books weren't selling, Nietzsche still had a handful of loyal supporters. One of these, Malwida von Meysenbug, had taken an interest in the troubled philosopher since his falling out with Wagner. In April 1882 she invited him to visit her famous literary salon in Rome. Boasting a glorious location overlooking the Colosseum, her residence attracted artists and intellectuals from all over Europe.

Meysenbug wanted, in particular, to introduce Nietzsche to a young woman called Lou Salomé, who, along with her mother, had been staying with Meysenbug for several months. In Meysenbug's letter of invitation to Nietzsche, she highlighted Salomé's impressive intellect, telling him: 'she strikes me as someone who has reached much the same philosophical conclusions as you'.[41]

Nietzsche had also heard about Salomé from Paul Reé, who had visited Meysenbug a few weeks earlier, and written to Nietzsche insisting he come to Rome to meet this extraordinary young woman. Rée didn't mention, however, that he had already fallen in love with her.

When Nietzsche finally arrived at Meysenbug's salon and met Salomé, he, too, was immediately taken. He relayed his first impressions in a letter to his friend Paul Gast:

> Lou is the daughter of a Russian general, and she is twenty years old; she is as shrewd as an eagle and brave as a lion, and yet still a very girlish child.[42]

He would later add:

> She [seems] amazingly well prepared for my way of thinking and my ideas.[43]

Salomé

Salomé, unlike Nietzsche, was born into a life of great privilege. Her father was a high-ranking officer in the Russian army, and the family had grown up 'in the very heart of Imperial Russia, directly across from the Romanov Winter Palace'.[44] Salomé's father, like many Russian officers at the time, had literary leanings, counting amongst his friends the acclaimed poets Pushkin and Lermontov.

As a child, Salomé charmed all around her, but none more so than her doting father. When she rebelled at pressure from her parents to learn Russian at school (she already spoke German and French in the home), her father quickly surrendered, agreeing to let her pursue studies in whatever she liked.

At the age of seventeen, Salomé wrote to Henrik Gillot, a Dutch preacher whose sermons were the rage of St Petersburg, and asked if he could provide her with private lessons. In her letter to Gillot, sent without her parents' consent or knowledge, she explained:

The person writing to you, Herr Pastor, is a seventeen-year-old girl who is lonely in the midst of her family and surrounds, lonely in the sense that no one shares her views, let alone satisfies her longing for a fuller knowledge.[45]

Gillot, a forty-year-old man with two young children, agreed to meet Salomé discreetly for private lessons. The pastor was surprised to find 'that the seventeen-year-old could quickly absorb anything he gave her'.[46] She read Descartes and Pascal in French, and even learned Dutch so that she could read Gillot's copies of Kant. Within months she was writing 'insightful notes on Kierkegaard, Rousseau, Voltaire, Spinoza, and Schopenhauer'.[47]

But then Salomé started to have fainting spells. It is unclear if these were due to exhaustion, exhilaration, or some incipient physical condition, but we know she hardly slept at all during this period as she frantically tried to absorb all the knowledge provided in these lessons. Later, in her memoirs, she would describe how she fell into a sort of trance whenever she was in her pastor's presence. When, on one occasion, she fainted on her tutor's lap, he was no longer able to hold back his feelings. In the quiet of his darkened study, he proposed to her, promising to leave his wife and children if she agreed to marry him.

Salomé idolized Gillot, but had never thought of him as a lover, let alone a husband. Even at that young age, she could see that marriage would lead to children, and the almost certain loss of the intellectual independence she so desperately craved.

When Salomé's recently widowed mother learnt of these developments, she immediately cancelled the lessons and forbade Salomé from ever seeing Gillot again.

Salomé took refuge in her bedroom, where she continued her studies at such a frenetic pace that her mother became quite alarmed. When she started coughing up blood, her mother decided it was time to remove her from St Petersburg, not only for her health, but to find a less fraught environment in which she could continue her education. The two women travelled to Zurich, at that time the only city in Europe with a university that accepted female students. During her studies in Zurich, Salomé fell ill again, at which point a mutual friend gave her and her mother a letter of introduction to Meysenbug, who invited Salomé to convalesce with her in Rome.

Another triangle

And so, in late April 1882, Salomé, Salomé's mother, Meysenbug, Rée, and Nietzsche had several memorable meetings in Meysenbug's salon. Rée and Nietzsche took it upon themselves to show Salomé the sights of Rome, from St Peter's Basilica to the many sunny outcrops of ruins scattered throughout the city. As each day passed, the three of them grew closer, their feelings fuelled by long, passionate discussions about poetry, music, and literature.

Nietzsche was delighted to encounter a woman with such breadth and depth of knowledge. He heard how Salomé had, in Zurich, complemented her earlier readings with studies in comparative religion, familiarising herself with the Tao-te-Ching, the Vedic scriptures, and the writings of Confucius.

Nietzsche found he had more in common with Salomé than just an insatiable hunger for knowledge. She, too, had lost her faith and was seeking answers elsewhere. And she, like him, had left her home country, propelled into exile by a combination of illness, scandal, and disillusionment. Nietzsche entertained the thought, despite his earlier vows, that he might have found – in the confident and free-spirited Salomé – a woman he could share his life with.

Once again, Nietzsche found himself in competition with a close friend and rival for the object of his affections. In a letter he wrote his friend Overbeck, he seems to be trying to reassure himself, as much as Overbeck, of the unproblematic nature of his latest triangular intrigue:

> Rée and I share the identical feelings toward our brave and valiant friend [Salome] and he and I have *enormous trust* in one another...on this point.[48]

There are conflicting accounts about the sequence of events that followed Nietzsche's introduction to Salomé, but according to at least one report, both Rée and Nietzsche proposed to her during that Roman spring. Whatever the truth, we know that Salomé advised both men she didn't believe in marriage, and that she preferred a more open arrangement in her relations with men.

The nature of Salomé's relationship with Nietzsche and Rée is magnificently captured in an infamous photograph taken at around this time. In this portrait, Salomé stands, slightly elevated, on a small chariot wielding a whip, whilst before her, in reins, stand her two admirers. The positioning for this photo, the only one that survives of the three of them together, was suggested by Salomé, who clearly had a mischievous sense of humour.

Salomé also made another, more serious, suggestion during this time. She proposed that the three of them set up an academic commune in the countryside, where they could live together and study, unconstrained by the strictures of society. This was a tremendously appealing proposition for Nietzsche for several reasons. It would not only give the stateless philosopher a place he could call home, it would provide him with a base to carry out his ambitious study plans. Over the next ten years, he planned to deeply immerse himself in the study of science to complement his readings in the humanities. He could think of no one better to share this journey with than the intellectually precocious Salomé. It also seems safe to assume that he hoped, in the near future, to be sharing more than ideas with her.

All these plans would have to wait, however, as Salomé and her mother were soon due to leave Rome for a previously arranged trip to the Italian Alps.

Monte Sacro

In May, Salomé and her mother were joined by Rée and Nietzsche in Orta San Giulio, a historic lakeside village in the alpine region of Piedmont.

Soon after their arrival, the four travellers took advantage of the glorious weather to hire a boat around Lake Orta and out to the monastery island of San Giulio. They also explored the ancient town's narrow, winding streets, and took several long treks in the mountains.

After a few days, Salomé's mother and Rée both needed a day of rest. Nietzsche took advantage of this opportunity to invite Salomé on a hike with him to Monte Sacro, a wooded hill with spectacular views of the surrounding countryside.

But Nietzsche and Salomé were gone for many more hours than one would expect for such an expedition, and they returned to a rather hostile reception. Salomé's mother was horrified that her daughter had ventured off for so long without a chaperone, and Rée fell into a sullen silence on seeing Nietzsche return in such a buoyant mood.

Nietzsche, however, was not in the least concerned about his travelling companions' feelings, as he had just experienced what he would later refer to as 'the most delightful dream of [his] life'.[49]

Despite the best efforts of both Nietzsche's and Salomé's biographers, we still don't know what happened that afternoon on Monte Sacro. Most have surmised that some sort of intimate exchange took place – whether it was some carefully chosen words, an embrace, or even a kiss, we will never know. When Salomé was asked directly about the incident many years later, she offered, rather cryptically:

I no longer recall whether I kissed Nietzsche on Monte Sacro, or not.[50]

We do know, however, that Nietzsche's demeanour changed dramatically from that day onwards. In particular, his hopes of a relationship with Salomé seemed to have become irrevocably inflamed.

When Nietzsche visited his friends the Overbecks in Basel a few days later, he was still 'in a state of jubilant animation'.[51] They had never seen him like this before – 'he talked incessantly, mostly about Lou… [l]ike a man who has caught sight of the promised land'.[52] Even his health problems had temporarily receded; he no longer complained of headaches, painful eyes, or aching limbs, and his skin seemed to shine with a new vibrant glow. He announced with great solemnity during this visit that the time had come for him to emerge from solitude.

Monte Sacro is certainly the sort of place in which one could imagine such a life-changing event taking place. Its beautiful baroque chapels, each housing a tableau portraying a moment in the life of St Francis of Assisi, have overawed thousands of pilgrims and visitors before and since Nietzsche and Salomé's fateful climb to the mount. Listed today as a World Heritage Site, one can see how its sacred silence, broken only by the song of the nightingales and distant shouts of oarsmen from Lake Orta below, might have inspired these two restless souls to temporarily abandon their usual defences.

A couple of days after this incident, the travelling party went their separate ways. Salomé returned to Zurich to continue her studies, Rée went to his family home in Stibbe in western Prussia, and Nietzsche – after his brief visit to the Overbecks in Basel – returned to Naumburg to stay with his mother.

Rivalry

Over the next two months, Rée and Nietzsche both sent Salomé a steady stream of letters, as each tried desperately to gain her exclusive affection. Rée, now feeling quite threatened by the turn of events at Monte Sacro, no longer pretended to be loyal to his rival, who, until recently, he had regarded as his closest friend.

Rée started using the informal *du* in his letters to Salomé, a familiarity that Nietzsche would never presume to take. In a long, rambling letter Rée wrote Salomé at the end of May, he told her she was the only person he loved in the whole world. In the same missive, he proposed a strange plan. He explained that his mother was willing to 'adopt' her as a daughter, so that she could come and live with him in Stibbe. He explained:

> When you are with my family and myself Nietzsche will grasp all the more quickly that you wish to reject the idea of being for a long time with him, particularly with him alone.[53]

Rée went on to tell Salomé he had not mentioned his 'adoption' plan to Nietzsche, as 'he is likely to see it as a maneuver to keep you from him'.[54] (Which, of course, it was.) Rée concluded with a confession that would have been obvious to anyone who had read his letter thus far:

> In my relationship to Nietzsche I am not altogether frank and honest, especially since a certain little girl from abroad appeared.[55]

Nietzsche trod a more balanced path, and in his correspondence with Salomé, at least, demonstrated a greater respect for his friend and rival. On 24 May he told Salomé: 'In everything, Rée is a better friend than I am or can be; please observe this difference.'[56] Nietzsche may have felt, since Monte Sacro, that he could afford to be generous – and even uncharacteristically humble. But he left Salomé in no doubt about his feelings with the last line of his letter:

> When I am entirely alone, I very often say your name out loud – to my greatest delight![57]

Nietzsche's newfound confidence would be short-lived, however. In June, he became quite alarmed on hearing that Salomé was planning a visit to Rée in Stibbe. Knowing that she would need to stop overnight in Berlin on the way there, he proposed to meet her in the Prussian capital, presumably with a hope that he could persuade her to permanently defer the rest of her trip. He wrote:

> My dear friend…
>
> Here is the latest plan I have conceived…I want to go to Berlin during the time when you will be in Berlin; once I have arrived, I will immediately withdraw into one of the beautiful deep forests in the neighbourhood of Berlin – near enough so that we can meet when we like, when you like…For sincerely, I would *very much* like to find myself alone with you, as soon as possible.[58]

On 16 June Nietzsche made a dash to Berlin to meet Salomé in the city's Grunewald forest, but it seems there was, at best, a misunderstanding. He waited there, on his own, for several hours before making the long trip back to Naumburg, knowing that Salomé was almost certainly on her way to Rée.

Bayreuth

In July Nietzsche came up with a plan to lure Salomé away from Rée's family home. He decided to invite her to the Bayreuth festival. Although Nietzsche had fallen out with Wagner, he knew the grand musical event – now renowned throughout Europe – would be difficult for Salomé to resist. He suggested she stay with him in the nearby village of Tautenburg after attending the festival. To his delight, she accepted.

Rée tried to talk Salomé out of this plan. He warned her that accepting such an offer would give the impression she was betrothed to Nietzsche. Salomé didn't share Rée's concerns, but to reassure him, she came up with an extraordinary proposal. She offered to keep a diary addressed to Rée for the whole of the trip that he could read when she returned.

Nietzsche arranged for his sister Elisabeth to act as a chaperone for Salomé during the visit. If Nietzsche was concerned about conflict arising between his sister, who could be rather possessive, and Salomé, he didn't show it. On the contrary, he wrote to Salomé before her arrival:

My sister...is mightily pleased by the thought of being in your and my proximity.[59]

In a subsequent letter, Nietzsche explained to Salomé why he wouldn't be attending the festival, but would be waiting to meet her and Elisabeth in Tautenburg after it was over:

I would like you to read, beforehand, my little work *Richard Wagner in Bayreuth*...I have had such experiences with this man and his work, and it was a passion which lasted a long time...The renunciation that it required, the rediscovery of myself that eventually became necessary, was among the hardest and most melancholy things that have befallen me.[60]

Salomé thoroughly enjoyed herself at the festival, but Elisabeth was appalled at the way she flirted with many of the men they met there. Elisabeth, no doubt, felt a little resentful at the ease with which her young companion ingratiated herself with the fashionable festival crowd. Salomé communed at length with the painter Paul Joukowsky about spirituality, and partook in a playful and very public intellectual joust with the philosopher Heinrich von Stein, where she displayed, according to one observer, 'astounding dialectical virtuosity'.[61] To Elisabeth's horror, Salomé also showed several of her new admirers the chariot photograph of her, Rée, and Nietzsche. Elisabeth thought this was incredibly disrespectful of her brother.

On the way from Bayreuth to Tautenburg, an argument erupted between the two women. It began with Elisabeth giving Salomé a lecture about the impeccable morals of her 'pure-minded' brother.[62] Salomé took great offence at Elisabeth's insinuations and made it clear that in her view her brother wasn't as blameless as she liked to think. The rest of the trip took place in stony silence.

Tautenburg

When Elisabeth and Salomé arrived in Tautenburg, Nietzsche introduced them to their lodgings in the homestead of the local pastor, Johann Köselitz, a few minutes' walk from where Nietzsche was staying. Nietzsche had explained to Köselitz, as he had to his increasingly sceptical sister, that Salomé was there primarily as a student, to prepare for the academic community they, along with Rée, planned to set up in the near future. It is highly unlikely Nietzsche still believed this was going to eventuate, but it was a convenient way to explain why he and Salomé needed to spend so much time alone in the Tautenburg forest. Nietzsche was, in fact, at pains to ensure their rendezvous did not become a 'topic of European gossip'.[63] He even wrote to Pastor Köselitz beforehand, asking him to 'please do the two of us the honour of keeping the concept of a love affair far distant from our relationship'.[64]

But such a façade did not last long. Nietzsche and Salomé did everything they could to exclude Elisabeth, so that for most of the time she was chaperone in name only. Nietzsche would later look back on the weeks in the summer of 1882 as the happiest of his life. An entry in Salomé's diary shows how much she, too, enjoyed this time with Nietzsche:

> We are...spending happy hours at the edge of the forest on a bench near his farmhouse. How good it feels to laugh and to dream and to chat in the evening sunshine when the last rays fall on us through the branches of the trees.[65]

In another entry that was highly unlikely to reassure Rée, Salomé described how:

> At the village inn, when I arrive wearing my cap and Nietzsche without Elizabeth, and where one sits under the linden trees with their big branches, [the townsfolk] consider us to belong together as much as do you and I.[66]

Later, Salomé spells out to Rée the stark differences she sees between him and Nietzsche. Rée works with a 'clock in the hand', whereas Nietzsche, like her, is totally obsessed with his work:

> Every emotion that is not related to it appears to him as a kind of unfaithfulness. You do not have your heart stuck in your brain and indissolubly connected with it to the same degree as Nietzsche.[67]

It was during these weeks that Nietzsche wrote his famous treatise on style for Salomé, advising her that good writing must 'entice the senses', and how, as a writer, 'one must learn to feel everything'.[68]

Elisabeth became increasingly concerned as she watched these events unfold. On one occasion, when Salomé fell ill and took to bed for the day, she came across her brother trying to talk to Salomé through the bedroom door.

Eventually, Elisabeth decided that she needed to intervene. She confronted Nietzsche with her views about Salomé, warning him he was consorting with a fallen woman, a wicked seductress, a manipulator. When it became evident that he was totally impervious to her concerns, Elisabeth accosted Salomé directly, accusing her of trying to take advantage of her brother. In a letter Elisabeth later wrote to one of her friends, she described how taken aback she was by Salomé's response, who declared:

> It was your noble, pure-minded brother who first had the dirty idea of a concubinate!' ... [w]ho has first dragged our idea of staying together into the dirtiest mud.[69]

Salomé then added:

> Don't think for a moment that I am interested in your brother or in love with him, I could sleep in the same room with him, without getting any wild ideas.[70]

According to Elisabeth's letter, the mutual incriminations and accusations escalated from there, continuing until 'late in the evening'.[71]

It is unclear whether Salomé's outburst reflected her true feelings. Either way, it had the effect of bringing her visit to a precipitous end. She packed her things the next day and proceeded straight to Stibbe to be reunited with a very relieved Rée.

Although Salomé had clearly felt a deep intellectual affinity with Nietzsche, she had also, undoubtedly, found him overwhelming, and, at times, even a little frightening. Her Tautenburg diary, in the last days, refers to his violent mood swings and strong emotions, and includes a reassurance to Rée that despite her appreciation of Nietzsche's prodigious intellect and imagination, 'in the depth of [their] beings', they were 'worlds apart'.[72] She told Rée that within Nietzsche she sensed 'many a dark dungeon and hidden cellar that does not surface in the course of a brief acquaintance, yet could contain his very essence'.[73]

Despite Salomé's reservations about Rée, for reasons that were almost opposite to her concerns about Nietzsche, she travelled soon afterwards with him to Berlin, where the two lived together as lovers for several years.

Salomé would go on to have an illustrious career as a renowned intellectual and author, and become one of the first female psychoanalysts. She became a respected colleague of Sigmund Freud, writing more than twenty books, including a groundbreaking treatise on female sexuality. She would also have several famous lovers, including the poet Rainer Maria Rilke.

Meanwhile, Nietzsche, who at the age of thirty-eight had believed he might have found the ideal life partner in Salomé, was left feeling alone and distraught. It was at around this time that he wrote his final letter to her:

> Lou, dear heart, clear the air! I want nothing else than a pure, clear sky...A lonely man suffers frightfully when he suspects something about the two human beings he loves.[74]

Thus Spake Zarathustra

When it became clear to Nietzsche that Salomé had disappeared out of his life forever, he retreated south once again, this time without any clear plan or purpose. He ended up in the small town of Rapallo on the west Italian coast. Although its mild sea air provided some relief from the wracking syphilitic pain in his limbs, he couldn't shake the grief that had taken hold of him ever since Salomé's departure.

Day after day, Nietzsche walked for hours through Rapallo's narrow streets. Many times he climbed the steps of the town's main landmark, the *Castello sul Mare*, a weathered stone fort that jutted out to sea. From the vantage point of this edifice, built centuries earlier to defend against Barbary pirates, he considered, more than once, hurling himself down into the wind-lashed waves below.

It was in the midst of this despair that Nietzsche's most famous work came to him. As he later explained:

My health was not the best; the winter cold and exceedingly wet, [but] it was during this winter and under these unfavorable circumstances that my Zarathustra came into existence.[75]

Nietzsche wrote continuously, day and night, for ten intense days, as he desperately tried to push any thoughts of Salomé out of his mind. During this frenzy of activity, he produced the text that would become his most celebrated work. Written in a dramatic, allegorical, almost Biblical style, *Thus Spake Zarathustra* opens with its protagonist declaring that 'God is Dead!'[76]

Something critical had died within Nietzsche since the loss of his much-beloved Salomé, and he was now announcing to the world that something had died in their lives too. He pointed out to his readers that the institution that had provided society with its moral direction up until now – the Church – had withered to a point where it no longer had any authority. He warned that Western civilization needed a new foundation if it was to avoid drifting into a state of meaningless despair.

Nietzsche's announcement that 'God is dead!' was a shot across the bow, a warning to society of the dangers ahead if it failed to find a replacement for the religion that had, for so long, been Europe's main source of truth, values, and meaning.

The *Superman* or *Overman* (*Übermensch* in the original German) was Nietzsche's term for the new type of human being that was needed if society was to survive and flourish in this post-religious era. Nietzsche saw the *Superman* as the future man who would embrace everything, creating his own life and a belief system greater than any yet existing. The *Superman* would reject what Nietzsche referred to as the slave morality of Christianity – he would not be weakened by pity,

111

charity, or humility. He would take up the call to his own greatness and resent nothing. Although Nietzsche hinted that such a person had not yet appeared, he cited various individuals he saw as coming close to this ideal – Socrates, Jesus, Caesar, Leonardo da Vinci, Michelangelo, Shakespeare, Goethe, and Napoleon. (There were no women in this list – as far as Nietzsche was concerned, a woman's rightful aspiration was to give birth to such a man.)

Out of the ashes of his grief, Nietzsche had produced in *Thus Spake Zarathustra* a phoenix – a prophetic literary and philosophical masterpiece – that not only diagnosed society's ills and prescribed a cure, but also reflected his own personal anguish at losing the love he had dared to hope for. His notion of the *Superman*, rising above all pain, didn't just provide what society needed, it provided the solace that the devastated philosopher so desperately needed during this, his darkest hour.

The Death of Wagner

The publication of *Thus Spake Zarathustra* in 1883 marked the beginning of the final and most mature period of Nietzsche's work, during which he explored the limits of morality in a post-religious world. Although the collapse of his relationship with Salomé was clearly a trigger for this work, one wonders if he would have arrived at this place, philosophically, if he hadn't first overcome the God-like hold that Wagner had over him.

As if to highlight this fact, Nietzsche heard in the winter of 1883 – whilst he was putting the final touches on *Thus Spake Zarathustra* – that Wagner had died suddenly of a heart attack.

Wagner created scandal even at the moment his death. According to the reports that reached Nietzsche, he had been seized with violent chest pains while in the middle of a heated argument with Cosima over his interest in another woman.

Despite the death of his idol-turned-nemesis, Nietzsche still felt the need, it seems, to exorcise himself of the effects of his earlier association with the composer. He threw himself into writing further pieces disowning the man who had loomed large not only in his mind, but in the wider consciousness of cultivated German society. In his essays *The Case of Wagner* and *Nietzsche Contra Wagner*, Nietzsche posthumously denounced Wagner for his anti-Semitism, and for what he saw as the composer's cowardly alignment with Christianity and the German nationalist *Völkisch* movement.

Having shaken off this last hold the old master had on him, Nietzsche went on to write what many consider his most important works – *Beyond Good and Evil* in 1886 and *On the Genealogy of Morals* in 1887. In these tracts, which were still only reaching a very limited readership, Nietzsche explored in more detail the question that had possessed him to write *Thus Spake Zarathustra*: Where to now given that the Church has lost its monopoly on the minds and hearts of men?

Although these works were more temperate in tone than Nietzsche's earlier pieces, one doesn't have to look far within them to detect the rage of a man struggling to come to terms with being rejected in love. Consider this outburst from *On the Genealogy of Morals*:

> '[M]arriage is a barrier and a disaster along [the] route to the optimal. What great philosopher up to now has been married? Heraclitus, Plato, Descartes, Spinoza, Leibniz, Kant, Schopenhauer – none of these got married. What's more, we cannot even imagine them married. A married philosopher belongs in a comedy, that's my principle.'[77]

bitter

113

Nueva Germania

Relations had become highly fraught between Nietzsche and his sister following her successful efforts to eject Salomé from of his life. In 1885 any remaining prospect of reconciliation was completely dashed when Elisabeth married Bernhard Förster, an avowed anti-Semite.

Förster had established a far right political party called the German People's League, which had recently published a document called *Die Sucht nach dem Germanischen Ideal* (*The Search for the Germanic Ideal*). This work had become extremely popular in some pockets of German society, despite its vitriolic and poisonous descriptions of Jews as a 'parasite on the German body'.[78]

In February 1887 Elisabeth and her husband set sail on a journey to Paraguay with fourteen other German families to set up an Aryan commune. Calling their settlement 'Nueva Germania', they hoped to sow the seeds for a new German master race.

Later that year, Nietzsche discovered that his own works were being used by Elisabeth and her husband to promote their views about Jews. Infuriated at this misrepresentation of his beliefs, Nietzsche fired off a letter to his sister, in which he let her know that he was cutting all ties with her:

> I've seen proof, black on white, that Herr Dr. Förster has not yet severed his connection with the anti-Semitic movement…Since then I've had difficulty coming up with any of the tenderness and protectiveness I've so long felt toward you. The separation between us is thereby decided in really the most absurd way. Have you grasped nothing of the reason why I am in the world? …Now it has gone so far that I have to defend myself hand and foot against people who confuse me with these anti-Semitic canaille; after my own sister [has] given the impetus to this most dire of all confusions. After I read the name Zarathustra in the anti-Semitic

correspondence my forbearance came to an end. I am now in a position of emergency defense against your spouse's Party. These accursed anti-Semite deformities shall not sully my ideal!![79]

Wandering

Like a wounded animal, Nietzsche dragged his ailing body and broken heart around southern Europe for several years, wandering aimlessly in a pattern that would endure until the end of his days. Forever seeking warmer weather to relieve his worsening physical ailments, he was also driven to keep moving by an inner restlessness that never left him.

Although there is no doubting the brilliance of Nietzsche's intellectual and literary gifts, there is still a sense of personal indignation, of the childish tantrum, in the works he wrote during this period.

Nietzsche raged in full flight in these works against God, against civilization, against the so-called enlightened liberals of his day. Sometimes he raged against women. One can still feel him smarting at the sting of being spurned by Salomé and betrayed by his sister in the following extraordinary passage:

> Woman! One-half of mankind is weak, typically sick, changeable, inconstant...She needs a religion of weakness that glorifies being weak, loving, and being humble as divine: or better, she makes the strong weak – she rules when she succeeds in overcoming the strong...Woman has always conspired with the types of decadence, the priests, against the "powerful", the "strong", the men.[80]

Nietzsche passed through St Moritz, Genoa, Zurich, Nice, and several other towns and cities in search of a peace that never came. His agitation was compounded by a realisation that his declining health would soon force him to give up that which he cherished above all else – his independence.

115

In 1888, his last year of writing, Nietzsche wrote no less than five books, including his unconventional autobiography *Ecce Homo*, which included chapters with titles such as 'Why I am so wise', 'Why I am so clever', and 'Why I write such excellent books'.

By the autumn of 1888, Nietzsche's syphilis had advanced to a point where he had almost no vision, making it impossible for him to engage in one of his favorite pastimes – walking in the outdoors. He decided to move to the northern Italian city of Turin, its even pavements of black granite much easier to navigate as the short days and long shadows of winter approached.

In this sacred city, famed for housing the burial shroud of Jesus Christ, Nietzsche secured himself an apartment high up in the atrium of the Galleria Subalpina, overlooking the Piazza Carlo Alberto. It was in this Piazza, on a cold and bracing late winter afternoon, that the syphilitic organisms circulating in Nietzsche's body for decades finally reached his brain. The wandering and searching of this lonely, forsaken philosopher was just about to come to an end.

Collapse in Turin

In January 1889 Cosima Wagner received three rambling and rather disconcerting letters from Turin. Each was signed off as being from 'Dionysius', but Cosima immediately recognized the hastily scrawled handwriting.

The first letter read:

> To Princess Ariadne, My Beloved,
> It is a mere prejudice that I am a human being. Yet I have often enough dwelled among human beings and I know the things human beings experience, from the last to the highest. Among the Hindus I was Buddha, in Greece Dionysius – Alexander and

Caesar were incarnations of me, as well as the poet of Shakespeare, [and] Lord Bacon. Most recently I was Voltaire and Napoleon, perhaps also Richard Wagner...However, I now, as Dionysius victorious, who will prepare a great festival of Earth...Not as though I had much time...The heavens rejoice to see me here...I also hung on the cross...

Dionysius.[81]

The next letter revealed a long-held secret that Nietzsche's unravelling brain could no longer keep safe:

Ariadne, I love you!

Dionysius.[82]

In Greek mythology, as Cosima would have known, Ariadne was rescued by Dionysius from the caddish and boorish Theseus, who had abandoned her on the Greek Island of Naxos.

Others received similarly deranged missives. The King of Italy, Umberto the First, was delivered one that read:

To my beloved son Umberto,
My peace be with you! Tuesday I shall be in Rome. I should like to see you, along with his Holiness the Pope.
(signed) The Crucified.[83]

On the same day, one of Nietzsche's few remaining friends, Franz Overbeck, received a letter from 'Dionysius' in which he declared he was 'having all anti-Semites shot'.[84]

Overbeck rushed to Turin to check on Nietzsche's welfare. On arriving, he found him rambling and incoherent, and in the grip of a terrible and frightening madness.

According to witnesses, Nietzsche had caused quite a commotion in the town's main square a few days earlier. A quiet winter's afternoon in the Piazza Carlo Alberto had been dramatically disturbed when the crazed philosopher, appearing from nowhere, ran up to a horse that

117

was being flogged by its rider. Before a crowd of dumbfounded on-lookers, Nietzsche threw his arms around the horse's neck, whispered some words of consolation in its ear, and then, in a fit of sobs and shouts, collapsed to the ground.

Overbeck arranged for his friend to be urgently admitted to an asylum in Jena. According to the institution's medical records, when Nietzsche arrived he explained to the staff:

My wife, Cosima Wagner, has brought me here.[85]

Nietzsche's Sister Takes Control

Nietzsche languished in the Jena asylum for four years, until 1893 when his sister returned from Paraguay to find her estranged brother had suffered a complete mental breakdown.

Elisabeth and her husband's Aryan commune had ended in disaster. German agricultural methods proved to be totally unsuitable for South America, and disease had spread rapidly amongst the settlers.

On 3 June 1889 Elisabeth had discovered her husband dead in their hotel room, surrounded by empty bottles of strychnine and morphine.

Elisabeth continued with the colony for another four years after her husband's suicide, until its complete collapse forced her to return home.

In addition to the shock of finding her brother wasting away in an asylum, Elisabeth received another surprise: her brother's books had suddenly become very popular. This was largely due to the efforts of Overbeck, who had published – at his own expense – Nietzsche's last five works, written in the year leading up to his breakdown.

Although Nietzsche was not able to appreciate it, his work was, at last, receiving acknowledgement after years of public indifference. As one German journalist noted in the quarterly literary magazine *Freie Bühne*, a few months before Elisabeth's return:

> Nietzsche [is] well on the way to becoming the fashionable philosopher, the great event of the time.

Elisabeth immediately sensed an opportunity.

She moved her brother out of the asylum and into her home, and set up a room at the front of her house where visitors could come and view the enigmatic philosopher. To make him look more exotic, she let his hair grow long and dressed him in a long white robe. As he stood in her front room, vacant and staring, some who came to catch a glance of this other-worldly figure compared his appearance to the Persian prophet Zoroaster, also known as Zarathustra. Others came away whispering in awe about the deranged thinker's 'mammoth head' and 'penetrating glance'.

Nietzsche's reputation grew even greater in the face of this side-show orchestrated by his sister. Rudolf Steiner reported after visiting the house:

> He [sits] enthroned…in solemn awfulness, unconcerned with us, like a god of Epicurus.[86]

Another visitor, Gabriele Reuter, described his experience after being granted an 'audience' by Nietzsche's sister:

> I stood trembling beneath the power of his glance, which seemed to rise from unfathomable depths of suffering…It seemed to me that his spirit dwelt in boundless solitude, endlessly distant from all human affairs.[87]

Nietzsche, robbed of his greatest strength – his brilliant intellect – was now totally dependent on his unscrupulous sister. And he was powerless to resist her well-organized scheme to associate his works with her right-wing agenda.

After ten years of inexorable mental decline, Nietzsche finally succumbed to the terminal stages of syphilis on 25 August 1900. Elisabeth moved quickly to establish herself as executor of all her brother's works. She edited his unpublished manuscripts to align them with her own anti-Semitic beliefs, and published them under Nietzsche's name with the title *The Will to Power*. Although scholars have since determined this should not be considered one of Nietzsche's works, at the time of its publication it had the effect Elisabeth was hoping for.

Elisabeth devoted the next thirty-five years of her long life to systematically reshaping her brother's legacy to suit her own ideological ends. She changed her surname from Förster to Förster-Nietzsche to more closely associate herself with her late brother, set up the Nietzsche Archives, and established a Nietzsche Institute in the family home.

In 1930 she lent her prestigious support, as the sister of Germany's then-favorite philosopher, to the newly established Nazi Party. By then, she had successfully forged a myth, accepted throughout Germany, that her brother's works were supportive of Adolf Hitler's vision of a racially pure, all-conquering German state. As a sign of his gratitude, Hitler provided significant amounts of financial support to her institute. An infamous black-and-white photograph from 1933 shows a deferential Hitler bowing and shaking the hand of the elderly Frau Förster-Nietzsche at the entrance of her home.

One of Elisabeth's hopes in setting up the Nietzsche Institute was to turn her brother into a revered cultural icon, standing shoulder-to-shoulder with Goethe and Schiller (the German equivalents of Shakespeare and Keats). In keeping with this vision, the Institute sold mass-produced plaster busts, statuettes, and small paintings of the esteemed thinker.

In this rush to turn Nietzsche into a secular saint, a figurehead for the precariously poised modern German state, nobody took any heed of the philosopher's last words, pronounced with booming clarity in his final work *Ecce Homo*:

> I do not want 'believers'…I have a terrible fear I shall one day be pronounced *holy*.[88]

In Seine Werke

During World War One, fourteen years after Nietzsche's death, all German soldiers under the Kaiser's command were issued with a copy of *Thus Spake Zarathustra*. British soldiers finding this strange book on dead, wounded, and captured enemy combatants naturally came to believe its author supported the German war effort.

These experiences, and Hitler's conspicuous bestowal of honors on Nietzsche's elderly sister for her late brother's work, left an indelible association in the public eye between Nietzsche and Nazism.

As a result, Nietzsche developed a reputation outside Germany, especially in English-speaking countries, as the philosopher whose thinking had led to two disastrous wars and, in the end, to Hitler's 'Final Solution'. Germany's propagandists had adroitly exploited Nietzsche's notion of the *Superman*, his celebration of master over slave morality, and his infamous declarations that 'God is Dead' and 'Whatever does not kill me makes me stronger', with catastrophic effect. It wouldn't be until much later that scholars would correct the record, pointing out Nietzsche's well-documented abhorrence of both nationalism and anti-Semitism. The truth was that Nietzsche was suspicious of all mass movements – he was more interested in how individuals could liberate themselves from the mob than what they could achieve by joining it. As he had presciently warned in *Beyond Good and Evil*:

Insanity in individuals is something rare – but in groups, parties, nations and epochs, it is the rule.

In recent years there has been a dramatic rehabilitation of Nietzsche's reputation, and a newfound appreciation of the relevance of his ideas to contemporary culture. Nietzsche's work is now seen as having anticipated many of the major intellectual movements of the twentieth century, including psychoanalysis, existentialism, post-structuralism, and postmodernism.

When scholars began revisiting Nietzsche, and exploring early commentaries on his work, they came across a text that, although highly significant, had been largely forgotten. Written in 1894, when the philosopher was deep in the throes of dementia, this book bore the unassuming title *Friedrich Nietzsche in seinen Werke* (*Friedrich Nietzsche in his Work*). This first attempt to give a comprehensive and faithful account of the philosopher's work didn't garner much interest at the time, although one of Nietzsche's closest friends, Edwin Rohde, did feel moved to comment, after reading it:

Nothing better or more deeply experienced or perceived has ever been written about Nietzsche.[89]

This book was actually one of the first biographical works on any subject to draw on the ideas of psychoanalysis; it argued that Nietzsche's philosophy had arisen out of a dualism inherent in his personality – between a forbidden, passionate, sensual aspect of himself and his brittle, protective exterior.

The author of this extraordinary work was Lou Salomé.

122

Chapter 4

Heidegger: Being and Loving

First of the Existentialists

Nietzsche's death in 1900 marked the dawn of a new and wondrous century – a century in which the horse and buggy would be replaced by the motorcar, the telegram by the telephone, and the local artisan by the assembly line. It would be a century of great advances in medicine, with cures found for diseases that had previously wiped out huge swathes of humanity, including the syphilis that had destroyed Nietzsche.

It would also be a century of two horrific world wars, in which new and terrible methods for mass killing were unleashed on civilian populations in Dresden, Hiroshima, and Nagasaki. It was the century of the Holocaust, and the age in which scientists would discover the destructive power of nuclear fission and fusion. For the first time in history, humanity would find the means to annihilate itself.

In short, it would be the first century in which science would have a greater impact than religion on the course of history.

With his declaration that God was dead, Nietzsche had encapsulated the crisis that would accompany this triumph of science over religion. Although science provided a better understanding of how the world worked, it didn't provide moral guidance on how to behave in this new world. Nietzsche had seen, with the decline of religion, how society was at risk of drifting into a meaningless nihilism in which nothing mattered. As we have heard, he believed a new type of person, and new values, were needed to replace the void left by religion's demise.

In bringing attention to this crisis in such a dramatic fashion, Nietzsche posed a pressing question to the philosophers who came after him. How were we to find meaning and purpose in a world in which God no longer existed? A group of thinkers known as the existentialists would try, in various different ways, to answer that question. The first of these was Martin Heidegger.

Heidegger was well placed to take up the mantle left by Nietzsche. The son of a church sexton in Germany's conservative and Catholic deep south, he studied theology as a young man, only to drop out following a 'crisis of faith', after which he moved on to the study of philosophy. After being appointed professor at the University of Marburg in the early 1920s, Heidegger immersed himself in developing a new system which explored how to live in the post-religious world heralded by Nietzsche. Heidegger's works would argue that even if God was dead, we could still create a life of authenticity by exercising our free will to make the right choices, no matter what circumstances we were thrown into in this world.

Late one morning in 1924, however, something happened in one of Heidegger's lectures that severely tested his ability to live up to his own principles.

When Heidegger met Hannah

Martin Heidegger was mid-sentence when his stream of thought was interrupted by the sight of a slim, dark-haired student arriving late into his lecture theatre in early November 1924. As she climbed the stairs to search for a seat, he found himself staring at her for a few moments before realising all the eyes of the class were upon him. He regathered his composure and, after pretending to be slightly irritated at the intruder's lateness, resumed speaking. He couldn't help noticing, however, as he glanced back in her direction, the incredible dignity and self-assuredness of this young student. He immediately sensed she was not like the others in his class. As she laid her books on her desk and looked up at him in silent anticipation, the other students looked to her, and then to him, expecting and possibly even hoping Heidegger would deliver the latecomer a rebuke.

But none came. The truth was that Heidegger was taken aback by the singular presence and beauty of this young *Fräulein* in the grey cashmere pullover. Her dark wavy hair and slight build stood out like an island against the sea of stocky Brunhildes that populated the rest of his class. The students of Marburg University, tucked away in this rural and conservative Catholic corner of southern Germany, were not used to seeing dark-haired people of Jewish descent, or any other ethnicity for that matter.

Heidegger resumed his lecture:

And so Aristotle – with his notion of *Being* – set up a way of thinking that has dominated how we see the world to this day. True, it has given us logic and the more recent wonders of science. But Aristotle's attempts to objectively catalogue all of existence – animal, mineral and vegetable alike – has had the unfortunate consequence of us also incorrectly perceiving humans – *ourselves* – as objects. Whereas the truth is that human existence is irreconcilably different to that of rocks or trees. It is different in several crucial ways...[1]

The eighteen-year-old Hannah Arendt had come a long way to hear Heidegger speak, from the Baltic city of Königsberg where another esteemed philosopher, Immanuel Kant, had delivered his famous lectures a hundred and fifty years earlier. Arendt would later acknowledge how critical this five-hundred-mile journey from Königsberg to Marburg had been for her early philosophical development. She had come solely to hear Heidegger, who had not yet published anything of note, but was quickly becoming renowned throughout Germany for his lectures. As Arendt would recall decades later:

> There was something strange about this early fame, stranger perhaps than the fame of Kafka in the early Twenties or of Braque and Picasso in the preceding decade, who were also unknown to what is commonly understood as the public and nevertheless exerted an extraordinary influence. For in Heidegger's case there was nothing tangible on which his fame could have been based, nothing written, save for notes taken at his lectures, which circulated among students everywhere. These lectures dealt with texts that were generally familiar; they contained no doctrine that could have been learned, reproduced, and handed on. There was hardly more than a name, but the name traveled all over Germany like the rumor of the hidden king.[2]

Arendt, like many Jews in Germany in the early 1920s (before anyone had foreseen the cataclysm yet to come) was desperate to assimilate, to become German, to join in that great heritage of cultured thought associated with Teutonic identity. The precocious young student was familiar with Kant, Hegel, and the more recent work of Friedrich Nietzsche. She adored the German composers Bach, Beethoven, and Mozart. Now, she found it hard to believe she was actually here, enrolled in the lectures of this great emerging mind, this 'hidden king', Martin Heidegger.

Conversely, Heidegger was struck by something about this northern outsider who, on entering his classroom, had derailed his train of

126

thought for the rest of that day. As he sat in his office that evening, he found it hard to focus. Unsettling images of this new arrival intruded on his consciousness – her dark, perfectly formed brow, her intelligent aquiline nose, her thin turned-down lips. He was struck most, though, by her quiet, confident presence. It was as if she shone with a different energy to that of other students. The way the other students looked at her, it seems they noticed too.

Heidegger determined that day that he had a duty to make this new student welcome. He decided he would invite her to his office for a meeting. Perhaps he could offer her some private lessons to help her catch up with the syllabus. She had, after all, missed the important first half of his lecture. It was the least he could do.

He looked at his watch. It was getting late. Time to get home to Elfride and the boys. He knew she would want to talk to him after her long day looking after Jörg and Hermann. She would want to talk about the news of the day, about politics, about what the government should be doing to deal with the terrible inflation ruining the country. But he didn't share Elfride's interest in the practical day-to-day world of politics and current affairs; he preferred to immerse himself in critiques of the ancient Greeks. He was quite happy in that distant world that for him felt so close. Besides, he felt he was onto something; a new critical perspective that he wanted to explore. It consumed him in a good way.

He reflected on how much better things had been at home lately. Even the troubles around their second son seemed well behind them now. Yes, he thought, his mind jumping back to his earlier concerns, he would definitely invite this new student to some one-on-one tuition. It was, he told himself again, the least he could do.

When Arendt received a letter from her professor a couple of months later, she was delighted and excited, but also apprehensive. Desperate for any opportunity to be accepted into this staid, close-mouthed town, she found herself, nevertheless, a little nervous at the prospect of being alone with the great thinker. Their meeting was scheduled for the early evening. Immediately after lectures that day, she headed back to her room, bathed, and changed her clothes. She wanted to look presentable for her first private encounter with the much-esteemed professor.

To her surprise she found the great man gentle and softly spoken in his office, totally at odds with the stern presence he projected in the classroom. He seemed genuinely interested in her, where she came from, her philosophical and cultural interests. She found herself quickly put at ease. She even shared a laugh at jokes the professor made during their first meeting. He told her he was impressed with her knowledge, with the breadth of her reading, and that he thought she had a keen and brilliant intellect that could take her a long way with the right mentoring. She gratefully accepted his offer to meet on a weekly basis for individual lessons.

Over the next few weeks, Arendt found herself feeling increasingly restless and distracted on days she was due to meet her mentor. Even the lectures she loved so much seemed to drag forever as she waited for the evening to come. As well as being flattered by her idol's attention, she felt relieved to have a confidante. In their first few meetings, her questions were all of a philosophical nature, but after a month or so she relaxed more in his company, and revealed more of her insecurities and anxieties, including how alone she felt in her new home town.

At the end of one of these tutorials, Heidegger suggested they go for a walk. It was late in the evening when this incongruous-looking pair – he, older, and larger in knickerbockers and a folksy dark brown peasant-coat, and she, young and slim, with bobbed hair, in her figure-hugging and fashionable Königsberg clothes – made their way through the near empty campus grounds. It was a chilly winter night but the sky was exceptionally clear, and a sharp silver moonlight spilt over the campus's dew-laden green grassy lawn.

It was during this walk that Heidegger first let Arendt know that his interest in her extended beyond the pedagogical. It would appear, however, from the content of a brief letter he sent her the next day that the evening had ended rather awkwardly. He wrote:

Dear Miss Arendt,

[T]he gift of our friendship [is] a commitment we must grow with. And it prompts me to ask your forgiveness for having forgotten myself briefly during our walk.[3]

It seems Arendt wasn't too troubled by her teacher's indiscretion, as she continued to meet him regularly. Although the purpose of their meetings was, ostensibly, for him to help her with her studies, it turned out they had much in common. They shared a passion for ancient Greek philosophy, German composers, and the recent literature of Rilke and Thomas Mann.

Heidegger and Arendt enjoyed their time together so much they didn't want the semester to end. But winter came quickly, and Arendt had to return home to her mother in Königsberg for the break.

During this period, Heidegger wrote a series of beautiful and poetic letters to his young charge. On 21 February 1925, he wrote:

[W]hen the new semester comes it will be May. Lilac will leap over the old walls and tree blossoms will well up in the secret gardens – and you will enter the old gate in a light summer dress. Summer evenings will come into your room and still the quiet serenity of our life into your young soul. Soon they will awaken – the flowers your dear hands will pick, and the moss on the forest floor that you will walk on in your blissful dreams...[4]

Flattered by these lavish letters, Arendt mustered the courage after her return in the new year to ask Heidegger if he would read a confessional piece she had written during their time away. *Die Schatten* (*The Shadows*) described the fears and uncertainties of her childhood, recalling the many frightening nights she spent as a girl cowering with her mother in fear as her father – an engineer who died of syphilitic madness when she was only seven – rampaged through the family home in terrifying outbursts of violent, insane rage. Hannah had never before felt safe to reveal these experiences to another.

Heidegger was full of praise for Arendt's writing, a response that brought her to tears. It was at that moment, in his office, that she surrendered to his embrace. Heidegger would later describe what happened that night as when 'the demonic struck me'.[5]

Soon afterwards, he wrote to Arendt:

Nothing like [that] has ever happened to me. In the rainstorm on the way home, you were even more beautiful and great. I would have liked to wander with you for nights on end.[6]

After this fateful night in Heidegger's office, the professor and his young student no longer tried to resist each other. Their furtive and secret affair became an all-consuming compulsion as they took elaborate measures to avoid detection by Heidegger's wife and the university authorities.

A set of unspoken rules of engagement developed around their erotic tête-à-têtes. The professor was the one in charge, deciding when they should meet, and whether it should be in his office or her attic apartment on campus. Arendt, it seems, was always deferential and respectful, even while making love. She never at any stage during the affair doubted her abilities, either as student or lover. In fact, according to one biographer, she found a certain satisfaction in submitting to her teacher's peculiar whims, desires, and demands. She sensed that he needed to be in control, and she found this vulnerability of his endearing. Paradoxically, it served to maintain her interest and it gave her a sense of importance and control.

After making love, they would, when time allowed, lie together in each other's arms and talk about their various concerns including, of course, philosophy, but also, inevitably, his marriage.

After spending more than a year under Heidegger's supervision at Marburg University, Arendt was expected, like other students, to move on to another university to broaden her educational experience. Having become quite attached to her new lecturer, however, she now did not want to leave. Heidegger upset her considerably by encouraging her to do so. He was becoming increasingly concerned that if she stayed in Marburg, somebody would discover what was going on. He was painfully aware that if their liaison became public knowledge, it could have a hugely damaging effect on his career. His oft-repeated expression of these concerns to Arendt caused building tensions, which sometimes boiled over into angry accusations and stony silences. As we shall hear, Arendt held out as long as she could, delaying her move to the spring of 1926, when she transferred to the University of Heidelberg.

Elfride

During this first year of Heidegger and Arendt's affair, Elfride Heidegger was very busy with their two young sons, born in quick succession soon after they married. She suspected her husband might be having an affair, but not with Arendt. At this point she wasn't even aware of Arendt's existence. She was concerned, rather, about what might be developing between Heidegger and her childhood friend

Elisabeth Blochmann. Ever since Elfride had introduced them to each other a few years earlier, she couldn't budge the feeling that a close tryst had developed between the two.

Blochmann came from an assimilated upper-middle-class Jewish family, and included philosophy among her many interests. From the day she was introduced to Heidegger, she looked up to him as a philosophical guide and mentor. Eventually becoming a distinguished academic herself, Blochmann would write to Heidegger frequently over the course of what became a long-lasting friendship.

In 1918, when the newly married Heidegger served at the front in World War I, he wrote as many letters to the young Blochmann as he did to his new wife. In one of these secret missives, written in a tortured prose for which he would later become notorious, he referred to what he saw as their special connection:

'It should be our duty to utter to congenial spirits that which in our innermost truth we experience as something alive and urgent.'[7]

It would turn out that Elfride's suspicions about Blochmann were well-founded. As well as being close friends and confidantes for the best part of sixty years, Heidegger and Blochmann were also lovers for at least a part of that time.

In his mid-thirties Heidegger was, it seems, at a peak with respect to both his philosophical and libidinal energies, for during that time he was not only in regular sexual congress with his wife and two lovers, he also started writing what would become one of the most important philosophical works of the mid-twentieth century.

A Shocking Revelation

In the early years of Heidegger and Elfride's marriage, some extraordinary events took place that help us to understand why he might have felt so free to take on other lovers.

Elfride Petri first met her husband-to-be in the winter of 1915–1916 in Freiburg, a picturesque medieval university town nestled deep in the Black Forest in Germany's south-west. The Lutheran daughter of a high-ranking Prussian officer, Elfride had enrolled at the university to study political economy.

Heidegger had just completed his thesis in philosophy, earning him the right to teach. Elfride met him at the first lecture he ever gave.

Heidegger immediately fell for this serious young student with chestnut hair, petite features, and downcast eyes. As he got to know her in the ensuing weeks, he discovered underneath her gentle and agreeable demeanour a strong and principled character that he would come to increasingly respect and admire.

Heidegger and Elfride were married on 21 March 1917 in Freiburg's main cathedral in a small ceremony conducted by Heidegger's close friend, the Catholic priest Engelbert Krebs. This was followed a week later by a Protestant ceremony hosted by Elfride's parents.

A little more than a year into their marriage, Elfride managed to convince Heidegger, who as a young man had studied for the priesthood, to abandon his Catholic faith and convert to Protestantism, a faith, which in her case, bordered on agnosticism. This was a significant step for Heidegger, whose connection with the Catholic Church went all the way back to his earliest years, when his father had been a sexton and cellar master for the family's local parish in Meßkirch, a tiny village sixty miles east of Freiburg. Elfride would later lament about Heidegger's conversion to Protestantism:

My husband has lost his religious faith, and I have failed to find mine.[8]

A couple of years after Heidegger and Elfride's wedding, two major events took place. The first was the happy news that Elfride had become pregnant with their first child, Jörg. The second was Heidegger's appointment as research assistant to Edmund Husserl, the highly acclaimed Chair of Philosophy at Freiburg University at that time.

Husserl had recently become renowned in philosophical circles for developing a new movement known as phenomenology, which had, as its primary idea, the notion that philosophers should sidestep the age-old problem of whether mind or matter comes first, and instead focus their efforts on studying the form and content of consciousness itself.

The phenomenological movement would later become associated with three giants of twentieth-century German philosophy – Husserl, Heidegger, and their close colleague and friend Karl Jaspers. All three studied at Freiburg University. As we shall hear, Heidegger would eventually distance himself from his associates, not just in philosophical thought but also politically and personally. Husserl, a Jew, would come to feel particularly betrayed by the developments yet to come.

It was during Heidegger's first year of working for Husserl that a highly significant event took place in Heidegger and Elfride's marriage, an event so explosive it threatened to tear the young couple apart.

Heidegger's research for Husserl required him to spend a lot of time away from home. It was early in 1920, three years into their marriage, after Heidegger returned from one of these trips, that Elfride told him some shocking news.

She revealed she was pregnant for the second time, but on this occasion he was not the father.

Elfride, during the long stretches at home with her first child, had suffered terribly from loneliness, and as she now tearfully related, she sought solace in the arms of an old childhood sweetheart, a medical doctor called Friedel Caesar. Caesar had taken to visiting Elfride in

Heidegger's absence, providing her with much-needed company and comfort until the inevitable had happened.

Heidegger's response to this news was surprising to say the least. Despite, or perhaps because of, the fact that this was the conservative rural south of Germany, his reaction was to immediately reassure his wife and tell her not to worry, that he would bring up the child as his own. He promised, in fact, to never mention it again. It was a promise kept, though his expectation that Elfride would never again mention the truth about their second son's birth was a burden she would find difficult to bear for the rest of her life.

Die Hütte

This bizarre and unexpected turn of events may help to explain why Heidegger felt free to conduct affairs with both Hannah Arendt and Elisabeth Blochmann. We will never know if this was the cause, but we do know that Heidegger started his affairs with both women soon after Elfride's shocking disclosure. Twenty years would pass before he would tell his wife about his affair with Arendt; it is unclear whether he ever told her about Blochmann.

In any case, one can understand Elfride's reluctance to raise her suspicions, given the incredible forbearance her husband had shown in response to her infidelity. Some have described this arrangement as an open marriage, but a tacit understanding to ask no questions, and tell no lies seems more likely.

The unusual circumstances surrounding the birth of 'their' second child Hermann, in August 1920, also helps to explain a special gift that Elfride presented her husband with soon afterwards. This gift was, in part, her way of expressing her gratitude to Heidegger for his forgiving and generous response to her indiscretion. It was also a gift that would contribute greatly to the evolution of Heidegger's first philosophical work.

In 1922 Elfride used her inheritance money to buy several acres deep in the Todtnauberg forest, a beautiful expanse of lush woodland eighteen miles south of Freiburg. In this secluded spot, she built a four-room cabin that became affectionately known as *die Hütte* (The Hut). Although they also kept a house in Freiburg, the Heidegger family stayed at *die Hütte* for long periods whenever they could; it would become for them a place of many treasured memories.

There was no road to *die Hütte*. The family could only get there by hiking through the heavily wooded forest in the summer months, or by skiing into it in winter. It would become, for Heidegger, a sacred place of solitude and inspiration where he wrote nearly all his philosophical works.

One side of *die Hütte* was lined with trees, the other with snow-covered slopes and valleys. In summer the family played outdoor games in the grassy clearing surrounding the dwelling. In winter's shorter days, the children skied and played in the snow whilst Elfride attended to household chores and Heidegger worked on his writing. In the evenings, the family would come together for *Abendbrot* in front of the fireplace.

Although *die Hütte* would later become an ideal location for Heidegger to write in, the bustle of family life with young children initially proved too distracting as he tried to complete his first major philosophical work. In the mid-1920s, he rented a room in a nearby farmhouse from a farmer called Johann Breder. In this room he wrote from morning to dusk, returning to the hut in the evening to be with his young family. There, by the fire, his family would partake in a simple supper of bread, cheese, *wurst,* and wine. After the children were laid to bed, Heidegger and Elfride would sometimes step outside the hut and, holding each other close, behold the dark, mysterious star-studded sky as it looked down on them and the stillness of their humble dwelling in the midst of the *Schwarzwald.*

Being and Time

In 1927 an important opportunity arose for Heidegger. Husserl announced his retirement as Chair of Philosophy at Freiburg University, and the university had begun to look for a successor.

To be seriously considered for the position, Heidegger knew he needed to publish something significant. This spurred him on to complete the book he had been writing for several years. He eventually published it in late 1927 with the title *Sein und Zeit* (*Being and Time*).

Being and Time not only secured his promotion, it went on to receive widespread acclaim. In the years that followed, it came to be regarded throughout Europe and beyond as one of the most important philosophical texts of its time.

Heidegger opened *Being and Time* with a dedication to Husserl, who for many years would mistakenly assume his pupil's book was a straightforward extension of his own work. It wasn't until Husserl read Heidegger's work some years later that he realised his apprentice had departed from him in revolutionary ways that he would never agree with.

Heidegger's ambitious first work was concerned with the true nature of existence, or what philosophers throughout the ages had referred to as *Being.* Heidegger's main contention was that two thousand years earlier Aristotle had made a fatal error in his conceptualisation of *Being* that had taken the whole history of Western thought, and Western society with it, on a wrong turn. Aristotle had seen *Being* as the sum total of everything that existed, and had proceeded to classify this existence into categories such as animal, vegetable, and mineral.

According to the Aristotelian view, on which modern science – and our modern view of the world – is based, the world is essentially made up of stuff (or matter). Heidegger asserted, however, that before we set about classifying everything that exists, we should have asked the question:

Who or what is this *Being* for whom these descriptions matter?

Heidegger pointed out that we, who are asking this question, are fundamentally different to the rocks, trees, and animals we are asking about. We differ from them in several fundamental ways. Firstly, we *ask questions* about existence. (Rocks don't do this.) Secondly, many of our heartfelt questions about existence – the most important questions we can ask – arise from an awareness that we are mortal, that one day our life will come to an end. We are also distinct from the rest of the universe in that we experience free will, and with it a sense of responsibility to make the right choices in our lives.

Heidegger argued that Aristotle had confused *beings* (all the separate things or objects that exist) with *Being* (what existence is really like for those of us asking questions about it). Heidegger also criticised the tendency in philosophy since Aristotle's time – and still evident today in science – to be preoccupied with *what we know* about the universe. Heidegger argued that, in practice, we don't relate primarily to the world through *knowing* it; our relation to the world is better characterised by what he referred to as *caring*. We care about our world and the people and objects within it. And, as Heidegger pointed out, we are generally more concerned with the immediate usefulness and relevance of these objects in our world, what he called their *instrumentality*, than with some abstract understanding of their nature and properties.

To illustrate his concept of *Being* – and distinguish it from that of his predecessors – Heidegger asked his readers to consider, in what has since become a famous example, a man grasping a hammer. Whereas an Aristotelian or modern-day scientific approach to the hammer would be to classify it according to its physical and other attributes (e.g., made of metal and wood, being of a certain size, being man-made, and so forth), Heidegger asks us to see the hammer in its natural relation to the *Being* for whom it is important.

Heidegger asks us to imagine the relevance of the hammer for a cobbler in his shed – to picture him reaching for this tool to tap some tacks into the base of a shoe. The cobbler takes pride in his trade. It is his livelihood. He knows that the money he makes from selling his shoes will be used to provide for his family. Heidegger insisted it makes more sense to see objects such as this hammer – and the wider world – in the context of their relevance for our everyday lives. He argued this is not only how we see the world, it is how the world really is. Heidegger contended that, even for philosophers and scientists, such a stance leads to a more accurate appraisal of the world than science's artificial and contrived bird's-eye view of objects suspended in space, the 'view from nowhere' as contemporary philosopher Thomas Nagel has since characterised it. For Heidegger, it makes no sense to separate the 'external' world from the *Being* asking questions about that world.

Also, as Heidegger points out, the cobbler – like all of us – and unlike other 'stuff' in the universe – knows that one day he will die. This awareness (even if it is only a dim awareness that he repeatedly tries to push away whenever it arises) spurs him on to try to provide enough for his family in the limited time he has left. He feels a pressure, generated by this awareness of his mortality, to make the right choices in his business, his relationships, and his life in general. He wants to exercise his freedom to live what Heidegger called an authentic life, one that he can later look back on with a sense that it was well-lived.

139

This central idea of Heidegger's – that we need to put ourselves as human beings back at the centre of our understanding of Being, of existence – would come to inspire many philosophers, psychologists, theologians, artists, and writers in the decades to come. His ideas would have a profound and revitalising effect on people in a wide range of disciplines. However, most who tackled the text of *Being and Time* would find it an exceedingly challenging read. On every page the reader found themselves faced with new words that Heidegger had invented, and maddeningly labyrinthine turns of phrase. Heidegger defended his writing style, arguing that the language we use in everyday speech is partly responsible for obscuring the true nature of *Being*, and to get underneath this we need whole new ways of expressing ourselves. He was unapologetic almost to the point of arrogance about the difficulties his work posed for the reader, provocatively declaring that:

Making itself intelligible is suicide for philosophy.[9]

Heidegger coined the term *Dasein*, which literally means 'being there', but is usually translated as 'being-in-the-world', to signify his central conception of us all being – like the cobbler in his illustration – inextricably tied up with the world and the objects in it, and at the same time aware of our mortality and of the responsibilities that come with our freedom.

Although Heidegger shared Husserl's interest in human consciousness, and his work has been grouped along with Husserl's as belonging to the movement called phenomenology, Heidegger's ideas were in many ways fundamentally different to those of his mentor. Whereas Husserl saw himself as scientifically developing a universal, objective, and timeless system to characterise and classify all aspects of consciousness, Heidegger's notion of *Being* – as suggested in the title of his monumental work – was inextricably tied up with his notion of time.

Heidegger saw that our experience of the world, of *Being*, is unavoidably shaped by the place and time in history into which we are thrown. He called this the *facticity* of our existence. For Heidegger, the main purpose of our short life is to exercise our freedom by making the right choices – and thereby create a life of meaning and authenticity – whatever historical circumstances we find ourselves in.

It is perhaps not surprising that concerns about making the right choices, whatever historical situation one finds oneself in, were coming to dominate Heidegger's thinking. At the age of thirty-eight the up-and-coming philosopher found himself in interesting circumstances – married, with two children, and secretly harbouring two Jewish lovers, in a Germany awash in a rising tide of rampant nationalism and anti-Semitism. Heidegger would soon be required to make some of the most difficult and fateful decisions of his life, decisions that would have repercussions long after he made them.

Although the publication of *Being and Time* in 1927 would ensure Heidegger a place in the history of continental thought for many years to come, his seminal work would soon be overshadowed – at least in his country – by another book published two years earlier, a book taking Germany by storm.

The name of this book was *Mein Kampf*, written by a political activist called Adolf Hitler.

The Rise of Nazism

Heidegger and Arendt's affair had been over for three years when Hitler first came to Freiburg in the summer of 1932.

Hitler had not yet gained power, but was touring the country rallying for support. As he entered the city, some people in the streets threw stones at his vehicle. Those who taunted him were shocked when he leapt out of his car brandishing a whip.

On the next day, 29 July, Hitler addressed a crowd of 50,000 people at the Freiburg football stadium. Elfride Heidegger, an enthusiastic supporter of the Nazi party, was there, along with her two sons Jörg and Hermann, aged thirteen and twelve. Elfride was proud of the way her boys looked in their pressed white shirts and ties – they had never been dressed so neatly. Like others attending the massive gathering, Elfride desperately wanted to believe the visiting speaker's promises that he could rescue Germany from its post-war nightmare and once again make it a strong, proud, and successful nation.

Martin Heidegger was not at the rally. Despite his wife's encouragement to attend, he preferred to concentrate on his academic work.

In the winter of 1932–1933, Hitler was appointed Chancellor of Germany. Immediately, the Nazi Party proceeded to suppress all political opposition, using a combination of legislation, mass arrests, and paramilitary violence and intimidation. Thousands of communist party members were jailed. Trade unionists had their offices destroyed – many were taken to the first concentration camps.

In 1933, in the midst of this extraordinary turmoil, Heidegger was promoted to the position of Rector – the German equivalent of Dean – at Freiburg University.

Heidegger would subsequently attract a lot of criticism for taking on a position which required him to enact the laws of the ruling Nazi regime, including, most controversially, the banning of Husserl and other senior Jewish academics from the Freiburg campus. But the circumstances regarding Heidegger's appointment, and the way in which he carried out his official duties, were not as black-and-white as some of his critics would later imply.

Heidegger's appointment to the position of Rector was, according to an interview I conducted with his ninety-two-year-old son in 2013, thrust upon him by a series of sudden and unexpected events, and even then he only took it on with a great deal of reluctance.

The position of Rector was originally supposed to have been taken up by Heidegger's friend, colleague, and neighbour, Willhelm von Möllendorff. The Möllendorffs lived just across the street from the Heideggers.

Heidegger's son Hermann recalls:

The Heidegger family lived at 47 Rötebuck Road and the Möllendorff family lived at 34 or 36. The families were friends despite the fact that Mrs Heidegger was interested in the National Socialists and Mrs Möllendorff in the Social Democrats.[10]

Möllendorff had been elected to the position of Rector by the Senate in December 1932, and was due to replace the retiring Rector Professor Sauer on 15 April 1933. But just before Möllendorff could take up his appointment, he was publicly attacked in the Nazi's local propaganda arm, the newspaper *Allemagne*. The *Allemagne* reported that Möllendorff had been a supporter of the Social Democrat Party, and questioned whether it was acceptable for one with such unpatriotic views to be appointed. The not-so-hidden threats of intimidation, exclusion, and even violence in such pronouncements were not lost on the university's academics, who became very anxious not only about their future, but the future of the university.

It was at around this time that Möllendorff put pressure on Heidegger to nominate instead of himself for the position of Rector. Möllendorff visited the Heidegger household many times during this period, as Heidegger's son recalls:

I remember very clearly at least three times I opened the door to Mr Möllendorff because he had to discuss something with my father. I have very vivid memories of Mr Möllendorff coming to our house, as I took him upstairs to my father and said goodbye to him

143

when he left. And what I found out after, what they actually discussed in the bedroom, was how things should proceed at the University, what was to be the next step. Because Möllendorff had been publicly attacked...they thought they really had to do something, and Möllendorff told my father that he [Heidegger] should become the new Rector.[11]

Other academics also approached Heidegger, asking him to nominate for the position so that the university wouldn't be vulnerable to attacks or closure by the Nazis. The outgoing Rector Professor Sauer also asked Heidegger to stand, promising his vote. Heidegger had, mostly as a result of the urging of his wife, voted for the National Socialists at the recent election, so was more likely than Möllendorff to be accepted by the Nazi government.

Although Elfride was a supporter of the National Socialists, she wasn't supportive of her husband becoming Rector. She thought he lacked the skills and experience for such a complex and demanding administrative post, and tried to convince him not to give in to the pressure of his peers. As Hermann Heidegger recalls:

My mother said 'you cannot do this, you're not suited for this, you shouldn't do this'.[12]

Regardless of his wife's protests, at the meeting of the University Senate on 21 April 1933, Heidegger was nominated and elected Rector unopposed.

Just prior to Heidegger's appointment, during the administration of the previous Rector Professor Sauer, a law had been passed that required all Jewish professors and lecturers in Germany to be immediately *urlaubed*. This translates literally as being 'put on leave', but in actuality it meant they were to be permanently excluded from university grounds. Edmund Husserl, as a retired but still visiting professor, was affected by this ordinance, and, along with all other Jewish staff, banned from the university grounds two weeks before Heidegger's appointment, not *after* as has been incorrectly reported by some commentators.

Heidegger's son claims that one of the first things Heidegger did on being appointed Rector was to request authorities reverse the ban on Husserl and three other Jewish academics. As Heidegger's son recounts:

Immediately after Heidegger took office, on the 21 or 22 April, he called Karlsruhe [where the Minister for Culture's office was located] and asked for the Jewish professors to come back, and on 28 April the Minister for Culture from Karlsruhe wrote to the Senate of the University of Freiburg that this order [from the 6 April] shall not apply, shall exclude, the following members of staff: Professor Coln, Professor Husserl, Professor Michael, and Assistant Brock...[The order] was still in force in that it said all Jewish professors and lecturers have to leave their office, but this shall not apply to the following, and they actually mentioned them by their names; and this was a direct consequence of his [Heidegger's] call.[13]

Less partial sources, such as *The Blackwell Companion to Philosophy*, have confirmed that Husserl's ban was, indeed, overturned during Heidegger's tenure.

Although the positive steps that Heidegger took to protect Husserl from the policies of the Nazi Party have been overlooked by some of Heidegger's fiercest critics, the fact remains that many of Heidegger's thoughts and actions during this period were highly suspect. The recent publication of his private diaries – the so-called 'black books' – has shed light on the fact that he, like his wife and many others in

Germany at the time, subscribed to views that, in the light of what happened next, seem chilling to us today.

In one such entry, Heidegger wrote:

World Judaism is ungraspable everywhere and doesn't need to get involved in military action while continuing to unfurl its influence, whereas we are left to sacrifice the best blood of the best of our people.[14]

It should be noted, in Heidegger's defence, that there is no evidence he or his wife supported the systematic killing of Jewish people that took place in subsequent years. The complexities around Heidegger's culpability or otherwise are further illustrated by the fact that on 29 April 1933, a day after Heidegger had succeeded in getting the Nazi ban on Husserl reversed, Heidegger's wife sent Husserl's wife a letter in which she sympathised with the difficulties being faced by the Husserls, including a recent anti-Semitic attack on their son. The letter reads:

Dear Frau Husserl,

In my name and the name of my husband,

In these very difficult times, I am writing you to say a few words. We would like you to know that every day we think of what you have done for us, and I would also like you to know that despite my husband having decided to take a different way, a different route in philosophical terms, he will never forget what he has received, what he has learnt from your husband. And especially I will also never forget how much you have been supportive and how much you have done for us in the very hard years after the war [World War I].

I have suffered extremely for the fact of not having been able to show you this thankfulness in recent times…We were really shocked what we read in the press recently about your son in Kiel, and we hope that this has only been a single incident or attack, as has happened many times in the past.

So please Mrs Husserl accept these lines as what they are, namely words of deep thankfulness to you and your husband,

Elfride Heidegger.[15]

The Death of Hindenburg

Despite the increasingly shrill political atmosphere taking hold of Germany and its institutions during this time, the years that followed were some of the happiest the Heidegger family ever experienced. Although he spent many hours locked away with his writing, Heidegger did take some time out to enjoy life with his family. As his son Hermann recalls:

> I remember we would go on boat trips...on different rivers in Germany. My father also sometimes brought colleagues on these trips, for example, Siegurd Janssen, a pharmacologist from Freiburg University, with whom we did a trip on the Danube. On one time [we] started at Bergheim and then went to Regensburg. And another time started from Ulm and then went to Passau. I [also] remember doing one of these trips on the Main River.[16]

As Elfride watched her sons enjoying these special times with their father, however, she found herself burdened with an increasing anxiety, for she knew the day was soon approaching when she would have to tell her second-born the truth about his birth. She had long ago promised herself that she would tell him before he came of age. That day came on 2 August 1934, as news bulletins around the world announced the death of President Hindenburg, widely seen as the last moderate politician in Germany with any hope of holding back Hitler's quest for total control. On this day, Elfride took the fourteen-year-old Hermann aside and solemnly told him that the death of

President Hindenburg, being a very important occasion, was one in which she wished to tell him something important about his origins. Elfride Heidegger then had the conversation with her son she had been dreading for more than a decade.

Herrmann would later recall:

> For me it was shocking. For my mother it was a relief. For me it was even more difficult because she told me I had to promise her that I would never tell anyone else about it until she died.[17]

Elfride forbade her son from ever talking about this with his 'father' Martin, a request that Hermann would dutifully obey for the rest of his life.

Arendt Under Pressure

It had now been several years since Martin Heidegger had seen his former student and lover Hannah Arendt.

Their affair had lasted from 1925 to 1928. Throughout these years they secretly met and made love – usually in Heidegger's office – whenever they could. When they weren't able to get together, they wrote to each other, Arendt sending her letters to Heidegger's university address so they wouldn't be detected by his wife. In the early years of their liaison, Heidegger found it exceedingly difficult to tolerate long periods of time without his young mistress, asking her to write whenever she could.

In the spring of 1926, in the wake of yet another argument about whether or not they should be living in the same town, Arendt finally packed up and moved to Heidelberg, accepting an invitation from Heidegger's colleague Karl Jaspers to study under him. Jaspers helped Arendt with her doctoral dissertation on the concept of love in the thought of St Augustine. Arendt's interest in St Augustine shows that her passionate interest in the German philosophical tradition, including its antecedents in medieval Christian thought, had not wavered despite the poisonous tide of anti-Semitism enveloping her country at that time.

Although Arendt had moved almost a hundred miles away, she and Heidegger managed to continue their affair for another two years. In a series of elaborate communications designed to avoid detection by the university, Heidegger's wife, or Arendt's tutor Jaspers, Heidegger and Arendt arranged to meet at railway stations and hotels in various small towns between their two cities whenever they could.

In early 1928, however, Heidegger travelled to Heidelberg to tell Arendt that he could no longer continue their affair. The reasons for Heidegger ending things are unclear, but we do know his career had just taken a huge leap forward with the publication of *Being and Time* and his appointment to the position of Professor at the University of Freiburg. He now had a lot less time to continue his long-distance affair, and a lot more to lose if it were discovered. We also know he was seeing more of Elisabeth Blochmann during this time; Blochmann even secretly visited him at *die Hütte* in 1929, a privilege Arendt never enjoyed.

A year after Heidegger and Arendt's affair ended, Arendt married the Jewish philosopher and journalist Günter Stern. Soon afterwards, she completed her dissertation, but because of her Jewish heritage the authorities refused to grant her *habilitation*, the final qualification needed to teach in German universities. Her reaction to this was to start researching anti-Semitism in Germany, a brave and risky step that would soon make her position completely untenable.

Although Arendt had effectively put herself into exile from Heidegger, she found it was not that easy to shake off the hold her former teacher had on her. Even getting married had not been enough to break the bind that Heidegger still had on her heart. Heidegger, it appears, had the same problem. In 1929 he managed to find a reason to visit Heidelberg, where he met with his beloved – and now married – ex-student. As the following letter – written by Arendt to Heidegger soon after this visit – shows, their feelings for each other had not been diminished by distance or Arendt's recent marriage:

> Dear Martin,
> You will probably have already heard about me from other random sources. That takes the naiveté of the message from me, but not the trust that our last reunion in Heidelberg once more newly and gratifyingly strengthened. So I am turning to you today with the same security and with the same request: do not forget me, and do not forget how much and how deeply I know that our love has become the blessing of my life. This knowledge cannot be shaken, not even today, when, as a way out of my restlessness, I have found a home and a sense of belonging with someone about whom you might understand it least of all.
> I often hear things about you, but always with the peculiar reserve and indirectness that is simply part of speaking the famous name – that is, something I can hardly recognise. And I would indeed so like to know – almost tormentingly so, how you are doing, what you are working on, and how Freiburg is treating you.
> I kiss your brow and eyes,
> Your Hannah.[18]

After a long break in any correspondence, in the winter of 1932, Arendt wrote to Heidegger saying she had heard distressing rumours – that she didn't believe – that he was becoming a Nazi and an anti-Semite. Heidegger's reply, written whilst he was frantically working with other academics at Freiburg University to determine how best to respond to Nazi Party pressures about the university's Rectorship, reveals in its extraordinary outburst the strain he was feeling at the time:

> This man who comes anyway and urgently wants to write a dissertation is a Jew. The man who comes to see me every month to report on a large work in progress...is also a Jew. The man who sent me a substantial text for an urgent reading a few weeks ago is a Jew. The two fellows whom I helped get accepted in the last three semesters are Jews. The man who, with my help, got a stipend to go to Rome is a Jew. Whoever wants to call this 'raging anti-Semitism' is welcome to do so. Beyond that, I am now just as much an anti-Semite in University issues as I was ten years ago in Marburg...To say absolutely nothing about my personal relationships with Jews (e.g. Husserl, Misch, Cassirer, and others). And above all it cannot touch my relationship to you.[19]

Arendt and Blochmann Flee

In 1933 Arendt was arrested and interrogated by the Gestapo. After being released from questioning she fled to Paris, where she befriended her husband's cousin, the philosopher and literary critic Walter Benjamin. Arendt joined Benjamin in providing aid to Jewish refugees streaming across the German border into France.

From 1935 to 1939 Arendt worked in Paris as Secretary-General of *Youth Aliyah*, an organisation created to rescue Jewish children from the Nazis. Originally founded by the wife of a Berlin rabbi in 1933, *Youth Aliyah* became much more active from 1936 after laws were passed banning Jewish children from German elementary schools. Arendt assisted with the secret smuggling of several thousand children out of Nazi-occupied countries into kibbutzes in Palestine. During this tumultuous period, Arendt divorced her husband Günter Stern after just eight years of marriage. It would appear her attempt to marry her way out of the restlessness that she had described in her letter to Heidegger had not been successful.

In early 1940, Arendt married German poet and Marxist thinker Heinrich Blücher. This would turn out to be a much happier marriage than the first, although, as later events would reveal, she had still not completely let go of her feelings for Heidegger. With World War II now in full swing, however, she would not hear from Heidegger for several years.

In May 1940 the French government started rounding up all Germans in France – whatever their origin or political affiliation – as foreign citizens of an enemy nation. This included a large number of German Jews who had fled the Nazi regime. Arendt, caught up in this net, was arrested in Paris and transported hundreds of miles south to Camp Gurs, where she was incarcerated as an 'enemy alien'.

Located on a flat, desolate, dusty plain in the country's south-west, Camp Gurs was known for its harsh conditions. The shadow of the Pyrenees on a bleak western horizon was the only feature greeting Arendt and her fellow inmates as they looked out each day beyond the wire. Their beds were no more than straw-filled sacks that they were ordered to shake out every morning. Other daily tasks, bellowed at them by stony-faced guards, included preparing the daily meal from dried salted fish, and emptying the overflowing cans of the camp's makeshift latrines. The invisible threat of dysentery loomed ever-present over the camp.

Within a few weeks, Arendt and her fellow detainees settled into their routines with a grim resignation. This turned to panic, however, when she and the other Jews in the camp heard that France had surrendered to Germany, and that the camp would soon be handed over to the Nazis.

Amidst the confusion of France's surrender, however, Arendt and some other detainees were able to escape. She later wrote of their good fortune:

> A few weeks after our arrival in the camp...France was defeated and all communications broke down. In the resulting chaos we succeeded in getting hold of liberation papers with which we were able to leave the camp...[I]t was a unique chance, but it meant that one had to leave with nothing but a toothbrush since there existed no means of transportation.[20]

Using illegal visas issued by an American diplomat, Arendt was able to flee, along with her husband, to Lisbon in neutral Portugal. Her friend Walter Benjamin wasn't so fortunate; after being arrested by Franco's forces in Spain and informed he would be handed back to the Nazis, he committed suicide with an overdose of morphine.

From Lisbon, Arendt boarded a boat, and with Benjamin's last manuscript *On the Concept of History* in her hand, she sailed to the country that would become her home for the rest of her days, the United States.

Meanwhile, Heidegger's other secret lover – Elisabeth Blochmann – was being targeted and persecuted. In the years following her graduation, she had enjoyed a highly successful career, becoming a talented and respected Professor of Pedagogy at Halle in eastern Germany. In 1933, however, she was dismissed from her post on account of her mother being Jewish. She then found herself in increasing danger as paramilitary thugs took to roaming the streets, terrorising the local Jewish population. Heidegger wrote letters of support to the authorities in Blochmann's defence, but after receiving no response he helped her escape to the Netherlands.

Fortunately for Blochmann, she found a safe passage to England before the Nazis marched into Amsterdam. She went on to become a British citizen and a respected scholar of education and philosophy at Oxford University. She would continue to correspond with Heidegger for the rest of her life.

Meanwhile, Elfride Heidegger proved to be right about her husband's inability to manage a senior administrative post. On 23 April, after only a year as Rector at Freiburg University, Heidegger submitted his resignation. However, during his term as Rector, Heidegger did join the Nazi Party – in the first week in fact – and would remain a party member until 1945. This action would lead to severe and lasting adverse repercussions for the controversial philosopher and his family for years to come.

Fallout in Freiburg

On a clear spring day in May 1940, the sunny city of Freiburg – jewel of the Black Forest and home to university students from all over the country – had sixty bombs dropped on it. The bombs landed beside the railway station, close to the most highly populated part of town. More than fifty residents were killed. When the fifty-one-year-old Heidegger and his wife and teenage sons came out of their home to survey the damage and assist those in need, they and Freiburg's other surviving residents soon discovered, to their horror, that the bombs had been mistakenly dropped by the German Air Force on its own people. (Freiburg was very close to the border with France, the intended target of the bombers.)

Five months later, on 22 October 1940, Nazi authorities ordered the deportation of all remaining Jews from Freiburg and its surrounds. Three hundred and fifty citizens of Freiburg, mostly women, children, and elderly who had not been able to flee earlier, were removed from their homes and, with the cooperation of the French Vichy government, interned across the French border. Husserl was spared this indignity, having passed away in 1938 at the age of seventy-nine. His widow Malvine also managed to escape deportation, having fled to Belgium soon after her husband's death.

The three hundred and fifty who were rounded up were placed in Camp Gurs, the same camp that Arendt had escaped from only a few months earlier. These last Jewish residents of Freiburg, however, would not share Arendt's good fortune. By this time, the Nazis had totally taken over the camp. Over the next two years, typhus and dysentery swept through the camp several times, killing scores of those detained within its fences. On 18 July 1942 those who survived were deported to Auschwitz and never seen again.

On 27 November 1944 a second fleet of bombers emptied their ordinances on Freiburg, but on this occasion the bombers – all three hundred of them – belonged to Allied forces. The beautiful medieval city was almost completely demolished by the attack, though its central gothic feature, the towering Münster cathedral, still stood intact and only slightly damaged after the bombing was over.

On that chilly autumn evening, the city's shell-shocked residents crawled out of their shelters to a morbid spectacle they would never erase from their memories – the corpses of their fellow residents strewn over streets and sidewalks, the screams of the mortally wounded piercing the dusty air, and, for hours afterwards through the night, the wailing and sobs of the bereaved and traumatised left behind.

Downfall

After the war, Germany was divided into four sectors: French, British, American, and Russian. The French took control of Freiburg and oversaw the process of local *denazification*, whereby the occupying forces set about trying to purge Germany of any remnants of National Socialism. Heidegger, as a member of the Nazi Party, was immediately stripped of his professorship and forbidden to teach or study.

The French investigations and trials took years to complete. All suspect persons were classified into five categories: major offenders, incriminated, less incriminated, *Mitläufers* (literally – those who walked with the Nazis), and exonerated or non-incriminated persons. In March 1949 Heidegger was declared a *Mitläufer*, a (non-incriminated) fellow traveller or follower of Nazism. As a result of this somewhat qualified clearance, he was allowed in late 1949 to resume his post at Freiburg.

Although Heidegger had his job back, his reputation was in tatters – both at home and internationally – as a disgraced Nazi collaborator who had sided with Hitler and his evil regime. Much was made of the fact that, in 1938, he hadn't even attended Husserl's funeral. His critics also pointed out that in the second edition of *Being and Time*, published in 1941, he had removed the dedication to Husserl, an action the philosopher would later claim was forced on him by his publisher.

Elfride found her husband's post-war fall from grace particularly difficult to bear. She had always been a woman for whom reputation and 'saving face' were important, aspirations that seemed impossible now. As details of the unspeakable atrocities committed by the Nazis became more apparent, the standing of those who had openly been members of the Party, such as Elfride and her husband, became more and more indefensible.

It seemed to Elfride that the days of her husband being appreciated for his ideas were over, and that all she and her family could look forward to was a life of shame, exclusion, and humiliation.

The Visitor

Less than a year after Heidegger was reinstated, however, an unexpected opportunity arose. This opportunity literally knocked on the Heidegger's door on the morning of 8 February 1950, in the form of a visitor. The visitor's name was Hannah Arendt.

As Elfride Heidegger beheld this person standing in her doorway, she experienced a confusing array of emotions. The most prominent of these was a 'swift and violent' jealousy. Her husband had only just told her about his affair with this woman, how they had been lovers for several years whilst Elfride was bringing up their young children. But, as her husband had also recently explained, Arendt was now a respected and influential scholar, and might be one of the few people in the world capable of restoring his standing in the international academic community.

Arendt had arrived in Freiburg only the day before. Though now based in the United States, she was currently touring Europe in her capacity as Research Director of the Commission on European Jewish Cultural Reconstruction, an organisation dedicated to recovering Jewish artifacts lost in the war. Right up until the day she arrived in Freiburg, she hadn't been sure if she would contact Heidegger. Like most of her colleagues who had fled Germany, she had heard the stories about Heidegger joining the Nazi Party, and had all but written him off as a traitor to not only herself and her people, but to the most basic standards of decency and integrity.

But on 7 February, after checking into her hotel in Freiburg, she found herself – out of a sense of obligation more than anything else –

157

shooting off a brief letter to her former lover and professor letting him know she was in town. Within hours, he was at the hotel. Arendt would later admit to Heidegger that an intense feeling came over her on being notified of his arrival:

> When the waiter announced your name…it was as though suddenly time had stopped.[21]

Heidegger invited Arendt back to his house that evening. Mrs Heidegger was out, he explained, but 'would have gladly welcomed her had she not had a previous engagement'.[22] It was at this point that Heidegger mentioned to his past student that his wife now knew about their affair. Neither Heidegger nor Arendt let this fact sour their reunion, however. As Arendt would later recall, even though twenty years, a world war and the Atlantic Ocean had separated them, '[f]or the first time in our lives we really spoke to each other'.[23]

By the time Elfride got home that evening, Arendt was back at her hotel. When Heidegger explained to his wife who had visited that evening, there was, no doubt, a tense conversation at the Heidegger household. Elfride now found herself in an impossible situation. Although she was, according to all accounts, beside herself with jealousy at any mention of Arendt's name, she was desperate to have her husband's reputation restored. And so, she agreed to her husband's request to receive Arendt as a guest at their home the following morning.

Arendt's second visit to Heidegger's house did not go well. The air in the Heidegger home was tense that morning, and not helped by a passing remark Elfride made about the difference between German and Jewish women. As Arendt reported back to her husband, Heinrich Blücher:

> This morning an argument with his wife. [E]ver since she somehow squeezed the story out of him, she apparently never stopped

making life for him hell on earth...I'm afraid his wife is ready to drown all the Jews as long as I am alive. Alas, she is stupendously stupid.[24]

Despite this fraught and most unpleasant meeting of husband, wife, and mistress, the truth was each of them had a need to continue this uneasy association. Heidegger desperately needed someone who could rehabilitate his reputation. For Elfride, too, this was an opportunity she didn't want to let go of, despite the terrible personal cost. No doubt her task was made more difficult by her sense that her husband's feelings for his past student had not been extinguished by the intervening years. As for Arendt, it seems that she quickly fell back under the same spell she had been under years ago as a young, and perhaps somewhat impressionable, undergraduate.

A month later, in March 1950, Arendt returned to Freiburg at Heidegger's invitation, for a longer visit of four days. During this visit, Heidegger spent a lot of time explaining, justifying, and contextualising his wartime behaviour to Arendt. From that time onwards, she would become one of his greatest defenders and advocates.

Although most of the subsequent meetings, and even the letters, between Heidegger and Arendt were closely supervised and scrutinised by Elfride, Heidegger occasionally managed to evade his wife's watchful eye to express to Arendt the ongoing feelings he still had for her. In May 1950, whilst away from the family home, Heidegger sent Arendt a letter in which he declared that when he was thinking or writing philosophy, he thought of her alone. He also dared to write that 'he dreamed about her living nearby and of running his fingers through her hair'.[25]

In 1952 Arendt returned for another European tour, this time to promote *The Origins of Totalitarianism*, the book that would bring her worldwide fame. This was the first work to observe that Nazism and

Communism, rather than being poles apart, had a lot in common. Heidegger, it seems, didn't cope well with having his adoring ex-student achieve such international renown. According to Arendt's letters back to her husband, Heidegger couldn't hide his discomfort at having to share the limelight with his former lover and philosophical apprentice. This was nothing, however, compared to Elfride's ongoing struggles. As Arendt reported back in a letter to Blücher:

The woman is jealous almost to the point of madness.[26]

Rebuilding

After these meetings with Arendt, Heidegger managed to slowly and gradually rebuild his standing in the philosophical community.

He wrote prolifically in the years following World War II, becoming concerned in his later works with technology and how it mediates a person's relationship with the world. Heidegger's arguments – initially formulated in the 1920s – that objects are most usefully understood in the context of our relationship to them, and how they affect our being-in-the-world, would be even more relevant in the age of computers, global air travel, the Internet, and smartphones that was to follow.

In old age, Heidegger's writing became more poetic in style. He came to the belief that such language captured our existence in the world much more accurately than any scientific or traditional philosophical terms ever could. Like Salomé before him, Heidegger also found much inspiration in the works of Nietzsche. In 1961, he published a two-volume work about his philosophical predecessor, whose original cry that we must make something of our lives without God had clearly left a deep impression on the 62-year-old Heidegger.

Arendt in Jerusalem

During the same years that Heidegger was reestablishing a name for himself, Arendt found her philosophical career going from strength to strength as she produced works that explored the themes of power, violence, dictatorship, and democracy. She became one of the West's most highly regarded critics of totalitarian systems, whether these occurred in Nazi Germany, Communist Russia or anywhere else in the world. As she observed:

> The totalitarian attempt at global conquest and total domination has been the destructive way out of all impasses. Its victory may coincide with the destruction of humanity; wherever it has ruled, it has begun to destroy the essence of man.[27]

In 1961 Arendt was again cast onto the world stage, when as a journalist for *The New Yorker* she was commissioned to cover the trial of Nazi leader Adolf Eichmann in Jerusalem. Eichmann had been discovered by Mossad, the Israeli Secret Service, hiding in South America, and in a daring operation Mossad had kidnapped him and flown him back to Israel to face justice, more than two decades after committing his wartime atrocities.

Arendt upset many of her Jewish compatriots when she reported that the Eichmann she saw in the dock was not the depraved monster many had made him out to be. She experienced him, rather, as 'terribly and terrifyingly normal'.[28] She was struck by how this perpetrator of horrendous crimes against humanity was in fact just a man, and a fairly ordinary man at that. In a phrase of hers that would come to be quoted more than any other, she notoriously described what she experienced, sitting in the courtroom, as the 'banality of evil'. She wrote:

> The sad truth is that most evil is done by people who never make up their minds to be good or evil.[29]

Whether she was also thinking of her friend Martin Heidegger when she uttered these words is unknown, but Arendt could certainly speak with authority on the subject, having experienced such evil personally years earlier when she had been on the receiving end of Nazi persecution. In her analysis of wartime events, however, Arendt wasn't content with simple rationalisations about the evil of the German people (and the inherent goodness of the Allies). Unlike many commentators at the time, she was interested in trying to understand how such unspeakable things had happened.

Arendt would continue to be a strong advocate for the Jewish people and a loyal friend of Heidegger for the rest of her life, a stance that would earn her considerable criticism.

Heidegger, on the other hand, never publicly explained – or apologised for – his membership of the Nazi Party, although he would later privately describe his actions to a colleague as 'die größte Dummheit meines Lebens' (the greatest stupidity of my life).[30]

An Unbreakable Bond

Throughout the 1950s, 60s, and 70s, Arendt and Heidegger wrote to each other regularly, the sentiments expressed in their letters leaving no doubt in any reader's mind the tender and loving feelings they continued to have for each other.

In 1966 Heidegger sent Arendt, for her birthday, a painting of the view he looked at every day from his study in *die Hütte*. With it he enclosed a poem, *Autumn*, by Friedrich Hölderlin. Arendt wrote back to Heidegger that this gift brought her 'the greatest joy'.[31] In her reply, she quoted Goethe to describe how she felt about their friendship:

To say that a thing endures means that there is something in the end that is the same as it was in the beginning.[32]

162

A year later, Heidegger sent Arendt – who had just turned sixty – a copy of his recently published work *The Origin of the Work of Art*. Inscribed on its inside cover were the words:

For Hannah,
in memory of meeting again,
Martin.[33]

In these post-war years, Heidegger and Arendt also met face to face on several occasions, although in nearly every case Elfride was never far away, acting as chaperone. Elfride endured these encounters with as much good grace as she could muster; Arendt had, after all, been responsible, more than any other, for restoring her husband's good name on the world stage. But Elfride still struggled with what seemed to her to be an unbreakable bond between Heidegger and his former student. As Arendt complained in a letter to Blücher:

After years of apparently nursing the hope that he would forget me, [Elfride's] jealousy [has] only intensified.[34]

Although there is no evidence that Heidegger and Arendt – both now married – resumed a sexual relationship after the war, they did continue, right up to the ends of their lives, to share an intimate world that was theirs and theirs alone.

In 1974 Arendt wrote her last letter to Heidegger. In it she reminisced about the day they first met, half a century earlier:

No one can deliver a lecture the way you do, nor did anyone before you.[35]

On 4 December 1975, as New York City experienced its first snowfalls of the season, one of its more famous residents, Hannah Arendt, died of heart failure, aged sixty-nine. She was buried at Bard College in Annandale-on-Hudson. Her simple, unadorned blue-grey granite gravestone, which can still be visited today, bears the unassuming epitaph:

Hannah Arendt Blücher
Born Hanover Germany
Oct 14 1906
Died N.Y. N.Y.
Dec 4 1975

Heidegger was to die only five months later. But before he did, the eighty-six-year-old philosopher did something quite surprising.

He asked for a private meeting with the priest Father Bernhard Welte. Although the content of their conversation is not known, it has been reported as relating to his relationship with the Catholic Church. Perhaps the rapidly fading philosopher felt the need to revisit his old faith to unburden himself of a guilty conscience. We will never know, as the words that passed between Heidegger and his confessor were never revealed.

We may, however, get a glimpse of what was discussed from the address given by Father Welte to those gathered at Heidegger's funeral a few months later:

> Martin Heidegger's path has come to its end. What may we say at this end, over his coffin, in light of his death? Once a whole world listened to him. Perhaps at the news of his death it will listen once more...
> He was always seeking and...[he] characterised his thinking as a path. He traveled this path without ceasing. There were bends and turns along it, certainly there were stretches where he went astray. [But he] always understood the path as one that was given to him, sent to him. He sought to understand his word as a response to an

indication to which he listened without respite. For him, to think was to thank, to make grateful response to that appeal.[36]

Heidegger was buried in Meßkirch, the tiny village in which he was born, in its church cemetery beside his parents and brother.

Chapter 5

Sartre: She Came to Stay

The French Connection

In the years after World War II, when Heidegger was trying to defend his wartime conduct, the public spotlight shifted to a philosopher whose relationship with Nazism showed no such ambiguities. Jean-Paul Sartre had, in fact, fought in the French Resistance against the Nazi occupation of his country.

Before the war, however, Sartre's main source of intellectual inspiration had been Heidegger and other German phenomenologists.

As a young man, Sartre had visited Berlin in 1933 to read the work of this new school and had been particularly taken with Heidegger's notion of existence – not just as some abstract concept, but as something relevant to all of us who struggle with questions of freedom, meaning, and authenticity. Sartre found himself captivated by Heidegger's observations that we are thrown into the world at a point in history beyond our control, and that we have to fashion the best life we can from this contingency.

And so, in the post-war years, as Heidegger struggled to salvage his name, Sartre launched the philosophy he called *existentialism* onto the world on the back of Heidegger's ideas. Sartre's declaration that each of us had to forge our own meaning from an inherently meaningless world resonated with many Europeans emerging from the senseless horror of two world wars. The widely publicised free-loving lifestyle of Sartre and his fellow philosopher Simone de Beauvoir only served to cement his popularity. Sartre and Beauvoir became overnight celebrities, as they and their small coterie of bohemian friends not only wrote about, but boldly *lived* their new philosophy of freedom on the bustling streets and boulevards of Paris's Left Bank. Sartre and his associates would generate many followers, a veritable army of beret-wearing existentialists dressed in black, smoking *Gauloises*, and writing in cafés as they emulated the pose and lifestyle of their philosophical heroes.

By the winter of 1946, Heidegger had become so concerned about Sartre twisting and misrepresenting his ideas that he published an open *Letter on Humanism*, in which he distanced himself from the French philosopher and his work. In the letter he made it very clear he did not endorse Sartre's existentialist philosophy, even though it was supposedly based on his ideas. In his typically enigmatic, almost incomprehensible prose, Heidegger accused the French upstart of 'taking *existentia* and *essentia* according to their metaphysical meaning' and therefore staying 'with metaphysics, in oblivion of the truth of Being'.[1]

Despite Heidegger's protestations, the epicentre of continental philosophy had by the end of World War II well and truly shifted from Germany – where it had prevailed for over a hundred and fifty years – to Paris, where it would remain for the rest of the twentieth century. Although the philosophy of Jean-Paul Sartre would later be dismissed by many academics as merely an extended footnote to the work of Heidegger, Sartre would soon become the most famous philosopher the world had ever known.

Words

I began my life as I shall no doubt end it: amongst books.[2]

So wrote Sartre in his Nobel Prize-winning memoir *Words*, of his literary, yet terribly lonely, start to life.

Born in Paris on 21 June 1905, Sartre spent his early years without the company of other children. His first friends were the dusty tomes in his grandfather's library, of which there were many. This start to life set the scene for a love of literature that would never leave him, but it also resulted in an emotional emptiness, an emptiness that he would spend most of his adult years trying to overcome.

When Sartre was fifteen months old, his father Jean-Baptiste, an officer in the French Navy, died from enteritis caught whilst sailing in southern seas. As Sartre would later explain, Jean-Baptiste was 'already wasting away with the fevers of Cochin-China [Vietnam]' when he met Sartre's mother Ann-Marie, 'married her, begot a child in quick time, me, and sought refuge in death'.[3]

A widow at twenty-three, Ann-Marie had to relocate, along with her baby Jean-Paul, back to her parents' house in Meudon, an outer suburb in Paris's southwest.

Sartre would later come to see his father's absence in a positive light, blessing him with the perfect circumstances to explore and enjoy, uninhibited by paternal limitations, a life of unreined creativity and freedom:

> Had my father lived, he would have lain on me at full length and would have crushed me. As luck would have it, he died young.[4]
> The death of Jean-Baptiste was the big event of my life: it sent my mother back to her chains and gave me freedom.[5]

The 'chains' that Sartre referred to were his mother's parents. His mother's father, Charles Schweitzer, ruled the household with an iron will. Originally from Alsace on the French–German border, his Germanic blood revealed itself in his large muscular frame and dominating presence. Schweitzer was renowned in his local community as a philosopher, theologian, and feared but respected patriarch. With his long white beard, Sartre would later quip that his grandfather 'so resembled God the Father that he was often taken for Him'.[6]

The Schweitzers treated Sartre's mother as if she were still a child, putting her and the young Sartre together in what had been the children's bedroom, and referring to the pair as 'des enfants'.[7]

Ann-Marie Sartre mollycoddled her little boy, letting his blonde locks grow long and dressing him in frilly clothes. She even had a pet nickname for this child she adored and constantly fussed over, referring to him as her little 'Poulou'.[8]

One of the earliest surviving photographs of Sartre shows him, at two, in a sailor's outfit standing on his mother's lap. With his long golden curls and cherubic features, the child gazing out of the photograph – securely held in the arms of his proud mother – looks more like Shirley Temple than a future philosopher.

A year after this photograph was taken, disaster struck again in the life of the young fatherless Sartre. He developed a nasty infection in his right eye. His mother took him to hospital, but the doctors seriously botched up its treatment, leaving him with no movement or vision in that eye for the rest of his life.

Not long afterwards, his grandfather, having had enough of his grandson being dressed and pampered like a girl, took him to the barber and had his hair cut short. When he arrived home, Sartre's mother ran weeping to her room. Before them all, his true ugliness unveiled for the first time, stood a stunted, grotesque, and gnomish-looking boy with a shaven head and wickedly turned eye.

The remaining years of Sartre's childhood were terribly lonely and empty. He had no playmates or friends. His grandfather didn't see any benefit in him playing with other children, preferring him to spend his days at home being tutored in classics, literature, or mathematics.

On the rare occasions the young Sartre came into contact with other children, he was invariably taunted and teased about his odd appearance.

Although the large, rambling house owned by Sartre's grandfather was devoid of the comfort of other children, it was populated with mountains of books in every room. From a young age, Sartre learnt to find some solace amongst these volumes. Their words and stories helped protect him from the pain and loneliness he was forced to endure as an ostracised, unpopular child.

In his memoir, Sartre recalls the first time he realised that the black squiggly lines in the books he was looking at were *words* – sounds with meanings. This realisation first came whilst watching his mother read. He was fascinated by the way she smiled, laughed, and sighed at these magic marks on the page. As his mother mouthed these words to him, the mystery of these markings was gradually revealed. From that time onwards, Sartre hungrily set to learning what these symbols meant, starting a voracious reading habit that would endure for the rest of his life.

Before long, Sartre was impressing his mother and grandparents with feats of precocious scholarship, reading aloud classics that should have been well beyond his years. The young master of the household lapped up the attention and adoration these performances evoked, but the truth was at this young age he derived little pleasure reading such worthy works. Sartre's mother sensed her son's need to escape from the stern and barren world his grandfather had created, and whenever she could she took him to the local newsagent to buy him what he really wanted – comics, serials, and magazines. Sartre had a particular liking for adventure stories set in America's Wild West – his favourites were the tales of Buffalo Bill. When he was eight years old, his mother bought him some puppets, and he started one of the activities for which he would later become highly renowned – writing scripts for plays.

As Jean-Paul got older, he rebelled more and more against the strict regimen of his grandfather, and he got into the habit of sneaking off to the newsagent to secretly purchase the latest 'boys-own' tales. The themes in these throwaway books – of heroes, dragons, and damsels in distress – greatly appealed to Sartre as a young teen, so much that he started trying his hand at writing such tales himself. It thrilled him, and gave him a sense of great power, to discover that through the magic of writing he could create whole worlds from his imagination. This love of writing, initially an escape from the unbearable loneliness of his childhood, would later in life become an all-consuming passion.

As well as finding solace in the written page, Sartre continued to find comfort in the close company of his mother, with whom he still shared a room. Even as puberty approached, he spent many long days out with her whilst Monsieur and Madame Schweitzer managed the household. A favourite haunt of his and his mother's was the local fair, where they would often go on rides or share an ice cream. Sartre would later confess that as a boy he thought of his mother more like an elder sister, a sister whom he might one day, when he grew up, be able to marry.

At twelve, Sartre received some devastating news. His mother announced that she had met someone and intended to remarry. Sartre immediately resented the new object of her mother's affections, an old navy comrade of his father's called Joseph Mancy.

The new blended family moved out to the town of La Rochelle on France's rugged, windy west coast. There, the friendless Sartre spent the most miserable years of his teens looking out over the wild and unsympathetic Atlantic Ocean.

Sartre's new stepfather was indifferent to his needs, and Sartre's suffering only increased during these years. He tried to fit in with the other teenagers on the dull town's grey streets, but the local youths didn't take kindly to this ridiculously short and strange-looking outsider with a hideously bloated eye.

Sartre's misfortunes worsened even further after a notorious incident at his new school. In a misguided attempt to gain some credibility with his classmates, he showed them a letter he had received from the town's local prostitute, in which she declared how much she had enjoyed having sex with him. Unfortunately for Sartre, the school authorities got hold of the letter, and during the subsequent interrogations he was forced to admit he had forged the document. Sartre's attempt to use his precocious storytelling talents to improve his social standing had badly backfired. He was expelled from the school, in disgrace with the authorities and the boys he had been trying to impress. News of this 'scandal' spread quickly, providing even more fuel for the bullies in Sartre's neighbourhood whenever they came across him.

Sexual Awakening

At fifteen the desperately unhappy Sartre convinced his family to let him leave La Rochelle and move to Paris, where he enrolled as a boarder at the prestigious Lycée Henri IV. Sartre thrived in this new environment, where learning and intellectual discovery were valued and encouraged. He started to read philosophy for the first time, beginning with Henri-Louis Bergson. Bergson, a critic of the dry scientific and rationalist trends dominating philosophy at that time, wrote about free will and consciousness in a way that fired Sartre's imagination.

At the age of eighteen, Sartre, who only a few years earlier had been torn from the only source of sensuality he had ever known – the loving arms of his mother – lost his virginity to a married woman in her early thirties. He later described this experience as if it were a chore that had to be ticked off, complaining:

I did it with no great enthusiasm because she wasn't very pretty.[9]

In 1924 the nineteen-year-old Sartre enrolled in the École Normale Supérieure, an institution that had already nurtured many of France's greatest thinkers, and would produce many more. But it wasn't just Sartre's appetite for intellectual stimulation that was gratified at this esteemed institution. The nearby Luxembourg Gardens were a popular gathering place for prostitutes, and Sartre and his classmates took to regularly sampling their services. He didn't, however, have much respect or empathy for these women who provided him and his peers with their first sexual experiences, later recalling that 'we felt that a girl shouldn't give herself like that'.[10] The sexism and hypocrisy of these remarks foreshadowed an attitude that would later be observed by many women who came in contact with Sartre.

In his early twenties, Sartre embarked on his first – and last – attempt at bourgeois respectability. He became engaged to Germaine Marron, a girl from Lyon. Sartre even approached the engagement in the 'proper' way, asking the girl's parents for her hand in marriage. Germaine's letters to Sartre during this period paint a picture of an effusive but naïve girl, in love with the idea of being in love. In one of her many long, rambling letters to her beau, she declares: 'I love you to the point of madness.'[11]

It would appear that Sartre didn't feel the same as his betrothed, as at the same time he was seeing another young woman who ignited passions his middle-class fiancée could never hope to achieve.

This woman's name was Simone, but not de Beauvoir. Simone Jolivet was a flame-haired courtesan who spent her spare time lounging around with Sartre and his classmates, all of whom she titillated to the point of distraction with her outrageous and unashamed sensuality. Sartre was her lover for a few years, but never her client. He wouldn't have been able to afford her services even if he wanted to; she only took on extremely wealthy clients, mainly lawyers and local politicians. The twenty-four-year-old's signature move was to stand naked reading a book in front of a fireplace as her client walked in. As Beauvoir, who later got to know Jolivet through Sartre, observed: 'her cultured mind, her proud bearing, and the subtle technique she brought to her task knocked town clerks and lawyers flat.'[12]

When the ENS held its grand ball that year, Sartre didn't take his fiancée to accompany him – he took his lover Simone Jolivet, who scandalised many a guest with her revealing costume. Soon afterwards she shocked even Sartre – and his classmate Paul Nizan – by gifting them with lampshades she had fashioned out of purple pairs of her own panties.

Jolivet had aspirations to be a writer, and Sartre agreed to help her in this quest. When, on one occasion, she complained that his letters to her were more like lectures, he wrote back to her in a scolding tone:

> Who has made you what you are? Who's trying to keep you from turning into a bourgeois, an aesthete, a whore? Who has taken charge of your intelligence? I alone.[13]

Sartre's fiancée was oblivious to his bohemian tête-à-têtes with Jolivet and others, and continued to make wedding plans for her and her paramour. But when Sartre – who had been spending more time revelling with his new free-spirited friends than studying – failed his first attempt at sitting his examinations, Marron's parents called off the engagement. Although Sartre was in truth much relieved to be released from this middle-class bondage, the news affected him more than he expected. He recalls:

Instead of joining my friends at tennis I went by myself to a meadow with a bottle, and I drank. I even cried.[14]

It was soon after the end of this always-doomed engagement, and almost two years into his faltering studies at the École Normale Supérieure, that Sartre met someone who truly was his match, a woman who would become his lover, favourite companion, and intellectual partner for years to come.

Thus Pissed Zarathustra

Simone de Beauvoir arrived at the École Normale Supérieure in 1928. She had just completed a degree in philosophy and literature at the nearby Sorbonne, and enrolled in the École Normale to complete her *agrégation*, a highly competitive and prestigious higher degree in philosophy that, if completed, would allow her to teach at any school in the country. She found herself immediately welcomed by all other students in her year, except for three.

These were the notorious Jean-Paul Sartre, Paul Nizan, and Rene Maheu, who made it abundantly clear they considered themselves superior to everyone else in the classroom. They had already established a reputation for provocative and outrageous behaviour. In one infamous incident, Sartre and his friends dropped water bombs from the school's roof onto unsuspecting students, shouting to those below Thus Pissed Zarathustra![15]

Beauvoir was quite impressed by these young mavericks' antics, not to mention the clever philosophical allusion they incorporated into their version of a schoolboy prank. But whenever she came across them in the classroom or courtyard, their body language was decidedly closed. Their conspiratorial chatter would quickly fall away when she approached, resuming only when she was out of earshot. Unbeknownst to her, however, these men had taken more notice of the newcomer than they were letting on. The questions she asked in lectures suggested a good grasp of philosophy and an impressively sharp intellect. Their initial bemusement at the girl they, in the early days, referred to as 'the badly dressed one with the beautiful blue eyes' came to be replaced by an ever-increasing curiosity and respect.[16]

In her memoirs, Beauvoir recalls the joys of returning to the ENS after her first spring break:

> The Easter holidays came to an end; in the gardens of the Ecole Normale, aflower with lilacs, laburnums, and pink hawthorn, I was delighted to meet my fellow-students again. I knew almost all of them.[17]

She adds:

> Only Sartre's little band, which included Nizan and [Maheu], remained closed to me; they had no truck with anybody else; yet only attended certain lectures, and always sat apart from the rest of us.[18]

Beauvoir goes on to describe her first impressions of this aloof and closely knit trio:

> Nizan was married and had travelled; he sported plus-fours and I found the eyes behind the heavy horn-rimmed glasses very intimidating. Sartre wasn't bad to look at, but it was rumoured that he was the worst of the lot, and he was even accused of drinking. Only one of them I thought seemed fairly accessible: [Maheu]. He too was married. When he was with Sartre and Nizan, he ignored me. [But when] I met him on his own, he would exchange a few words with me.[19]

As it turned out, Beauvoir would strike up a close friendship with Maheu. They took to studying together in the Bibliothèque Nationale, and sitting side-by-side in lectures.

It was shortly after this that Sartre made his first move. Knowing that Beauvoir was deeply immersed in writing a thesis on the seventeenth-century philosopher Leibniz, he asked Maheu to pass to her, during a class, a rather crude drawing he had sketched of Leibniz surrounded by bathing beauties. Beauvoir would later recall how, on receiving this portrait, she had blushed like a teenager.

A few weeks later, Maheu informed Beauvoir that he, Sartre, and Nizan would be most honoured if she could join their weekly study group. Beauvoir was thrilled to be invited into this mysterious club, and found her excitement building as the day of their first meeting approached:

> I was over the moon, [but] so nervous I don't think I slept at all the night before. I know that I prepared for the first study session as if I were going to take the examination itself. I was terrified they would not find me brilliant but only a silly girl who knew very little and could not think.[20]

The location for the gathering was Sartre's room in the nearby student residences of the *Cité Universitaire*. On Monday, 8 July 1929 Beauvoir arrived with Maheu, and met Sartre properly for the first time. At first she was taken aback at the sight that greeted her – Sartre and Nizan crouched together in a rather squalid and extremely cramped bedsit:

> Sartre greeted me in a worldly manner: he was smoking a pipe. Nizan, who said nothing, had a cigarette stuck in the corner of his one-sided smile and was quizzing me through his pebble lenses, with an air of thinking more than he cared to say.[21]

Beauvoir was directed to the only empty chair in the room, unceremoniously backed onto Sartre's unmade bed. The room smelt of stale food, and was generally in disarray, with notes, books, and papers scattered all over the floor, and overflowing ashtrays scattered throughout the room.

The men encouraged Beauvoir to present her annotated readings of Leibniz. She complied with their request, but within a few minutes they interrupted her, complaining that Leibniz was intolerably boring, and that they should talk about Rousseau instead. Sartre then launched into an exposition of Rousseau's work so erudite it left Beauvoir breathless. She would later reflect:

> I was intelligent, certainly, but Sartre was a genius.[22]

From that day until the day of her final exam, Beauvoir spent nearly all her spare time with these three new friends. She felt she had found, amongst these fellow dilletantes, these lovers of literature and philosophy, an intellectual home where she truly belonged. Their iconoclastic attitudes would be deeply influential in shaping her own stance as a young woman towards not only philosophy, but also authority, freedom, relationships, and sexuality:

> When they were all together the three 'comrades' didn't pull their punches. Their language was aggressive, their thought categorical, their judgments merciless. They made fun of bourgeois law and order...they jabbed a pin in every inflated idealism...[E]very kind of soulfulness, the 'inner life', the marvellous, the mysterious, and the precious, all fell under their lashing contempt; on every possible occasion – in their speech, their attitudes, their gestures, their jokes – they set out to prove that men were not rarefied spirits but bodies of flesh and bone, racked by physical need and crudely engaged in a brutal adventure that was life.[23]

A Dutiful Daughter

It had only been through a series of family misfortunes that Beauvoir found herself in the position, highly unusual for a young woman in the 1920s, of being able to study philosophy.

In the early 1900s, just before she was born, Simone's father Georges Bertrand de Beauvoir had parked the family's modest savings in what had appeared at the time to be an astute and safe investment – Russian railway stocks. But after the communist revolution in October 1917, he lost everything, including any possible dowry for his daughters. As he repeatedly lamented to Simone and her younger sister Helene: 'you girls will never marry – you'll have to work for a living'.[24]

In a curious parallel with the trajectory of her future soul mate Jean-Paul, Simone would later reflect that her father's bankruptcy was one of the best things that ever happened to her. His financial troubles allowed her to avoid the conventional path into marriage expected of women of her generation, and to indulge her interests in literature and philosophy.

Simone had not always been so independently minded. Born in 1908 to Georges and Françoise, she was, at the beginning, a timid and serious fair-haired child who followed all the rules, both at home and at school. Indeed, she was noted by her teachers to be a model pupil in both her application to studies and her conduct in the classroom. At the age of ten she was sent to the *Cours Adeline Désir*, a private Catholic girls' school in Saint-Germain-des-Prés, where the focus was very much on prayer, catechism, piety, and deportment. She went through a deeply religious phase during this time, and for a while even had aspirations to become a nun. There was very little in the way of formal academic studies at this traditional girls' school; the lessons were mainly devoted to etiquette, knitting, crochet, and playing the piano.

In adolescence, however, the precociously intelligent Simone had a crisis of faith, and shocked many around her – including her devoutly Catholic mother – by declaring that she was an atheist.

In her late teens, Beauvoir started devouring philosophical texts, and surprised her family even further by announcing she wanted to undertake formal studies in philosophy at one of the state's elite colleges. This caused great consternation amongst the nuns at her school, who told her a state school was 'nothing better than a licensed brothel'.[25] Her mother, too, tried to counsel her against the move, warning her that the study of philosophy mortally corrupts the soul'.[26]

Simone sensed, however, that she did have some unspoken support from her father, a self-declared atheist who had long held his own ambitions to be an artist, but for family and financial reasons had been unable to heed this inner calling. All throughout her childhood, Beauvoir's father had been impressed and intrigued by his daughter's bright and inquiring mind, often boasting to his friends: 'Simone thinks like a man'.[27]

To assuage the concerns of her mother about the moral dangers of a coeducational college, Simone agreed to a compromise. After passing her *Baccalauréat* exams at seventeen, she enrolled in an all-girls Catholic institution on the outskirts of Paris where she was, at least, able to study classics and mathematics. It didn't take long, however, for her to feel constricted in this environment, and on turning eighteen she defied her mother and enrolled for a degree course at the prestigious Sorbonne, only the ninth female in history to do so. Once within its hallowed halls, she set to pursuing her dream of sitting the *agrégation*, the nation's most gruelling and competitive examination in philosophy.

Torn Between Two Lovers

On a sweltering summer's day in July 1929, Beauvoir, Sartre, Nizan, Maheu, and many other of France's brightest young minds sat the *agrégation* examinations that they had spent months assiduously preparing for. The results were posted soon afterwards on university noticeboards. Of seventy-six who sat, only twenty-six passed. In first place was Sartre. Close behind – in second place nationally – was Beauvoir. Her achievement was all the more extraordinary considering Sartre had been preparing for many more years, and had failed at his first attempt the previous year. At twenty-one, Beauvoir was the youngest student to have ever passed the elite exam. That night Sartre took his runner-up out on the town, and as they celebrated, he made her a promise:

From now on, I'm going to take you in hand.[28]

By this time, Beauvoir had started to attract increasing interest from several young men on campus. Leading these suitors were the eccentric Sartre and his extremely handsome – but married – friend René Maheu. Both found themselves helplessly drawn to this awkward, yet intellectually brilliant, girl who had descended, as if from nowhere, into their all-male class.

In the August summer holidays, Paris all but closed down for the month. Beauvoir joined her family for their annual vacation in Limousin, a quiet rural settlement 200 miles south of Paris. Beauvoir had been there every year with her family since she was a young child, but on this occasion – when she received a visit from a young man – it became clear to her parents that their eldest was a child no longer. The young man, who had caught the overnight train all the way from Paris, was her fellow graduate Jean-Paul Sartre.

Within a few hours of Sartre's arrival, Beauvoir found herself on the grass with him in a buttercup-strewn meadow, just out of sight of her family's holiday home. It was then that Sartre explained to her that he had decided he was never going to marry or be tied down in any way. He told her he wanted to commit himself to living freely for the rest of his life, that he refused to let his life be limited by the expectations of family or society. He expressed a hope that she, too, would not let herself be burdened by marriage, and would choose to live a life of freedom. Beauvoir felt a strange elation on hearing Sartre's bold words. At that moment she knew she had found someone with whom she could truly share life's adventure. He reached over to kiss her, and she didn't resist. Within minutes, however, they were interrupted by a shout. It was from Beauvoir's parents, who had spent hours looking for their missing girl. At the time of discovery they were fully clothed, but rapturously ensconced in each other's arms. Beauvoir's father looked uncomfortable as he advised Sartre that he would have to leave, that people in the town had already started talking. Sartre quietly responded that he would leave, but only after finishing the philosophical discussion he was having with Monsieur Beauvoir's daughter.

Two weeks later, Maheu, too, visited Limousin, but he came in secret without Beauvoir's parents knowing. He booked a hotel room in the town, and Simone managed to slip out of the family home to visit him. She was much more physically attracted to Maheu than Sartre but she couldn't help notice that he didn't evoke the same feelings of closeness and excitement that she had had experienced with Jean-Paul. Although Beauvoir managed a couple of rendezvous with Maheu during his three-day visit, she was still a virgin when he left.

That state of affairs would not, however, last long.

After Maheu left, Beauvoir had the rest of her summer holidays to think about what she really wanted in life. It occurred to her that

Maheu's bourgeois hypocrisy in seeing her behind his wife's back was the very opposite of Sartre's courageous, honest approach to life and love. At that moment it became clear to Beauvoir it was 'Sartre and no one else' that she desired.[29]

On her return to Paris in September, Beauvoir moved into an apartment owned by her grandmother. It was on the fifth floor of a building on the Avenue Denfert-Rochereau in Montparnasse. It was here, on 14 October 1929, that she and Sartre had sex for the first time, setting in train one of the most extraordinary relationships of the twentieth century.

After a few weeks of 'feverish caresses and lovemaking', Sartre came the closest he ever would to proposing to Beauvoir.[30] On a bitingly cold autumn day, whilst sitting next to each other on a park bench in a public garden, Sartre suggested: 'let's sign a two-year lease'.[31] With this phrase Sartre wasn't suggesting they live together (incredibly, they never would), but that they extend their relationship for another two years. Beauvoir was happy with the informality of this offer – she had long ago accepted she was unlikely to marry. And she had already indicated to Sartre that she, like him, was willing to risk all to live a life of freedom unencumbered by the shackles of bourgeois convention.

It was on that fateful day that Beauvoir also agreed to Sartre's suggestion that, from that day on, the two of them would be free to love whomever they wanted, but would stay true to each other by being honest and forthcoming about all their other liaisons.

Raymond Aron

It's good to be back.[32]

Sartre sat across from his friend Raymond Aron in the *Bec de Gaz* on rue Montparnasse, taking in the familiar street scene he had missed so much. The year was 1932, and Sartre had just spent two years in the port city of Le Havre on the Atlantic coast in his first teaching position since graduating from the ENS. Beauvoir had also been posted outside Paris, in the city of Rouen in Upper Normandy. Despite being sent to different locations, he and Beauvoir had visited each other often, catching the train to each other's towns.

Sartre had enjoyed his solitary walks on Le Havre's rugged beaches. In the soothing sounds of the Atlantic's crashing waves, he had found a peacefulness he hadn't known before. He had also enjoyed teaching the sons and daughters of farmers and fishermen, finding their eagerness to learn and lack of pretentiousness refreshing. Although he had appreciated the novelty of the slower provincial pace, he was glad to be back in the city of lights. He loved its bustling streets, its bookshops, its brasseries, and theatres. Even the puddles of spring rain on its sidewalks, with their reflections of the Left Bank's colourful shops and cafés, seemed to be welcoming him home. It was good, too, to be back with old friends. He hadn't seen Aron since their days together at the École.

As the clouds cleared on the horizon, Sartre took in the sun setting behind his companion, lighting up *Les Invalides* in a pink-orange glow. The waiter arrived with their aperitifs.

Sartre continued the reminiscing he had started earlier: 'It was so exciting then, when we were studying for the *aggrégation*. Looking back, Plato, Rousseau, even Leibniz seem much more exciting than what I've been doing.' He laughed. 'I can't spend the rest of my life teaching bored kids in regional lycées. I'll go insane.'

Aron smiled. 'You should consider a visit to the French institute in Berlin, where I've just been. The Germans have developed a new philosophy they call phenomenology. Have you heard of the work of Heidegger? Or Husserl?'[33]

Sartre shook his head. His curiosity was now well and truly aroused.

Aron continued, 'According to them, you can make a philosophy from anything, from everyday life.' Aron picked up his apricot cocktail: 'You could make a philosophy out of this glass if you wanted to.'[34]

The pedestrian traffic passing the café had started to pick up as Sartre sat back in his chair, contemplating what Aron had said. Some early theatre-goers in their evening wear had taken their place at a nearby table. Sartre absent-mindedly watched the café's waiter chalking out the dinner menu on a sidewalk blackboard. The lights of slowly passing cars fused with that of street lamps reflecting softly off wet cobblestones, breaking up the blanket of darkness that was descending over the city.

The idea of going to Berlin appealed greatly to Jean-Paul. *I must talk this over with Beauvoir,* he thought.

Berlin

A year later, Sartre arrived in the German capital. With Aron's help, he had managed to get a scholarship at the French Institute, right in the centre of Berlin.

Just prior to Sartre's arrival, in 1933, Hitler had been appointed Chancellor of Germany. Large flags bearing swastikas fluttered from government buildings, and Nazi soldiers marched through the streets. But Sartre took little heed of such fanfare – he was more interested in German phenomenologists than the country's politics.

Sartre soon settled into a steady routine, spending his mornings in Berlin's impressively resourced public libraries reading everything he could get his hands on about the new German philosophers. He found himself drawn to the works of Husserl and Heidegger, and the way their philosophies concerned themselves with, as Aron had said, everyday experiences in the everyday world. Sartre found these works a revelation, a welcome contrast from the dry abstract preoccupations of Plato, Kant, and other traditional philosophers he had been exposed to at the École.

In the afternoons, Sartre went for long walks along the river Spree, surveying the city's wide-open boulevards, its grand museums, and its fine examples of neoclassical architecture. In the evenings he worked away at the second draft of his first novel, a novel he had already spent years writing. It was in Berlin that he thought of adding a new dimension to his work-in-progress; he would incorporate into it themes from the new philosophies he was learning about. Five years later, this much-rehashed novel would be published as *La Nausée* (*Nausea*). The idea of using fiction as a medium to bring philosophy to life would become, in subsequent years, a hallmark of Sartre's work.

Whilst in Berlin, Sartre wrote every week to Beauvoir, who was still posted to her teaching position in Rouen. He told her he hoped to find a German lover while in Berlin, but his clumsy grasp of the German language was making it difficult. As he would recall several years later in his *War Diaries*:

> In order to seduce, I counted on my power of speech alone. I can still recall the trouble in which I found myself in Berlin. I'd set off determined to experience the love of German women, but I soon realised I didn't know enough German to converse. Stripped of my weapon, I was left feeling quite idiotic and dared attempt nothing – I had to fall back on a French woman.[35]

The French woman, as he faithfully explained in his letters to Beauvoir, was Marie Ville, the wife of one of his colleagues at the French institute. Marie was young, dreamy, and ethereal – the type of woman Sartre would be attracted to time and time again. Sartre regaled Beauvoir with exotic tales of his outings with the sensual and adventurous

Marie. Together they explored the decadent netherworld of Berlin's nightlife – a world of cabaret, homosexual bars, transvestites, female wrestlers, and art-house theatres – and a world that, unbeknown to them, would soon disappear as the Weimar Republic shuffled towards its final days.

A Visit from Beauvoir

In February 1934 Beauvoir – perhaps just a little concerned at how much fun her partner was having – decided on impulse to visit him in Berlin. Putting her job at considerable risk by falsely telling her employer she was ill, she slipped away to spend a couple of weeks with her beloved. In her autobiography, Beauvoir would later insist she felt totally comfortable with Sartre's new affair. This might, however, have been partly due to the fact that on her arrival Sartre told Beauvoir he didn't see it lasting much longer with Marie. Beauvoir recalls:

> [T]his was the first time since we had known one another that Sartre had taken a serious interest in another woman; and jealousy is far from being an emotion of which I am incapable, or which I underrate. But this affair neither took me by surprise nor upset any notions I had formed concerning our joint lives.[36]

Olga

On her return to Rouen, Beauvoir's increasing sense of isolation wasn't helped by the next letter she received from Sartre, in which he related how much he was continuing to enjoy his outings with Marie Ville. Like Sartre, Beauvoir tended to feel claustrophobic and ill-at-ease after too long in a provincial setting, and she now started to wonder how much longer she could cope with being away from both her partner and her home city of Paris.

Until, that is, she started having an affair with one of her students.

The seventeen-year-old Olga Kosakiewicz initially made very little impression on her twenty-five-year-old teacher. Dreamy, vague, and distractible, the Russian-born boarder usually sat up at the back where she contributed little to Beauvoir's baccalaureate class. In fact, the only thing Beauvoir had noticed about this student was the annoying way she let her stringy blonde hair fall across her face. No one was more surprised than Beauvoir when, after the students were asked to write an essay on Kant, Olga's effort shone above all the rest. A few days later, Olga caught her teacher's attention again, but this time for a different reason. Beauvoir noticed, at the end of class, that she was sobbing. As the other students filed out, Beauvoir asked her to stay back to talk about whatever it was that was troubling her. It didn't take long for Beauvoir to determine that this sullen, pale, skinny teenager had no confidence and no friends. As the girl wiped her eyes, Beauvoir offered some encouraging words about how impressed she had been with her recent essay. When Beauvoir saw what little effect these comments had on the girl's misery, she found herself suddenly moved by pity to suggest that perhaps they could meet that Sunday outside of school and talk some more.

That weekend, over a coffee in Rouen's *Brasserie Victor*, Beauvoir learned that Olga was the daughter of Russian aristocrats who had fled Russia for France soon after the revolution. Settling in L'Aigle, a small town in Lower Normandy, her parents had set up a sawmill business that had been struggling in recent times. Unsure what to do with their uncommunicative and directionless daughter, they sent her to school in the region's capital in the hope she might develop an interest in something and make some much-needed friends. But Olga wasn't coping well with being so far from home.

Beauvoir offered to take this lost soul under her wing and help her with her studies. Impressed by the literary aptitude she had shown in her essay on Kant, Beauvoir introduced her young charge to the works of her favourite authors – Proust, Stendhal, and Baudelaire – and encouraged her to try her hand at doing some more writing.

Olga would later recall being in awe of her teacher from her very first lesson. Unlike the other teachers at the *Lycée Jeanne d'Arc*, Beauvoir wore make-up and elegant suits, and exuded a confident, urbane style. Olga's fascination only increased when her teacher dropped hints about her independent and unconventional lifestyle.

Olga's rapidly building infatuation wasn't eased at all by the innocent pastimes Beauvoir invited her to participate in. At Beauvoir's behest, they met several times after school to play chess, cards, and table tennis. Beauvoir continued to lend Olga books from her personal library. She also answered, in a matter-of-fact way, her wide-eyed student's questions about her bohemian lifestyle in Paris and her open relationship with Sartre. Beauvoir, who was a keen hiker, also arranged for the two of them to take some long walks in the countryside outside Rouen.

It gave Beauvoir much pleasure and relief to see her student's spirits lifting. Their emerging friendship also helped to assuage the nagging doubts that plagued her the whole time that Sartre was in Berlin.

Cherry Brandy

In the summer break of 1934, Olga returned to her parent's house in Normandy, whilst Beauvoir enjoyed a much-anticipated holiday in Germany and Crete with Jean-Paul. During the trip, Beauvoir did not, however, forget her young friend, writing to her often. In one of her letters to Olga, she insisted it was time for her to stop addressing her as '*Mademoiselle*':

> You are much too close to me for this formal word to be suitable any longer.[37]

In the same letter, Beauvoir confessed:

> I'm deeply attached to you, but didn't know to what extent until you left. I miss you, almost painfully. Not only are you one of the most admirable people I know but you are one of those people who enrich the existence of those around them, and who leave a big emptiness behind them.[38]

After Olga returned, she and Beauvoir spent all their spare time going out together to drink, listen to music, and dance. Olga was a fabulous dancer and taught her older friend some moves. They soon got into the habit of finishing these evenings in one of their hotel rooms, where they would get drunk on cherry brandy. One night, Olga tripped and fell after leaving Beauvoir's room, and spent the rest of the night passed out at the bottom of the stairs. It was soon after this that Beauvoir, having already crossed the line from teacher to friend, crossed another. When Beauvoir awoke on that particular morning with Olga at her side, and remembered everything they had done, she was surprised to find she didn't feel perturbed at all. In fact, it was the happiest she had felt for a long, long time.

L'Hotel du Petit Mouton

Beauvoir was not the only one to succumb to Olga's charm. In October 1934 Sartre – having completed his scholarship in Berlin – caught the train to Rouen to visit Beauvoir. He was immediately impressed by the sight that greeted him at the platform – next to his partner stood a tall, blonde teenager who seemed just as excited as Beauvoir to see him.

Sartre, now based back in Le Havre, visited Beauvoir almost every weekend in the months that followed. But it soon became clear to Beauvoir that it was not just her he wanted to see. Beauvoir couldn't help but notice how distracted Sartre seemed whenever Olga was in the room, how his eyes tracked her every move.

Beauvoir moved from the shabby railway hotel in which she had been staying to the more charming and rustic *Hotel du Petit Mouton*. She arranged for Olga to move into the same hotel, and helped her set up her own room. Beauvoir and Sartre bought Olga a shelf-full of philosophy books, and both undertook to provide private lessons to the girl they started to refer to as 'the daughter of the Cossacks'.[39] The twenty-nine-year-old Sartre, the twenty-six-year-old Beauvoir, and the eighteen-year-old Olga soon became an inseparable unit. Every weekend they came together at the *Petit Mouton*, blissfully blurring the boundaries of teacher, student, friend, and lover. As Beauvoir would later recall:

> Olga's enthusiasms swept away our provincial dust with a vengeance: Rouen began to take on a glimmering, iridescent appearance. She would open the door to us with great ceremony, offer us Jasmin tea and sandwiches made from her own recipe, and tell us stories about her childhood and the Greek countryside in summer. We in turn told her about our travels, and Sartre went through his entire repertoire of songs. We made up plays and in general behaved as if we were twenty again.[40]

Despite the sensual, bohemian atmosphere that prevailed in the *Hotel du Petit Mouton* that spring, Olga managed, incredibly, to resist Sartre's attempts to seduce her. This was certainly not due to a lack of trying on Sartre's part. Olga recalls:

[He] had something of a medieval knight about him. He was very romantic.[41]

Sartre had, in fact, become hopelessly obsessed. His infatuation with Olga would torture him for the next two years as he repeatedly tried, unsuccessfully, to win her over. Apart from one tormenting kiss soon after they became acquainted, all his efforts were in vain. The increasingly confident Olga, however, grew to relish the attention she was getting from her teacher's partner, who in her presence was now behaving more like a helpless schoolboy than an up-and-coming philosopher.

Beauvoir's joy at the fun they were all having together soon soured as Sartre's lustful preoccupation with their new friend became unrelenting and all-consuming. Beauvoir would later recall that 'the agony which this produced in me went far beyond mere jealousy'.[42]

Polyamory in Paris

In June 1936 Sartre and Beauvoir both managed to get teaching posts back in Paris, and Sartre – after two long years of futile and fruitless grasping – was finally able to leave his feelings for Olga behind.

Back in Paris, however, Beauvoir and Sartre became involved in several other love triangles. In fact, a pattern emerged in which Beauvoir would seduce one of her students, and then hand her over to Sartre to feed his seemingly unquenchable desire for new flesh.

Bianca Bienenfeld was only sixteen when she approached Beauvoir – now teaching at the illustrious *Lycée Molière* in Paris – and asked her how she could progress to studying philosophy at university.

In a replay of her behaviour with Olga two years earlier, Beauvoir suggested they meet in a café to talk, and before long they became close friends. The young Bianca, like her predecessor, became fascinated when Beauvoir told her about her relationship with Sartre, how they planned to never marry or have children, and how they took on other lovers and were never jealous of each other. As Bienenfeld recalls in her memoir, she became captivated:

> From the very first months I identified myself ardently with Simone de Beauvoir. I did everything to get closer to her, to such an extent that my classmates later made fun of the speech habits I'd picked up from her...Around June, even before graduating from high school, I knew I wanted to get a degree in philosophy and teach, just like her.[43]

Soon, Beauvoir and Bienenfeld were spending every Sunday together. After Bienenfeld graduated from high school, the two women went on a hiking trip in the Morvan region in Burgundy, where it rained non-stop for five days. They stayed in tiny rustic *pensions* sharing a bed.

'It was during this trip that we began, shyly at first, our physical involvement',[44] recalls Bienenfeld. She was soon telling Beauvoir that she would never love anyone else as much she loved her.

By the time Bianca turned eighteen, her and Beauvoir's affair had reached a new level; they were now making love several times a week. It was at this point that Beauvoir introduced her to Sartre, who within a few days was able to lure the awestruck teenager up to his room at the *Hôtel Mistral* in Montparnasse.

After Sartre slept with Bienenfeld – and described his conquest in lurid detail to Beauvoir – Beauvoir's enthusiasm for the charms of her young student quickly faded. When the three of them next got together at the *Café Rouge*, Bienenfeld's attempts to conscientiously share her affections with both her lovers became decidedly awkward. As Beauvoir recalls:

She took [both] our hands, squeezed them, let them go, took them again, being careful to share herself evenly. She [did] not realise that effusions of tenderness work with two but not with three.[45]

Although Beauvoir would never, even years later, identify herself as lesbian or bisexual, she did admit to Sartre in a letter around this time that she had 'developed a certain taste for such relations'.[46]

In 1939 Beauvoir bedded another one of her students, the seventeen-year-old Natalie Sorokine, whom she would later rather disparagingly describe as 'a blond in heavy shoes…prone to jealous fits and insouciant temper tantrums'.[47] When Beauvoir's brief affair with this pupil was on its last legs, she introduced her to Sartre, who took no time at all to seduce her.

One of the more chilling aspects of this pattern of sequential seduction carried out by Beauvoir and Sartre during these years was how soon Sartre would shoot a letter off to Beauvoir after each conquest, describing it in shameless detail. These letters were written in a way that seems intended to arouse both Sartre and Beauvoir's voyeuristic appetites. Sartre wrote these letters while his bed was literally still warm from the body of his latest lover. In one such letter, after seducing the twenty-year-old actress Colette Gilbert in 1938, he told Beauvoir:

It's the first time I've slept with a brunette, actually black-haired, Provençale as the devil, full of odours and curiously hairy, with a little black fur patch at the small of her back and a very white body, much whiter than mine…Very lovely legs, a muscular and absolutely flat stomach, not the shadow of a breast, and, all in all, a supple, charming body.[48]

Showing scant concern for Gilbert's dignity or privacy, Sartre continues to recount the seduction with a blow-by-blow dialogue:

Around midnight she suddenly became very nervous, pushed me away then drew me back and finally said:

194

'It bothers me that I'm not yours. I would like you to enter me.'

'You want me to try?'

'You're going to hurt me, no, no!'

But I tried gently. She moaned...After a moment she said louder:

'No more, no more, let me be, please!'

I stopped and said to her, 'but you're no longer a virgin.'[49]

Consequences

The arrival of World War II didn't slow down Sartre and Beauvoir's bed-hopping. If anything, the lovers they took on increased, as if in protest at the clampdown of freedoms taking place elsewhere in Europe.

By 1943, however, the consequences of their exploits were starting to catch up with them. The parents of Natalie Sorokine complained to school authorities that Beauvoir had not only breached her professional duties as a teacher by having sex with their daughter when she was only seventeen, but had groomed her to be preyed upon by her immoral and depraved partner Jean-Paul Sartre. The parents wanted Beauvoir charged with abduction of a minor. Beauvoir was not charged, but the education department upheld the complaint, and formally suspended Beauvoir from teaching for the rest of her life.

The following year, after the liberation of Paris, Beauvoir came across Bianca Bienenfeld, who, like so many others of Jewish heritage, had spent the last few years in hiding. It had been five years since Beauvoir and Sartre's ill-fated liaison with her, and Beauvoir was shocked and dismayed at the state in which she found her once bright, attractive student. Beauvoir learned that soon after their three-way collapsed, Bienenfeld suffered a nervous breakdown from which she had never recovered. A horrified Beauvoir wrote to Sartre:

She's suffering from an intense and dreadful attack of neurasthenia, and it's our fault, I think. It's the very indirect, but profound, after-shock of the business between her and us. She's the only person to whom we've really done harm, but we have harmed her…She weeps all the time – she wept three times during the dinner, and she weeps at home when she has to read a book or go the kitchen to eat…At times, she really looked quite mad – bottling things up, anxious, but with moments of repressed tenderness and mute appeals that tore at my heartstrings. It's important to see a lot of her, and I'm going to try because I'm filled with remorse.[50]

She Came to Stay

In the same year that Beauvoir's teaching career ended in ignominy, her career as a writer took off.

In August 1943 after thirteen years of writing and rewriting, Beauvoir finally published her first novel *She Came to Stay*. Sartre had been encouraging her to write a novel based on real-life experiences, and this was the result. A thinly disguised account of her love triangle with Sartre and Olga, the book became an overnight sensation, its racy passages of seduction, jealousy, and intrigue providing a welcome distraction for Paris's war-weary residents. The early pages of the book titillated its 1940s readers with a detailed account of Beauvoir's seduction of Olga.

In the book, Olga's name had been changed to Xavière, and Beauvoir's to Françoise, but scenes such as the following – on the dance floor of a city bar late one night– provided readers with a taste of what Beauvoir experienced in the early days of her first same-sex affair:

[Xavière] certainly enjoyed attracting attention, and was deliberately holding Françoise tighter than usual, and smiling at her with flagrant coquetry. Françoise returned her smile. Dancing made her

196

head spin a little. She felt Xavière's beautiful warm breasts against her, she inhaled her sweet breath. Was this desire? But what did she desire? Her lips against hers? This body unresisting in her arms?[51]

Beauvoir had achieved instant notoriety by putting her polyamorous lifestyle on display for all to see. But she had also provided one of the first accounts of existentialism in action. She had demonstrated what it was like to live according her and Sartre's new philosophy, a philosophy which held that meaning and purpose in life could only be found through the fearless embrace of freedom.

Beauvoir found the praise of her novel from both the public and critics difficult to believe. In her memoirs, she recalls:

One literary columnist, discussing new books from Gallimard, referred to me as "the firm's new woman novelist." The words tinkled gaily around in my head. How I would have envied this serious-faced young woman, now embarking on her literary career, if she had possessed any name other than my own – but she *was* me![52]

In *She Came to Stay*, the main character struggles with feelings of jealousy and insecurity as she tries to honour a pact she has made with her partner to have an open relationship. Beauvoir lays bare, with unflinching honesty, what it was like to have Sartre as a partner and lover. This was the first ever real-life account of a famous philosopher in the bedroom, as a lover, and Beauvoir revealed the man she loves to be a self-centred, sadistic, and deeply flawed human being.

It says something of Sartre's character, however, that when asked by Beauvoir to read a draft of the novel, he gave his immediate approval and encouraged her, commenting that he thought she had portrayed him most accurately.

Being, Nothingness, and Nausea

Beauvoir wasn't the only writer experiencing fame and adulation during these years. Sartre published his first novel, *Nausea*, in 1938 to glowing reviews. Sartre's first literary work, like Beauvoir's, had taken years to complete. After redrafting it to incorporate the philosophical ideas he encountered in Berlin, he rewrote it three times and, after initially experiencing rejection, finally got it published just after his thirty-third birthday.

Sartre's first work had other parallels with Beauvoir's. It was highly autobiographical, and portrayed Sartre in a most unflattering light. It was as if Sartre could see his own failings as a person – his lust, his self-absorption, his insensitivity to others – but had no ability, or desire, to do anything about them.

Nausea tells the story of Antoine Roquentin, a professor of philosophy in an unnamed town on France's Atlantic Coast, who is trying to get back together with his ex-lover, a delicate and rather innocent young woman called Anny. Anny rejects Roquentin's overtures, as she finds him distant, aloof, and frustratingly difficult to connect with. Roquentin is acutely aware of his own shortcomings, and finds himself spending more and more time in his own head, preoccupied with negative and self-defeating thoughts. Sartre's protagonist comes across as a lost, dissatisfied, and gloomy character alienated from the world, other people, and himself. With Roquentin, Sartre created the first existentialist anti-hero, the type of character that would inhabit much literature and cinema in coming years. He was the first in a long line of fictional outsiders set adrift in an empty world devoid of meaning and purpose.

In a famous scene towards the end of *Nausea*, Roquentin, after years of aimless meandering, has an epiphany in which he realises that his thoughts, his worries, the ideas in his mind, are just fleeting illusions in contrast to the hard, cold, undeniable reality of the already-existent world around him. This realisation comes to him unbidden, and all of a sudden, while he is sitting on a park bench, consumed in gloom about all his life's problems. As he stares at the gigantic gnarly spreading root of a chestnut tree before him, he sees existence, as if for the first time, as it really is:

> I no longer remembered that it was a root. Words had disappeared, and with them the meaning of things, the methods of using them, the feeble landmarks which men have traced on their surface. I was sitting, slightly bent, my head bowed, alone in front of that black, knotty mass, which was utterly crude and frightened me. And then I had this revelation.
>
> It took my breath away. Never, until these last few days, had I suspected what it meant to 'exist'...If anybody had asked me what existence was, I should have replied in good faith that it was nothing, just an empty form which added itself to external things, without changing anything in their nature. And then, all of a sudden, there it was, as clear as day: existence had suddenly unveiled itself. It had lost its harmless appearance as an abstract category, it was a very stuff of things, that root was steeped in existence.
>
> ...It was no use my repeating: 'it is a root' – that didn't work any more. I saw clearly that you could not pass from its function as a root, as a suction pump, *to that*, to that hard, compact sea-lion skin, to the oily, horny, stubborn look. The function explained nothing...That root, with its colour, its shape, its frozen movement, was...beneath all explanation.[53]

With these words, written in his early thirties, Sartre had completely reversed the philosophical position of his childhood days, as described in *Words*. As a child, Sartre had clung to the world of books, ideas, and the imagination to help him cope with the stark, desolate, frightening reality of the world. In *Nausea*, however, Sartre renounces this world of words to face, for the first time, the immovable, irreducible truth of the external world.

Sartre was an unusual philosopher in that he mostly presented his ideas in works of fiction, in a long string of critically acclaimed novels and plays yet to come. In 1943, however, he published a more traditional work of philosophy that formally laid out his ideas. This work's title, *Being and Nothingness*, clearly acknowledged his debt to Heidegger.

In *Being and Nothingness* Sartre proposed a new philosophical framework to account for and reconcile two different aspects of existence – the external world and our own private experiences of consciousness. Sartre contended that *Existence* (all that exists) comprises two entities: *Being*, which consists of the material world and everything in it, and *Nothingness*, which Sartre saw as the primary quality of consciousness. Sartre noted that consciousness – or thought – cannot be located in space and has an inherently negative nature in that it typically wants to change the current situation, to negate what currently exists. Our minds are nearly always living in the future, thinking about how things could be different to how they are at present. Sartre believed this ineffable nothingness, or consciousness, we humans experience is the most important aspect of our existence. For Sartre, this nothingness *is* freedom. Sartre explained that our lives have no inherent meaning or purpose, but by harnessing our freedom to choose we can create meaning, and create an authentic and fulfilling existence for ourselves.

Sartre, like Heidegger before him, realised that awareness and freedom come with a heavy burden of responsibility. This burden is viscerally captured by Sartre when Roquentin, on being confronted with the meaninglessness of his existence, experiences a dizzying sickness in his stomach. This moment in the novel – and the novel's title – were inspired by Sartre's reading of a passage from Nietzsche's *Thus Spake Zarathustra,* in which Nietzsche proclaimed that most people tremble with nausea when challenged to embrace their fate and say 'yes' to life.

Existentialism is a Humanism

On a hot and balmy afternoon in the autumn of 1945, in a dusty and airless room on Paris's Left Bank, Jean-Paul Sartre gave a speech that cemented his position as Paris's most celebrated philosopher.

In the days leading up to the event, posters in the Metro, and on café and shop noticeboards, announced that the forty-year-old philosopher would be giving a lecture called 'Existentialism is a Humanism'.

Some of those drawn to the lecture had read *Nausea* or *Being and Nothingness.* Many others had read Beauvoir's bestseller *She Came to Stay,* that bared the bohemian life of free thinking and free love that Sartre, Beauvoir, and their friends had been enjoying between the wars.

The existentialists had by now well and truly captured the public's imagination with their new philosophy that one could live by, rather than just read or write about. There was much excitement in Paris's artistic and intellectual circles at the prospect of hearing Sartre speak in public for the first time. The fact that he wasn't an academic, but a failed high-school teacher who had dropped out to become a writer, only added to his allure. Many who attended were disillusioned by recent events in their country and were hungry to hear about a new way of living and being in the world.

Sartre's audience in the dusty hall was electrified with excitement even before he started to speak. The room was packed wall-to-wall, with many standing on chairs or straining on tiptoe to get a glimpse of this odd-looking, diminutive intellectual with a turned eye, thick glasses, and uneven teeth. Sartre's voice was quiet but laden with authority as he delivered his manifesto to the hushed, expectant crowd. He began:

> There is no determinism, man is free, man is freedom. Nor...are we provided with any values or commands that could legitimize our behaviour.[54]

With this opening, Sartre voiced the unspoken thoughts of not just those in the room, but of many in Europe towards the end of 1945. Religion had long ago lost its credibility, but now science – with its recent contributions to the development of ever more fearsome killing machines – had failed to fill the vacuum left behind by religion's demise. Nietzsche's dire warnings about a lost and directionless society following the death of God were ringing true. There was a sense amongst many that Europe's political leaders, having wreaked two horrific wars on their subjects in the space of one short generation, could no longer be trusted to lead.

In this famous speech, Sartre asked questions that were already on many people's minds. If we were no longer able to rely on the church, or science, or our political leaders, to whom or what could we turn?

As the afternoon sun streamed in through the windows of the dusty, jam-packed hall, Sartre told his audience that the answer to this new predicament lay within each and every one of them. We could only create meaning and purpose in our lives, he insisted, through our own individual decisions and actions. By making the most of our freedom.

'Man', he declared, 'is nothing else but what he makes of himself. That is the first principle of existentialism.'[55]

As those present strained to hear over coughs, murmurs, and shuffles of the sweating, heaving mass packed together on that oppressively humid afternoon, Sartre expanded at length on his idea that with the loss of God, the Church, and even science to guide us, the onus of responsibility to make our lives worth living fell squarely on our own shoulders. He closed his address with words that would become a much-quoted catchcry of his new philosophy:

Man is condemned to be free.[56]

Fame

The next day, reports of Sartre's speech were on the front pages of all Paris's newspapers. One headline shouted: 'Too many attend Sartre lecture. Heat, fainting, police'.[57]

According to these reports, the lecture was a sensation. Chairs had splintered under the weight of people clamouring to get a view of Paris's celebrity philosopher. Many had fainted in the crowded and airless room.

The main message of these reports, a message that filtered through to the population at large, was that existentialism was a philosophy of hope, but one that emphasised individual responsibility. In the wake of devastating news about concentration camps in Europe and atom bombs in Asia, the godless but hopeful spirit of existentialism resonated with many people's sense of what was needed to move forward. Humanity's future was now in its own hands.

That autumn, Paris flourished with the reopening of jazz bars, cafés, bistros, and salons. A new breed of Parisian appeared on the streets – in particular on the Left Bank – thin, chain-smoking, earnest-looking types, clutching copies of *Being and Nothingness* which they read conspicuously in sidewalk cafés. Suddenly, 'existentialists' were everywhere, hanging out at their favourite haunts by the Seine, reading, scribbling, and sipping coffee as white-shirted waiters flitted between tables under awnings in the late afternoon sun. The tree-lined boulevard of Saint-Germain had come back to life. This post-war bustle of existentialist hope, freedom, and opportunity, tempered with a new realism, would electrify Paris's streets for years to come.

With existentialism well and truly in vogue, Sartre and Beauvoir found themselves accorded the status of celebrities. The press stalked this short man and upright handsome woman wherever they went, whether promenading through their favourite streets in Montparnasse, or on the boulevards and avenues of the Left Bank. Newspapers were full of stories of their daring, open, immoral way of life. Bookstore windows everywhere displayed their latest works. Even the signs atop Paris's theatre-houses would soon be emblazoned with the billings of Sartre's latest play.

During these years, Sartre and Beauvoir settled into a routine well-known to their friends and admirers. Living apart in separate hotels, they wrote on their own for several hours each morning. If Sartre had a new lover staying from the previous night, he would make it clear that she should leave promptly so that he could get on with his work. After their morning hours of writing in solitude, Sartre and Beauvoir met for lunch to discuss their progress, exchanging drafts for each other's review and critique.

After lunch, Paris's most famous couple strolled through one of their favourite precincts – Montparnasse, St-Germain, or the Latin Quarter – before returning to their hotels to work through the afternoon.

In the evenings they met up with friends at the *Café de Flore, Les Deux Magots,* or another of their favourite haunts. At the height of their fame, their guest list included Albert Camus, George Bataille, Arthur Koestler (with whom Beauvoir had a memorable one-night stand), and Pablo Picasso. Picasso and his mistress Dora Marr regularly invited Sartre and Beauvoir to the artist's Paris apartment for lunch. Beauvoir recalls:

> Picasso always welcomed us with sparkling vivacity, but though his conversation was gay and brilliant, we didn't exactly talk with him. It was more a case of his holding forth solo.[58]

As the 1940s came to a close, the newspapers and airwaves were again full of praise for Sartre as his *Roads to Freedom* trilogy of novels appeared in Paris's bookstores. *The Age of Reason, The Reprieve,* and *Iron in the Soul* chronicled, with a disarming honesty but gloomy attention to psychological detail, the lives of characters based on Sartre and his real-life friends, and the different ways each responded to the Nazi occupation of France and other events of World War II. Each character struggled in their own way to respond to these extraordinary historical circumstances. As Sartre later explained:

> My intention was to write a novel about freedom.[59]

A Convenient Philosophy

Sartre, who as a child had suffered terrible loneliness, now found himself – in his forties – adored and in the constant company of lovers. He had left behind the desperate longings of his childhood to create a philosophy of freedom that conveniently ensured he would never have to suffer the pain of loneliness again. His new philosophy dictated that he exercise freedom in all his affairs, including love and sexuality. Thanks to existentialism, this once frightened and lonely child had grown into a celebrity philosopher, never again far away from the comfort and sensuality of another's touch.

Despite all his other liaisons, Sartre would repeatedly assert that his greatest love was always for Beauvoir. She remained his closest and most intimate confidante.

One wonders if Sartre's pact with Beauvoir, that allowed him to have as many lovers as he wished, provided a bulwark for him against any fears he had, conscious or unconscious, that she might abandon him, as his mother had done all those years ago. Sartre's insistence that Beauvoir be free to take on other lovers could also be seen, in a round-about way, as his way of avoiding the pain of abandonment he experienced in his younger days. If he was *allowing* Beauvoir to have other lovers, it was at least in some way under his control.

Although Sartre managed to develop a philosophy that, in effect, solved the problem of his childhood loneliness by ensuring a regular and inexhaustible pipeline of lovers, the truth was he was neither happy nor satisfied. At around this time, he confessed to Beauvoir that he actually felt cheapened and empty after each new conquest. Seduction had become a compulsion for him, a habit he felt unable to control or resist.

Sartre the freedom-seeker was quickly becoming a prisoner of his own uncontrollable needs and desires. He confided to Beauvoir that he didn't actually have a high sex drive – there was something deeper, more mysterious, and more out of his control that drove his Don Juan-like behaviour.

Sartre also felt a great degree of obligation to those lovers with whom he had a relationship for any extended period of time. Consequently, rather than finding a life free of burden, he found himself, as time went on, accumulating an increasing number of women who were emotionally and financially dependent upon him.

Mother and Son

In October 1946 an opportunity arose for Sartre to resolve some of the effects of his traumatic and lonely childhood. His mother – now in her sixties – found herself alone again after the death of her husband

Joseph Mancy, the man who had been so cruel and indifferent to Sartre during his teenage years. Sartre's mother bought an apartment on Rue Bonaparte in St-Germain-des-Prés, and invited her forty-one-year-old son to move in with her. Sartre moved in immediately, and lived with his *maman* for the next sixteen years. They were joined in the small apartment by another figure from Sartre's past, his mother's faithful maid Eugénie, who insisted on referring to the now-famous philosopher by his childhood pet name of 'Monsieur Poulou'.[60]

Although Sartre was now, so to speak, back in the arms of his much-missed mother, it didn't retard his now well-entrenched pattern of trying to seduce every woman he encountered.

Changes

Beauvoir did, however, notice one change in Sartre soon after he moved in with his mother. It was becoming increasingly clear to Beauvoir that the love of her life was losing interest in her sexually. It was almost as if the sensual aspect of his relationship with her was no longer needed now he had his mother back in his life. When Beauvoir asked Sartre about this change, he acknowledged, with a frankness that had characterised their relationship right from the beginning, that her intuition was correct. He confessed to her, by way of an explanation that certainly didn't make her feel any better, that for him the thrill of sex was no longer so much about physical pleasure, it was about the thrill of the chase, the almost sadistic conquest of another.

This revelation triggered painful memories for Beauvoir. When her mother was in her mid-thirties – the same age at which Beauvoir now noticed Sartre losing interest in her – her father had lost interest in her mother and started to frequent prostitutes, much to the distress and shame of Beauvoir's mother and the rest of the family.

Despite this significant and, for Beauvoir, painful shift in their relationship, Sartre and Beauvoir remained partners in every other sense of the word. Throughout these difficulties and beyond, they continued to see each other, and assist each other's writing projects, almost every day. Every summer they travelled abroad together, though they often took their lovers along with them.

Decades later, a sixty-nine-year-old Sartre would open up even more to Beauvoir about his sexuality and shed further light on why he was unable to continue a physical relationship with her. In a taped interview Beauvoir conducted with him as part of their commitment to honestly document their existentialist experiment with total freedom, Sartre even managed to startle Beauvoir with the graphic account he gave of his compulsive, stunted eroticism, an account that suggested he had not progressed very far emotionally or sexually since his deprived and lonely adolescence. As the sexagenarian philosopher explained to his partner and interviewer:

> I was more a masturbator of women than a copulator...For me, the essential and affective relation involved my embracing, caressing, and kissing a body all over...As I was reasonably well equipped sexually my erection was quick and easy, and I often made love, but without very great pleasure. Just a little pleasure at the end, but pretty feeble...I should have been quite happy naked in bed with a naked woman, caressing and kissing her, but without going as far as the sexual act.[61]

Algren

Although by the late 1940s Sartre had stopped sleeping with Beauvoir, he remained, as we have heard, her closest companion. He actively encouraged her not to mope about the changes in their relationship, but, in the spirit of their existentialist philosophy, to embrace her freedom and take on new adventures and lovers.

Which is exactly what she did.

In 1947 the thirty-nine-year-old Beauvoir was invited on a speaking tour of the United States. Naturally, she accepted, thrilled at this beginning of a new chapter in her literary career.

During the Chicago leg of her tour, she met the intense, brooding, blonde-haired writer Nelson Algren.

Algren's number had been given to her by people she met in New York City. On her second night in Chicago, feeling hemmed in by sterile hotel-room walls, she mustered up the courage to call him. It turned out to be a good decision. On their first night together, he introduced her to Chicago's nightlife, taking her to a dazzling array of wine bars, jazz clubs, and strip joints. Beauvoir had never before encountered Algren's type, a hard-drinking, gambling, chain-smoking writer of gritty fiction who was most at home amongst bums, prostitutes, and drunkards.

Algren's attentions in the coming days boosted Beauvoir's self-esteem, which had taken quite a battering with Sartre's announcement that he no longer desired her. Algren impressed Beauvoir so much that she would base one of the main characters of her next novel, *The Mandarins*, on him. In its pages, she immortalises the night she and Algren first slept together:

> Suddenly, he was no longer awkward or modest. His desire transformed me. I who for a long time had been without taste, without form, again possessed breasts, a belly, a sex, flesh; I was as nourishing as bread, as fragrant as earth. It was so miraculous that I didn't think of measuring my time or my pleasure; I knew only that before we fell asleep I could hear the gentle chirping of dawn.[62]

After Beauvoir returned to France, their affair continued for several years, with each flying across the Atlantic to visit the other when time and money allowed. During the long months they were apart, they wrote many letters heavy with words of longing. In one letter, Beauvoir gushed to her New World lover that 'writing to you…is like kissing you. It is something physical'.[63] Algren, who found the separations more difficult than Beauvoir did, replied somewhat curtly that 'no arms are warm when they're on the other side of the ocean'.[64]

But Algren became increasingly annoyed that whenever Sartre needed Beauvoir she would drop everything and fly back to France. Eventually, Algren got tired of playing second fiddle and ended the relationship.

In later years, Algren became extremely bitter about his relationship with Beauvoir, especially when he discovered that she had shared vivid details of their affair with Sartre. The last straw came when he read Beauvoir's 1954 novel, *The Mandarins*, and found in it a rather unflattering character called Lewis Brogan who was clearly based on him. Many of the most private and intimate moments he had shared with Beauvoir were splashed throughout the novel. Lewis Brogan observes in a scene towards the end of the book:

You can't love someone who isn't all yours.

In the last interview Algren gave to the press many years later, he clearly still hadn't let go of what had, for him, been an unforgivable betrayal. As he explained:

I've been in whorehouses all over the world and the woman there always closes the door…but this woman flung the door open and called in the public and the press…I don't have much malice towards her, but I think it was an appalling thing to do.[65]

The Second Sex

In 1949 Beauvoir published what many would later see as her greatest work, *The Second Sex*. It opened with the observation:

One is not born, but later becomes, a woman.

Beauvoir's description of woman – in the eyes of society – as secondary to man, and the hurdles this places in front of every young girl as she starts out in life, helped to launch feminism's second wave. Beauvoir was again creating controversy, this time for speaking the truth about the effect on women of living in a society in which, for centuries, men had held dominion:

It is required of women that in order to realise her femininity, she must make herself object and prey, which is to say she must renounce her claims as a sovereign subject.[66]

The Second Sex generated the most heat, however, for its unprecedented discussion of women's bodies, of female sexuality, and of topics such as contraception, lesbianism, and abortion. The Vatican immediately banned the book. Beauvoir was heckled on the street, and received a barrage of hate mail accusing her of a range of sins including, of all things, repressed frigidity. In some of the nastier letters, men made crude suggestions about how they could cure her of such a problem.

Beauvoir coped with the barrage of hate remarkably well. It helped that she knew Sartre fiercely supported her bold, honest exploration of sexuality, a topic also dear to his heart. It had been Sartre, in fact, who first planted the idea that led to her writing *The Second Sex*. She had mentioned to him she was considering writing a memoir, and he suggested perhaps she should first explore what it means to be a woman.

In later years, Beauvoir would follow through on her initial impulse, writing a comprehensive four-volume autobiography; this would also be the subject of much critical acclaim. The volumes, published over a fourteen-year stretch from 1958 to 1972, were *Memoirs of a Dutiful Daughter*, *The Prime of Life*, *Force of Circumstance* and, finally, *All Said and Done*.

A Younger Man

As mentioned, Beauvoir paid a high price for having the audacity to write openly about female sexuality in the conservative and chauvinistic 1950s. After *The Second Sex*, her notoriety reached such a pitch that she dared not venture out of her apartment for fear of being harassed.

Paradoxically, the years in which Beauvoir was most lambasted for her views on sexuality were those in which her own love life had languished. Following her acrimonious break-up with Algren, she went through an extended period of sexual inactivity, loneliness, and self-doubt.

By 1952 the forty-four-year-old Beauvoir found herself facing the fate she described so eloquently in *The Second Sex*, whereby every woman discovers, on reaching a certain age, that she is no longer considered worthy of a man's desire.

Beauvoir was shocked and delighted, then, when a mutual friend told her that the twenty-seven-year-old film director Claude Lanzmann had mentioned that he found her very attractive. Soon afterwards, Beauvoir received a call from Lanzmann. He asked her if she would like to see a movie.

'Which movie?' she asked.

'Whichever one you like', he replied.[67]

Beauvoir surprised herself when, after putting the phone down, she collapsed in a flood of tears.

After the film, Beauvoir and Lanzmann spent the afternoon in a café. She found it hard to take her eyes off the young lean man sitting across from her. She learned that Lanzmann, who was Jewish, had been active as a resistance fighter in World War II, at the time only a teenager. He flirted with her mercilessly that afternoon, his 'crystal blue eyes' steadily returning her gaze through the cloud of cigarette smoke that issued from his nose and mouth.[68] When Beauvoir tried to fend him off, pointing out he was seventeen years younger than her, he replied that he did not think of her as old at all.

They met for dinner the following night, and afterwards returned to Beauvoir's apartment in Rue de la Bûcherie on the Left Bank. The next morning, the young filmmaker had to leave for Israel – he had bought his ticket and arranged the trip well before his tête-à-tête with Beauvoir.

During the weeks he was in Israel, he and Beauvoir wrote each other every day.

When he flew back in to Paris, Lanzmann caught a taxi from the airport straight to Beauvoir's apartment. There, as he would later re-call:

[I found her] eyes, her arms, her mouth, her hands moving over my body as though to recognise it, the long, slightly tremulous embrace of our reunion.[69]

From 1952 to 1959, Beauvoir and Lanzmann lived together, but, as Lanzmann recalls, he had to share her:

'One evening was reserved for Sartre, the next for me.' He adds, 'We also often had dinner together, sometimes the three of us.'[70]

Lanzmann was very fond of 'the sultan of Rue Bonaparte', his pet term for Sartre, and didn't suffer from the jealousy that had created

213

problems for Nelson Algren.[71] As Lanzmann explained in an interview years later when asked about their relationship:

> Why should we have had any jealousy between us? When I started my love affair with Simone de Beauvoir, she had no sexual relationship at all with Sartre. They did not make love. That would have been unbearable for me – I could never share a woman I loved.[72]

In fact, Lanzmann had only admiration for Sartre – he loved the free-flowing conversations he had with Sartre and Beauvoir over long lunches in these years. He would later describe Sartre as 'magnificent, a philosophical genius – a truly great thinker'. He recalls that '[e]very time you left a meeting or conversation with Sartre, you felt this special sense of being capable of doing anything, such was his special charisma'.[73]

Decades later, Lanzmann produced what some hailed as the most important film ever made. His groundbreaking nine-hour epic, *Shoah*, released in 1985, was the first ever documentary of the Holocaust. Using first-person testimony from a long cast of survivors, it remains today one of the best foils against those who would try to dismiss or deny what happened to Europe's Jewish population in the lead-up to and during World War Two.

Three Mistresses

As Beauvoir became happily ensconced in her affair with Lanzmann, Sartre's life was becoming more and more complicated. By 1953 he had accumulated three mistresses, all of them highly dependent on him.

The first was Wanda Kosakiewicz, Olga's younger sister, whom Sartre had pursued as his consolation after Olga turned him down. It had taken Sartre more than a year of persistent haranguing and cajoling before Wanda had eventually, unlike her stronger-willed sister, succumbed to his charms.

Now, more than a decade later, he couldn't disengage himself from her.

The happiest days of Sartre and Wanda's affair had been from 1939, when they first slept together, to 1943, when he gave her a leading role in his play *No Exit*. Sartre became most upset, however, when Wanda started sleeping with the play's dashingly handsome director, Albert Camus, during rehearsals.

Although Wanda's fling with Camus was brief, Sartre was deeply hurt, and his relationship with Wanda would never be the same again. He continued to offer her roles in his plays, though, and from 1946 onwards he started paying her a monthly allowance. She would remain his lover for many years, and be financially supported by him for the rest of her life.

More recently, Sartre had started sleeping with Michelle Vian, wife of Boris Vian, one of Paris's most celebrated jazz trumpeters. When Sartre first met this hip young couple in 1949, their marriage was already on rocky ground.

Their troubles had begun just after the liberation of Paris, when Boris's band became increasingly popular, and women started throwing themselves at him after his performances. When Michelle expressed her frustrations to her husband about his frequent philandering, he angrily suggested she leave him alone and get her own lover. She resisted his suggestion, desperately wanting to stay faithful, but one evening, in a fit of rage and despair, she slept with the band's sixteen-year-old clarinetist.

This development didn't help the stability of the marriage or the band. Boris and Michelle's relationship was hanging together by a thread when Sartre befriended the couple. In May 1949 Sartre invited the beautiful, black-haired Michelle out on a secret date. During this outing, she found him the perfect gentleman, and was deeply moved at how interested he seemed to be in her troubles. By February 1950 the thirty-year-old was pregnant to Sartre and booking herself in for an abortion. Boris started to complain to all who would listen that Sartre was destroying his marriage. The Vians finally divorced in 1952.

Michelle would have another two abortions to Sartre, and remain his lover until his dying days.

Sartre's third love affair during this time took the incestuous polyamory of his circle to a whole new level. The forty-eight-year-old Sartre swooped on Claude Lanzmann's sister, Evelyne, the slim, blonde, twenty-three-year-old whose marriage to a man called Serge Rezvani had just fallen apart. Evelyne, like Wanda, was a budding actress, though with considerably less talent. She had been spectacularly unsuccessful in getting any acting work, even after getting a 'nose job'. (Her first drama teacher had told the young Jewish hopeful that she would never get cast 'with that Semitic nose of hers'.)[74]

Evelyne was long-legged and extremely tall, a feature she liked to exaggerate even further with high heels, dyed platinum blonde hair, and short clingy dresses. Sartre, at only five foot two, did feel somewhat self-conscious at her side, as he confided to Beauvoir:

> I thought other people looked upon me as a figure of fun, being the lover of such a tall girl...But sensually I liked it very much.[75]

Sartre not only provided Evelyn with acting parts in his plays, he offered to pay her accommodation costs, as he did with many of his 'girls'. He relocated her from her hotel room in Montmartre to a more convenient location, a two-bedroom apartment at 26 Rue Jacob, only a five-minute walk from his home in Rue Bonaparte.

Middle Age

Sartre became extraordinarily busy as he approached middle age. As well as writing numerous plays and essays, he co-founded and co-edited, with Beauvoir, the political and literary magazine *Les Temps Modernes.*

During these years, Sartre settled into a daily routine that began each morning in the book-filled apartment he shared with his mother. From his desk, crowded with manuscripts, notes, and overflowing ashtrays, he looked out over the railings of his balcony to the bustling street below. After a coffee and several cigarettes, he would hanker down for several hours to work on his latest project.

After a long lunch with Beauvoir, whom he still saw every day, Sartre worked through the late afternoon and into the evening. Around midnight, he would stop and telephone each of his three mistresses in turn, and reassure them that he was not sleeping with other women.

In his early fifties, Sartre found it increasingly difficult to continue the hectic pace he had come to expect of himself. But then he discovered something that could help. Amphetamines. Mass-produced synthetic stimulants had only become widely available in the post-war period, and Sartre made the most of this fact. He was soon in the habit of taking up to fifty pills a day to maintain the legendary literary output he had become renowned for, and to, as he put it, 'switch on the sun on in his head'.[76] He also consumed, on average, two packets of cigarettes a day as he tapped away at his typewriter. Not surprisingly, his health started to decline during this time. His physical state wasn't helped by the fact that he intensely disliked, and totally avoided, all fruit and vegetables. His diet during these years consisted mostly of sausage, coffee, amphetamines, and French cigarettes.

This gruelling routine was, however, interrupted every September and October, when he and Beauvoir took a holiday abroad, often bringing their lovers and friends with them. But these were their months, primarily, for enjoying each other. Their intimacy, though no longer physical, was stronger than it had ever been. Each was still the other's main confidante and source of validation and inspiration. Beauvoir felt much less insecure about Sartre's other lovers now their relationship had lasted so long and weathered so much.

In 1956 they had a particularly memorable holiday in Rome. Beauvoir rented separate rooms for them in a hotel near the Trevi Fountain, around which they sat every afternoon soaking up the ancient Mediterranean sunshine. Even though they were on holidays, they still kept up a writing routine. After getting together early every morning for a coffee (Sartre's standard order was three double espressos), they returned to their rooms to write from eight in the morning till midday. After a light lunch they returned to their writing from five in the afternoon to nine in the evening, after which they would go out to enjoy the Roman nightlife and catch up with their Italian friends, most of whom were communists.

It was during this trip to Rome, in 1956, that Sartre, Beauvoir, and their friends heard about Soviet tanks rolling into Budapest, suppressing a peaceful political protest and killing hundreds of people. Sartre was horrified. For years he had been the West's most famous and vocal supporter of Soviet communism. Up until this event, he had espoused a belief that communism – with its aim of liberating citizens from oppression – was a natural partner of existentialism. But after the Soviet's ruthless suppression of the uprising in Hungary, Sartre let it be known publicly that he had changed his views. He unreservedly denounced the Soviet actions, and explicitly distanced himself from not only Soviet communism, but from the French Communist Party, which at the time was still a large and influential player in French politics.

Sartre at Sixty

By the time Sartre reached sixty, he had an even larger stable of women. Incredibly, he had at least five ongoing lovers at this time.

In addition to Wanda, Michelle, and Evelyne, all of whom he continued to see regularly and provide for financially, he had started a passionate affair with Lena Zonina, a Russian woman he had met on one of his many visits to Moscow.

Zonina was a journalist and translator, and member of the Soviet Writers' Union. Sartre first met her on the tarmac of Moscow airport on 1 June 1962. The Soviet government had invited Sartre as part of a post-Stalinist push to open up cultural exchange with the West, and Lena had been appointed as his official guide and interpreter. Despite heavy criticism from the French philosopher, the Soviet regime still saw Sartre as a potential ally during the Cold War, given his regularly voiced support for Marxist principles, and the fact that he was a fearless and influential critic of the United States.

Lena lived in a modest Moscow apartment with her young daughter. Like two of Sartre's other mistresses, she was a divorcee. Lena actually looked a little like Beauvoir, tall, with dark brown hair that she liked to pull back in a turban. She also had a white woollen jacket similar to one worn by her Parisian counterpart. But for Sartre, she represented something far more exotic than his usual companion. He idolised her spartan Russian existence, her dilapidated flat, and her loyalty to her troubled country's romantic and revolutionary past.

Beauvoir appeared to have no concerns about Sartre's affair with Lena. In fact, she usually accompanied Sartre on his visits to Moscow, and got on well with his Russian lover. As Beauvoir recalls:

> There was a bond between us that is hard to define – an understanding, an instant communication...It was a great pleasure,

walking about with her or sitting in her flat, talking and drinking vodka.[77]

Sartre became obsessed with Lena – he visited the Soviet Union eleven times just to see her. On one visit he even asked Lena to marry him, but she refused. Agreeing to this would have meant leaving her beloved country, something she would never contemplate.

Later, there were suggestions, never proven, that Lena was a KGB operative employed by the Russian government to seduce Sartre and keep him within its grasp.

Sartre's fifth lover during this time was Arlette Elkaïm, a statuesque nineteen-year-old Jewish–Algerian woman with raven-black long, straight hair. She had originally come to Sartre as a psychotherapy patient. Quite bizarrely, Sartre – who had no formal training as a therapist – had started taking on clients for a new type of treatment he had invented, based on existentialist philosophy. Very soon into this treatment, the philosopher–therapist and his nineteen-year-old patient became lovers. In an even more bizarre twist to this entanglement, Sartre soon afterwards legally adopted Elkaïm as his daughter. This strange arrangement had benefits for both parties. The emotionally troubled Elkaïm had disowned her own 'tyrannical' father, blaming him for her mother's suicide a few years earlier. And Sartre had recently realized, after a discussion with his publisher, that he needed a legal heir to take care of his affairs posthumously.

Sartre also tried to convince another of his psychotherapy patients, Liliane Siegel, to sleep with him, but she declined. She did, however, become his close friend and associate. Siegel, in fact, played a key role in the philosopher's final years, doing her best to procure other women for Sartre whenever she could oblige.

In his sixties, Sartre continued to visit each of his lovers at least once a week, providing financial and emotional support. Each of them suspected Sartre was seeing other women, but he continued to reassure each of them this wasn't the case. Beauvoir, of course, knew about them all in keeping with what was now a forty-year-old pact. Sartre cynically referred to the visits to his lovers as ward rounds, with himself being 'the district nurse'. As he complained to a friend who worked as a psychotherapist:

> You're lucky. Sick people come to your rooms, and they pay you.
> In my case, I'm the one who does the rounds, and I pay them.[78]

The Greatest Achievement

Sartre's compulsive need to seduce, a need that had consumed him ever since his mother had abandoned him at the age of twelve, accompanied him to the end of his days. At sixty-one, during a visit to Tokyo with Beauvoir, he managed to seduce their petite and very attentive interpreter Tomiko Asabuki. As Beauvoir observed to Sartre in a letter soon after:

> In almost every journey we've made or that you've made, there's been a woman who turned out to be the incarnation of the country for you.[79]

At sixty-six, Sartre's unhealthy living habits finally caught up with him. He had a stroke that left him paralysed for ten days. Two years later, in 1973, he had a second stroke that rendered him almost completely blind, and totally dependent on others. His days as a writer were over. The thing he loved to do most had been permanently taken away.

His unrelenting need to seduce young women, however, showed no signs of abating. Incredibly, at seventy, the frail and blind Sartre

took on yet another lover, a young woman in her twenties called Helene Lassithiotakis. She had turned up on his doorstep, asking if he
remembered her from lectures she had attended.

But soon after becoming Sartre's lover, the young Helene had a
psychotic episode, and then gained twenty kilograms as a side effect of
antipsychotic medication she was prescribed. This never stopped Sartre from visiting her and supporting her financially, even though they
stopped their physical relationship soon after she became unwell.

In his last years, Sartre was regularly visited by the romance writer
Françoise Sagan. She took him out to fine restaurants, where she
would cut up his food and feed him.

The aforementioned Liliane Siegel, Sartre's former psychotherapy
patient and now close confidante, managed to find quite a few women
who were willing to not only have lunch with the ageing philosopher,
but to grant his requests to be groped under the table while they told
him salacious details about their sex lives. The explicit nature of these
conversations even shocked the usually unflappable Siegel.

At seventy-four, Sartre boasted 'there are nine women in my life'.[80]
However, a few years earlier, he was quoted in an interview admitting
a greater truth:

> There are several women in my life…although in a sense Simone
> de Beauvoir is the only one.[81]

In another interview, towards the end, Sartre was asked if he had
been 'macho' in his relationship with women. He replied, after a long
and thoughtful pause, that he did not believe he had been so with
Beauvoir.

Sartre's sentiments were mirrored by Beauvoir, who would later
describe her relationship with Sartre as the 'greatest achievement in
[her] life'.[82]

222

Fifty Thousand at a Funeral

On a grey morning in late April 1980, 50,000 people poured onto the streets of Paris for the funeral of Jean-Paul Sartre, the city's most revered and celebrated intellectual. Never before or since have so many gathered to pay their respects to a philosopher. Braving the cold and drizzle, the crowd extended as far as the eye could see, shuffling in a hushed silence behind a rain-streaked black hearse.

Beginning its journey at the Broussais Hospital in Rue Didot, the funeral car slowly edged its way through the crowds that had brought Paris to a standstill. Many looked down from windows high above the streets that bordered the procession; some clambered onto monuments or statues to get a glimpse of their idol as he passed.

Politicians, academics, students, dignitaries, and workers alike lined the French capital's streets to pay homage to their much-loved philosopher-king.

When the hearse arrived at Montparnasse cemetery, the respectful silence that had prevailed up to this point gave way to jostling and shouts as the press and other onlookers surged to get a view of the casket. Microphones on long poles hovered over the silent coffin as it was carried to the grave. Journalists and members of the public held their cameras up high, frantically trying to catch one last glimpse of the philosopher before he was laid to rest.

Newspapers around the world would report on the funeral the next day. One described how in the commotion 'several were injured and many fainted as the crowd trampled over graves to reach the site where Mr Sartre's body will lie'.[83]

The same article described how 'Mr Sartre's longtime companion, writer Simone de Beauvoir, had to be helped through the throng, and one man slipped and fell into the grave shortly before the coffin was lowered into it.'

After the casket was eased into its final resting place, between the graves of two other men of letters – Charles Baudelaire and Guy de Maupassant – the crowd suddenly went quiet again, and, as if on cue, the rain started to fall more heavily. At the graveside, in the mud, knelt the lonesome figure of Simone de Beauvoir. The waiting press ceased all movement, and left a deferential distance between themselves and Sartre's lifelong companion.

The seventy-two-year-old Beauvoir, elegantly wrapped in black dress and bone raincoat, her hair pulled back severely, closed her eyes, shutting out the crowd and the rain. She tossed a handful of dirt and a posy of flowers on the coffin as it descended to the earth. Her best friend and partner of fifty years was gone. Memory after memory of all the times they had shared came to her now, unbidden, as if to comfort her in her moment of need.

Beauvoir would later proudly tell interviewers that she and Sartre had read every single work of each other's before publication. Her next – and last – book would be the only exception to this rule. Addressed to her departed best friend, it would be called *Adieux*.

Together, Beauvoir and her partner had forged a brand new philosophical movement that had captured the imagination of the post-war generation. They were the first celebrity philosophers since Voltaire, inspiring waves of followers with their bohemian lifestyle of living in cheap hotels, writing in cafés, and freely loving whomsoever they desired. They had left an indelible mark on twentieth-century culture, bringing philosophical ideas into the mainstream, and into the awareness and lives of everyday people.

On 14 April 1986, six years after the death of her beloved partner, writer, feminist, and existentialist philosopher Simone de Beauvoir died at the Cochin hospital in Paris. *Le Nouvel Observateur* acknowledged her pioneering feminist role with a headline that read:

Women, you owe her everything![84]

Beauvoir was buried next to Sartre at the *Cimetière du Montparnasse*. Their joint grave can be visited to this day, where one will always find it garlanded with fresh flowers and messages of love from the daily stream of visitors who come from all around the world to pay their respects.

Chapter 6

Foucault: A History of Sexuality

At Sartre's Funeral

At the news of Sartre's death, fifty-two-year-old Michel Foucault was asked by one of his students whether he would be attending the great philosopher's funeral. 'Of course,' he replied. Along with every other intellectual and artist in Paris, he wouldn't dream of missing it.

And so, the next day, the Professor of The History of Systems of Thought – a title he bestowed upon himself on his appointment ten years earlier to Paris's prestigious *Collège de France* – joined the huge throng of mourners that filled Paris's streets on that overcast April day.

Even amongst the crowd of thousands making their way towards Montparnasse cemetery, Foucault stood out, cutting a towering figure with his bald head, black skivvy, and dark suit jacket. Along with the students and associates who accompanied him, he was pulled along by the momentum of the crowd for several hours. When they eventually arrived at the cemetery, he turned to his friends and announced, with a nod to Sartre's coffin:

> When I was a young man, he was the one – along with everything he represented, the terrorism of *Les Temps Modernes* – from which I wanted to free myself.[1]

Foucault had never accepted Sartre's existentialist philosophy. Nor had he been impressed with Sartre's sympathy for Marxist ideology. He didn't buy Sartre's idea that each of us is free to create our own lives. Foucault and his fellow structuralists – Levi-Strauss, Lacan, and Barthes – would argue that we are not as free as we imagine ourselves to be. They believed our experiences of self and identity are constructed by external social and cultural structures largely beyond our control. Foucault's genius would lie in artfully revealing these hidden structures, and demonstrating how they had been bolstered throughout history to serve the needs of those in power.

Foucault's career-long determination to dethrone Sartre as the father of French thought echoed an impulse that had begun earlier in his life. As a young teenager, he had felt a burning need to break free from the shackles of his father's stifling and oppressive bourgeois mentality.

A Stifling Childhood

Michel Foucault was born in 1926 in the nondescript provincial town of Poitiers into a socially conservative upper-middle-class family that he found intolerable from a very young age. Foucault hardly saw his father, a surgeon who worked long hours until late into the night. Although Foucault's father was highly respected, his son found him unbearably pompous and aloof. Foucault's father assumed his son would follow his lead and study medicine.

But Foucault was closer to his mother, who was naturally more sympathetic to her middle child's sensitive temperament.

Foucault's high school years took place in the midst of World War II. Foucault would later attribute his fascination with history to some of his experiences during these years, including the day of the

Normandy Landing when teachers and other students burst into his classroom cheering and shouting that the Allies had landed.

Foucault also experienced the shame and shock of hearing that other pupils' parents had been arrested or shot for being Jewish, or – after the war – for betrayal and collaboration with the Nazis. He soon learnt not to ask other students questions about their families, sensing this was a taboo topic in a France ruled by rapidly shifting alliances.

As Foucault grew older, his mother could see that his inquiring and sensitive mind would not cope well with the rigours of medicine. She convinced her husband that, as Michel's older brother had already started medicine to ensure continuance of a family tradition, Michel should be granted some latitude in his studies.

Foucault was incredibly relieved when, at the age of nineteen, his parents allowed him to move to Paris and board at the *Lycée-Henri-IV*, the same school that Sartre had studied at twenty years earlier. It was here that Foucault began his lifelong study of history and philosophy.

Escape to Paris

In the ivy-clad sandstone buildings of the Lycée-Henri-IV in Paris's Latin Quarter, Foucault found not only a new world of history and philosophy, but also an older man who, unlike his father, he could look up to and respect. This man was his teacher, Jean Hyppolite.

Foucault had never met a man like Hyppolite before. Hyppolite had taught himself German just so he could read and comprehend Hegel's *Phenomenology of Spirit*. At the time, Hegel was not well known in French academic circles, but Hyppolite was able to transmit his enthusiasm for the German thinker in a way that Foucault and his co-students found captivating. A contemporary of Foucault's recalls the much-loved Hyppolite 'hunched behind his lectern', holding forth with a manner that was 'cheerful, cluttered, dreamy [and] shy, [often] drawing out his sentences with pathetic sighs'.[2]

Hyppolite had a lively light in his eyes that Foucault had never seen in the pinched and shut-down face of his father. Foucault would later recall of Hyppolite's lectures:

[In] this voice that kept on stopping, as if meditating was part of its rhythm, we heard not just the voice of teacher, but also something of Hegel's voice, and, perhaps, even the voice of philosophy itself.[3]

Hyppolite had, along with other notable thinkers of his time – including Bergson, Sartre, and Merleau-Ponty – attended the École Normale Supérieure, and Hyppolite encouraged Foucault to work hard so that he could have an opportunity to do the same. In introducing Foucault to Hegel's writings, Hyppolite whetted his student's interest in both history and philosophy, and helped him to develop his earliest ideas about the relationship between these disciplines. Within a few years, Foucault would draw on this foundation to formulate a unique *historiographical* approach that would systematically question and critique accepted narratives, and expose how established histories had been used by vested interests to maintain their power.

Hyppolite went out of his way to spend as much one-on-one time as he could with Foucault at the Lycée-Henri-IV, recognising in this awkward and intense young man a promising and prodigious talent.

Under Hyppolite's guidance, Foucault felt valued for the first time in his life. Unfortunately for Foucault, this feeling would not last long.

Diagnosis: Homosexuality

Hyppolite's faith in his star student was vindicated by his results in the ENS's entrance examinations. In 1946 one hundred students were selected to enter France's most prestigious centre of higher learning. Of that hundred, Foucault was ranked fourth. Foucault had shown he possessed the intellectual acumen required to join Sartre and other notables who had walked the corridors of the ENS before him. But from his first day there, it also became obvious to him – and others – that he didn't fit in.

Although the École was a hotbed of liberalism open to a wide range of ideas: phenomenology, existentialism, Marxism, Maoism, even feminism, there was one thing of which it was still not very tolerant: homosexuality.

Although he had experienced the occasional crush as a schoolboy back in Poitiers, it wasn't until he got to the École that Foucault became consciously aware of his sexuality. His awakening was helped by his discovery of Paris's beats and underground bars. Most of these places were unmarked, poorly lit venues characterised by a furtive and desperate anonymity. There was no such thing as gay pride in Paris, or any other western city for that matter, in the late 1940s. Homosexuality was still seen as a deviant, disgraceful affair. Foucault soon learnt that the experiences he yearned for were ones that, as Wilde had bemoaned a few decades earlier, 'dare not speak its name'. In the statute books, such experiences were still listed as a crime.

Foucault's classmates at the École Normale would later remember him as an aloof, irritable, and even frightening individual. He didn't mix with others, spending most of his time in the library or in his room. One student recalls passing a tormented and angry-looking Foucault in the corridor and asking where he was going, to which he replied 'to kill myself'. Stories such as this spread quickly throughout the student body, and most learnt to give their odd and curmudgeonly colleague a wide berth.

It soon became routine for Foucault, as darkness fell, to slink off to nameless establishments where, in shadowed corners of dingy bars, he would seek out other men in shrouded silence. Many of these men were married; hours earlier they had mumbled unconvincing excuses to their wives before taking off into the night. Like Foucault, they didn't yet have a word for their behaviour or their secret lives. At the time there were very few portrayals of homosexuality in literature, film, or theatre. Men such as Foucault and his anonymous associates had no social identity with which they could scaffold their self-worth against society's harsh disapproval.

On returning to his sleeping quarters after these illicit outings, Foucault would sometimes rock and howl with shame throughout the night, much to the disturbance of his fellow boarders.

One morning, Foucault was found lying on the floor of his room with bleeding wounds from a razor slashed across his chest. His father was called immediately. On finding his son in a state of mute and tortured despair, Foucault's father made urgent arrangements for a psychiatric consultation.

The psychiatrist, a bland yet kindly fellow, did not take long to make a diagnosis. He explained to Foucault's father that his young son was suffering from a classic case of homosexuality. The good doctor reassured Monsieur Foucault, however, that there were a range of treatments available to cure his son's malady.

Foucault managed to escape the psychiatrist's clutches, but the experience of having his sexuality diagnosed as a mental illness provided him with a very personal focus for his future scholarly inquiries. He had just experienced first-hand how 'truths' can be convincingly constructed by those in power and used to oppress the voiceless and disempowered. For the next few years, Foucault focussed the lens of his brilliant and analytical mind on the history of psychiatry as an institution.

Madness and Civilisation

In 1960, more than ten years after he had arrived at the ENS, Foucault completed the thesis for his doctorate. At 943 pages, this sprawling and monstrous manuscript was twice the size of the average submission. *Madness and Civilisation: A History of Insanity in the Age of Reason* presented a systematic and searing critique of the foundations of psychiatry. In constructing this masterful work, he had drawn on a wide range of historical, philosophical, and literary texts, uncovered and painstakingly analysed over many years.

Even though it had already taken him a decade of arduous research, writing, and rewriting to get to this point, Foucault knew the biggest challenge to achieving his doctoral degree still lay ahead. He would have to defend his thesis before a jury of specially selected examiners in a brutal public ritual that had long been part of the ENS's tradition.

It took Foucault another twelve months to prepare himself for this ordeal. His first task was to find a *rapporteur*, an academic who was willing to sponsor his thesis and sit on the jury.

Foucault approached his old mentor Hyppolite to ask if he could perform this role. To Foucault's disappointment, Hyppolite declined. His former teacher felt he lacked the credentials to evaluate such a heady and unconventional blend of history, psychiatry, and philosophy. Hyppolite did, however, suggest to Foucault an alternative, his colleague Georges Canguilhem, who he thought might be more qualified for the task. Canguilhem had degrees in philosophy and medicine, was a professor of both, and had written several papers on the history of science.

Foucault managed to secure a brief meeting with Professor Canguilhem in the vestibule of the Sorbonne's old amphitheatre. Foucault was only given a few minutes before the distinguished academic had to head into a lecture.

Canguilhem asked Foucault to succinctly outline what his thesis was about.

Foucault explained that the main argument of his work was that the Enlightenment, with its idolisation of *reason*, had created a need for *madness* – which up until then had been left alone and ignored – to be more clearly defined so that it could be controlled and suppressed. Foucault briefly expanded on his corollary; that psychiatry, which had only arisen as a new medical specialty during the Enlightenment, had been invented to carry out this task.

The professor, known for his gruff and impatient manner, was unimpressed. He replied:

If that were true it would [already] be known.[4]

To Foucault's surprise, however, Canguilhem agreed to read his thesis. On reading the work, Canguilhem experienced what he would later describe as a 'real shock'. Not only was the scholarship of a high quality, the dazzling rhetoric Foucault used throughout his work made his subversive arguments irresistibly compelling. Canguilhem found himself totally drawn in by the work's intricate and beautifully woven arguments.

He agreed to be Foucault's *rapporteur*.

Canguilhem did suggest Foucault tone down some of the language and more provocative claims within the text. Foucault was adamant, however, that he would not adjust the document's strident tone.

Uncharacteristically, Canguilhem did not press the point.

The Defence

On 20 May 1961 thirty-five-year-old Foucault tried to ignore the but-
terflies in his stomach as he walked down a corridor in the École he
had never been down before. This dimly lit passageway led to the Salle
Louise-Liard, a room reserved for the defence of the ENS's most important theses.

Foucault pushed open the heavy door at the end of this corridor,
and was greeted by a large, sombre space with dark timber walls. A
murmur of anticipation rippled through those seated inside as he entered, swathed in his black and blue academic gown. A hundred on-
lookers were packed into the regally styled theatre. Word had spread
that today's speaker could be expected to deliver something out of the
ordinary.

Foucault climbed three small steps leading to the dais on which he
was to speak, and took his place behind the lectern. Before him, in the
front row, sat his three judges. Behind them, higher up on overhang-
ing seats, stared back a crowd of staff, students, and external visitors.
Although a large clock on the opposite wall showed it was just after
one thirty in the afternoon, the room's small high windows and
opaquely coloured hardwood walls conspired to create a soft low light,
like that of a late winter twilight.

Foucault knew something about the background of each of the
three judges that faced him, but he also knew their assigned task, with
the possible exception of Canguilhem, was to find every flaw they
could with his presentation, to interrogate him mercilessly. As far as
the ENS's upper echelons were concerned, nothing was more important than demonstrating the ability to use reasoned argument to
defend one's ideas under pressure.

His judges were a philosopher, a historian, and a psychiatrist. Although Canguilhem, the philosopher, had agreed to sponsor Foucault's

thesis, he was anxious to hear his colleague's opinions, realising they might not share his enthusiasm. He was also highly mindful he needed to appear as rigorous and searching as his fellow jurors in his questioning.

To Canguilhem's left sat the jury's chair, historian Henri Gouhier. He had been an obvious choice to adjudicate this thesis, not only because of his expertise in the history of philosophy, but because he had the longest tenure of any academic at the École. The third judge, Daniel Lagache, was a respected professor of psychiatry from the Sorbonne.

A nod from the chair indicated to Foucault it was time to begin. Last-minute coughs and snatches of conversation from the audience gave way to a sudden silence as all eyes turned on Foucault. A thin beam of light streamed down from one of the room's translucent windows onto the candidate's face. He cleared his throat and began.

According to one account, 'Foucault's voice rose: tense, nervous, unfolding in rhythmic, staccato sequences'.[5] Within a few minutes, however, the candidate found his stride and was disarming his audience with not only the audacity of his arguments, but with a stylish and masterful delivery. As one observer recalls, 'every statement was as polished as a diamond'.[6]

The panel couldn't help but be impressed by the brilliant oratory of Foucault in full flight painting a picture of 'madness' in the seventeenth century, before the advent of psychiatry. He unearthed historical documents that revealed how, during the Enlightenment, hordes of people who didn't fit in with the Age of Reason's values – lepers, the poor, the homeless, epileptics, prostitutes, and other deviants and rebels – were rounded up and confined in large buildings throughout Paris. One of the largest buildings used for this confinement, the Salpêtrière, would later become one of Europe's most respected hospitals. But, Foucault insisted, it would only become known as a hospital *after* the many unfortunate souls languishing within its walls had been assigned one of the newly invented diagnoses of psychiatry.

The École had never encountered a thesis like this. For many in the audience, Foucault's ideas seemed outlandish, unbelievable, and outrageously provocative. In 1961 psychiatry was a highly respected institution. The movement known as anti-psychiatry, in which psychiatry's views of the world would be questioned and its abuses of power exposed, was born in the Salle Louise-Liard in that moment.

As Foucault neared the end of his defence, he summed up his central idea:

Madness was not a fact of nature, but rather a 'fact of civilisation'.[7]

He closed with a final observation:

To speak of madness one must have the talent of a poet.

In the eerie quiet that followed, everyone in the room heard Canguilhem's response:

But you, sir, have it.[8]

A long and strident applause ensued. Many in the audience rose to their feet, an unusual response after an academic presentation.

Foucault knew, however, that none of this meant he was certain to pass. He still had to face the onslaught of questions that would now come from the jury. Chairman Gouhier raised his hand to quell the audience and launched into the first of his many questions for the candidate, who suddenly looked very vulnerable in his exposed position on the stage.

Gouhier was the toughest of the three interrogators. He meticulously trawled through Foucault's defence, pointing out factual errors, logical inconsistencies, and unjustified exaggerations he had detected in Foucault's presentation. Foucault parried and responded as best he could, his efforts drawing the already mesmerised spectators in even further. The two other jurists followed with questions, which, though delivered more gently, still presented the candidate with considerable challenges.

After more than two hours on the podium, the chair informed Foucault that his cross-examination was over. He was still, however, required to stand for what seemed an eternity as his judges huddled together, sharing their deliberations. Eventually, after a few final whispers and nods, the panel stood. The audience, once again, fell deathly quiet. The chair glanced at his fellow panellists to confirm they were ready, and announced:

> The jury has decided to award the candidate, Monsieur Michel Foucault, with the college's highest academic title of Doctor of Letters.

The chair then added, as if to underline the significance of what all had witnessed:

> With a very honourable mention.[9]

Many who attended Foucault's defence that day talked about it for years to come. Not only had they been treated to an intellectual feat of staggering proportions; they had been entertained and transported in the process.

A few days later, Foucault received a written report from the jury. It read:

> M. Foucault is extremely well-read and possesses a strong personality and rich intellect. His exposition was remarkable for its clarity, its ease, and the elegant precision of a thought that knows where it's going, advances unhesitatingly, and is, one feels, in control of itself.

The next sentence, though, expressed a doubt, a residual unease in the judges' minds:

But apparent here and there is a certain indifference to the drudgery that always accompanies the most elevated work.

This ambivalent tone continued further along in the report:

M. Foucault is, of course, a writer, but M. Canguilhem criticised the rhetoric of certain parts, and the president thought he was too concerned with creating an 'effect'. There is…a spontaneous tendency to go beyond the facts.

In conclusion, the report stated:

The fact remains we are in the presence of a principal thesis that is truly original, by a man whose personality, whose intellectual 'dynamism', whose talent for exposition all qualify him for higher education. That is why, despite reservations, this degree was awarded unanimously with highest honours.[10]

This mixed response would be echoed many times throughout Foucault's career. When an abridged version of his thesis was published as a book the next year, it generated passionate but highly polarised responses. Some hailed Foucault as a prophet of a new type of cultural history. Others, in particular those in the psychiatric establishment, were quick to condemn its author as completely lacking in any scientific credibility.

Daniel Defert

At thirty-four, Foucault secured a position teaching philosophy at the University of Clermont-Ferrand, a smallish city in the Auvergne region, about four hours' drive south of Paris. Although he returned to Paris every weekend, Foucault soon started to feel frustrated and restless in this provincial setting which was, for him, a bit too similar to the one he endured as a child.

Foucault soon developed a reputation for being abrasive and contrary, and one of the more difficult members of staff at Clermont-Ferrand. His academic talents, however, towered above those of his peers, and in 1962 he was appointed head of the department.

By 1963 Foucault had started a passionate physical relationship with one of his students – the handsome, well-built twenty-three-year-old Daniel Defert. Foucault created controversy by quickly appointing his young lover to a position on the university staff. When asked by senior administration to explain why he had appointed Defert over an older female applicant who appeared better qualified, he replied: 'Because we don't like old maids here.'[11]

Foucault's relationship with Defert would turn out to be similar, in many ways, to that of his predecessor Sartre. Although Foucault would stay in a partnership with Defert for the rest of his life, there was nothing in that partnership that forbade Foucault from taking on as many lovers as he wished.

Although it can be presumed that Foucault's polyamorous activities might have challenged Defert at times, Defert would also take Foucault out of his comfort zone, albeit in a different way. Defert introduced Foucault to a world in which he initially felt very out of place – the world of political activism. Up until this point, Foucault had a modest profile as a thinker and writer of new ideas, but his reputation as an activist – a public champion of various causes – was yet to come. Defert managed to cajole his older partner, who was most comfortable in the library, onto the streets, into the hurly-burly of public protests, sit-ins and civil disobedience. As Defert recounts:

> I think that Michel became attached to me during this period because of the militant life I was leading.[12]

Like a number of other politically active students in France during this period, Defert was a committed Maoist. He and his comrades found great inspiration in the writings of Mao Zedong, whose *Little Red Book* was, at that time, selling more copies in Paris than any other city outside China. Just as Sartre's Marxist sympathies had made him slow to acknowledge the excesses of Stalinist Russia, Defert and his fellow Maoist revolutionaries had a blind spot when it came to the purges of the Chinese leader. For Defert and other left-wing students whose bedrooms sported a poster of the charismatic Chairman smiling down on them, Mao's ruthless deeds could be justified as part of a heroic class struggle against the crimes of capitalist oppressors.

In the years that followed, Foucault's increasing participation in radical political actions, instigated and encouraged by his lover, would propel him to new heights of recognition and notoriety. Before long, photographers would be scrambling for position to capture iconic images of the philosopher whenever he spoke publicly or led a protest. His arresting physical appearance and natural charisma would prove irresistible to a French media in search of its next celebrity philosopher.

For now, however, Foucault remained relatively unknown, ensconced in the early days of a sensual romance with his new lover Defert in the regional outpost of Clermont-Ferrand. He still had a full head of hair, an aversion to anything that could be seen as self-promotion or grandstanding, and was focussed, more than anything, on completing his next book, which would again critique an institution that had caused him pain in his younger years.

The Order of Things

In his second major work, *Naissance de la Clinique* (*Birth of the Clinic*), Foucault broadened his target of attack to include the whole medical profession. In this work, Foucault provided a detailed but provocative account of the history of medicine, charting its rise in respectability in

240

modern times. He described how the relatively recent construction of scientific systems of medical knowledge and proliferation of what Foucault referred to as medical *discourse* legitimised medicine and gave it enormous power. Foucault pointed out that this discourse comprised not only the language of medicine, but also unwritten rules about who could use this language.

Foucault's first two works had a common theme and method, both laying bare the relationship between language, knowledge, and power. Throughout his career, Foucault would continue to examine society's most powerful institutions and how these have used language and knowledge to maintain their dominance. Foucault saw language, or discourse, as the medium through which power produces speaking subjects. As a structuralist, he saw structures of power as more primary and influential than individual subjects. Here his thinking had broken with Sartre's conception of us all as solitary individuals making free choices in a neutral universe. For Foucault and the structuralists, the universe wasn't an empty stage we act upon, it comprised a network of invisible but powerful cultural forces that determines not only how we behave, but our very identity, the way we conceive of ourselves.

Foucault's powerful new approach to critiquing history would be much imitated in the years that followed. Many writers and academics would, inspired by Foucault's example, devote themselves to examining, unpacking, and retelling history in a way that exposes how those in power maintain their control. Foucault had created a new type of discourse, one that could be used by the powerless to challenge the powerful.

In 1966 Foucault published his third book, *The Order of Things*. More than any other, it documented his unique methodology and provided an overview of his revolutionary historiographical approach. This work secured structuralism as the most fashionable theory in town, dislodging Sartre's existentialism from what had previously seemed an unassailable position.

The book's subtitle, *An Archeology of the Human Sciences*, pithily summarises the intention of Foucault's life's work, to interrogate texts that have unquestioned authority in modern society – including the texts of history, psychiatry, medicine, science, and philosophy itself. In *The Order of Things*, Foucault explicitly acknowledges his debt to Nietzsche, who a century earlier in *The Birth of Tragedy* had tried to do a similar thing with the texts of the ancient Greeks.

In *The Order of Things*, Foucault argues that although society has, throughout the ages, undergone shifts in what it values most – whether it be Beauty, Truth, God, Reason, Freedom, or Knowledge – in each phase of history those in power have constructed institutions, power structures, and language systems to co-opt the current ideal and thereby maintain their position of dominance. He points out that this is usually done with such a clever and insidious subtlety that those being disempowered are scarcely able to notice what is taking place. Blatant displays of power or violence are not needed, he argues, for oppression to be effective. A personally laden example of this, for Foucault, was the construction and classification of homosexuality as a mental illness. This construction by those in power, whilst hiding behind a seemingly humane and scientific veneer of respectability, had been frighteningly effective in removing the voice and legitimacy of homosexual people without those in power having to even declare their intentions.

Although *The Order of Things* was written with an academic audience in mind, it became a surprise bestseller in France during the summer of 1966. Like Sartre's *Being and Nothingness* a generation earlier, it was *the* volume to be seen with, conspicuously carried around by young people in cafés, parks, even on the beach. When French people

242

turned on their televisions that summer, they would often be greeted by Foucault's striking Easter Island visage answering questions from an interviewer about his book. For the first time in history, a philosopher – through the new medium of television – was reaching into people's homes while they sat and ate their evening meal.

Tunisia

Later that year, Defert was called up for national service, and informed Foucault he would be posted to Tunisia. Although the newly independent North African nation was no longer a French colony, French forces continued to be stationed there at the request of the country's right-wing government. Foucault managed to get a position at the University of Tunis, allowing him to accompany his young partner to the volatile Mediterranean state. The two of them were determined to make the most of Defert's involuntary posting, and to do what they could to turn it into a memorable adventure.

Foucault found a small rental property on a hill overlooking the Mediterranean, and during Defert's off-duty hours the two of them spent many long hours lounging around on Tunisia's beaches and sampling the local hashish. A photograph from that time shows the happy suntanned couple sharing a pipe.

The holiday atmosphere would not last long, however. Foucault and Defert had arrived in a country simmering with civil unrest. Demonstrating students with nationalist, Marxist, and Islamicist sympathies were already engaged in violent clashes with the new government. Although Foucault didn't support all the protesters' causes (in particular, their anti-Israel stance), he couldn't help but admire their passion and courage in the face of sickening repression by government forces. He found ways to actively assist the rebels, sheltering some who were on the run from authorities, and allowing his house to be used to print political leaflets. In doing so, he put himself at considerable risk.

The students, however, viewed Foucault with considerable suspicion. To them he was an outsider hailing from the country they saw as their worst oppressor. Defert, too, found himself in a difficult position; although he was there as a representative of the French military, his radical Maoist sensibilities rendered him highly sympathetic to the revolutionary efforts of protesting students.

In the mid-sixties, calls for revolutionary change by disaffected students were not just happening in Tunisia, of course, but all over the world. The most dramatic of these was just about to take place in France's capital. Student activists in Paris, their courage and bravado fuelled by the anti-authoritarian writings of Foucault and others, were in the midst of launching an extraordinary social movement that would come within a hair's breadth of taking France to full-blown revolution, two hundred years after the first had shaken the country. This nationwide uprising, which began on the newly radicalised campuses of Paris's universities, would later become known as 'The Events of May 1968'.

May 1968

The events of May 1968 grew out of an increasing frustration amongst many young French people with what they saw as the outmoded conservatism and hypocrisy of their country's leaders, personified by the post-war president Charles de Gaulle. The rebels were inspired by a variety of ideologies, including Marxism, Maoism, anarchism, post-structuralism, feminism and, last but not least, the newly flowering sexual liberation movement. The initial protests, confined to university campuses, caused little concern for the authorities. The mood of the long-haired, denim-clad students taking part in these protests was playful, festive, and at times, even ironic, with slogans such as 'I'm a Marxist – of the Groucho kind' plastered on university walls.[13] What took everybody by surprise was the way in which these demonstrations snowballed so rapidly, spilling out onto the streets into massive displays of civil disobedience involving all sectors of society. Within weeks of the original demonstrations, hundreds of thousands of angry workers would be downing tools, threatening to bring the whole French Republic to a standstill, and striking terror into the country's political leaders.

The initial trigger for these events occurred in March 1968, when 150 university students occupied the newly built University of Nanterre outside of Paris in a protest against government policies regarding university funding. University administration called the police, who dispersed the demonstrators in this initial protest without incident.

Over the following weeks, however, ongoing conflict between activists and the university administration led to a series of rapidly escalating protests.

On 2 May the University of Nanterre's administration, fed up with ongoing challenges to its authority, shut down the university and threatened to expel student leaders who had been agitating for change.

The next day, students at the Sorbonne on Paris's Left Bank convened a snap protest in sympathy with their compatriots in Nanterre. Police were called to the Sorbonne to physically remove the protesters, but what happened next caught the authorities completely by surprise. France's national union of university students, the *Union Nationale des Étudiants*, called for a show of solidarity against the police, and within twenty-four hours 20,000 protesters, including large numbers of teachers and university staff, converged on the Sorbonne and occupied it in a massive display of defiance and solidarity.

Barricades

Four days later, on 6 May, authorities in high schools throughout France were confronted with a spectacle they had never encountered before. Student leaders, in uniform and wielding megaphones, urged their classmates to show solidarity with their university comrades by attending a demonstration at the Arc de Triomphe the next day. Thousands of high school and university students, teachers, workers, and others turned up at the rally, at which speaker after speaker aired a list of grievances against the government that included, amongst other things, inadequate university funding, conditions of workers, and the war in Vietnam. The mood of the protesters was angry, determined, and as far as the authorities were concerned, ominous. The rally's leaders demanded that all charges against previous protesters be dropped.

The de Gaulle government, rattled by the increasing scale of these protests, tried to deescalate the situation by ordering the withdrawal of all police from the Sorbonne campus, and reopening the Sorbonne and Nanterre universities. This olive branch, however, was quickly trampled underfoot by an increasing tide of anger that spread to include a substantial proportion of the French population.

On 10 May Paris's Left Bank became the scene of a demonstration even larger than that at the Sorbonne the week before. Not only was this protest much larger, its participants were better organised. Urged on by chanted slogans, a crowd of thousands moved to march across the Seine. Their progress, however, was blocked by an equally well-prepared cordon of heavily armed police.

In response, the protesters did something that hadn't been done on the streets of Paris for over two hundred years. They started erecting barricades. Within a couple of hours, a towering barrier of twisted metal, wooden furniture, street signs, and burnt-out cars teetered precariously between the heaving crowd of protesters and row upon row of police in formation.

Defert was on leave from his military service in Tunisia, and on a visit back to Paris during the week all this was taking place. In fact, he found himself on the Left Bank, amongst the large crowd of onlookers watching these events play out. On seeing the barricades go up, he ran back to his apartment and phoned Foucault in Tunisia to relay to him what was happening. Defert set the telephone receiver next to a radio, so that the two lovers, although more than a thousand miles apart, could listen together to the live news reports of the night that would later be known as the 'Night of the Barricades'.

The phalanx of protesters that had taken occupation of Paris's Left Bank collectively held its breath as it waited for the next move from the increasingly confounded and bewildered police. Cries of 'Liberté, Égalité, Fraternité!' from the crowd reminded those huddling behind their barricades that they weren't the first of their country to put their bodies on the line for freedom and justice. As far as they were concerned, the cause they were fighting for had a long, patriotic, and noble history.

As the sun set over the city with no sign of the police either advancing or retreating, the protesters decided to dig in for the night. Blankets and steaming soup were distributed amongst the thousands who stayed. The strum of a stray guitar in some small circles, accompanied by young voices, added to the feeling of camaraderie that spread through the crowd as night descended.

A little after 2 a.m., however, the protesters were woken by violent winds and the deafening racket of helicopters overhead. Chaotic scenes broke out as people scrambled for cover beneath their barricades.

Within seconds, they found themselves exposed by sweeping search-lights, and their bodies shaking from the boom of loudspeakers ordering them to yield. Before they had time to even think about their next move, they were overcome by waves of baton and shield-wielding gendarmes. In the highly uneven battle that followed, hundreds of protesters were left bloodied and bruised, some with serious injuries. Scores of others were arrested and taken into custody.

The World Watches

These dramatic events were broadcast on radio into living rooms throughout the country. Family members were awoken in the morning's early hours to be told of pitched battles on Paris's streets involving their sons, daughters, brothers, and sisters. The next day, television and newspaper images showed whole streets of France's cherished capital destroyed and in disarray. Student leaders on television told of sickening police brutality and violence. There was talk that undercover police had acted as *agents provocateurs*, throwing Molotov cocktails and setting cars alight, and then falsely accusing student agitators of these criminal acts.

Over the next two weeks, as the protests escalated, Foucault did everything he could to keep track of events in his home country. Television had just arrived in Tunisia, and French newspapers, although available, were always delayed by several days, so for the most part he relied on radio broadcasts and long telephone calls from Defert. Like Hegel two hundred years earlier, Foucault spent each day eagerly awaiting news of the revolution to his west.

But Foucault wasn't the only one sympathising from afar. Writers, actors, singers, and other public figures from around the globe, in the

United States particularly, voiced their support for the Parisian revolutionaries.

The log of demands submitted to the government grew longer, bolder, and more detailed each day. The students wanted to be actively involved in the running of their own universities, but they also had broader aspirations for society in general. Their rallying cries and placards reflected a rising wave of resentment against the older generation, a generation that had too easily surrendered to, and then colluded with the Nazis during World War Two, a generation who more recently had dragged France into two vicious colonial wars in Indochina and Algeria, and who continued to treat women, students, workers, and anyone not in the ruling class as second-class citizens. There was a dangerous and revolutionary sentiment in the air, a sentiment that had been noticed – and was causing great alarm – amongst the members of the ruling de Gaulle government.

On 13 May an astounding one million people attended a rally and marched through Paris's streets. The police conspicuously stayed away, on orders from a government fearful of triggering an all-out revolution. De Gaulle's Prime Minister George Pompidou did, however, address the angry crowd, announcing that all arrested and imprisoned protesters would be released and that the Sorbonne university, which had been shut down since the night of the barricades, would be reopened. This announcement backfired badly for the government, however, as students responded by immediately stampeding back to the Sorbonne in their thousands, reoccupying its buildings and immediately declaring it an 'autonomous people's university'.[14]

Meanwhile, workers throughout the country had started occupying factories. On 14 May an aviation plant near Nantes in west France was shut down by workers sitting down en masse on its factory floor. A large Renault parts plant near Rouen was taken over by workers and closed down, rapidly followed by other factories and warehouses.

A chain reaction of wildcat workers' strikes, independent of any directives from unions, randomly erupted all over the country. France was now well and truly on its knees; its leaders, even those running the unions, seemed to have lost all control.

A Surprise Invitation

During the third week of this tumultuous month, Defert continued to keep Foucault informed by long-distance telephone. Every morning brought a headline surpassing that of the day before. By 16 May more than fifty factories in France had come to a standstill. On 17 May 200,000 workers were on strike. Twenty-four hours later that number multiplied tenfold to two million laying down their tools. By the following week ten million workers, two-thirds of the French workforce, had walked off the job. Union leaders, who had made little progress in trying to reclaim authority over their members, were jeered at when they proposed a claim be put to the government for a thirty-five per cent increase in the minimum wage. Workers made it clear they didn't just want wage rises – they wanted to own the factories. They also wanted de Gaulle to resign. Many students, workers, and others believed they were on the verge of creating a new society.

What wasn't mentioned in the newspapers, and, in fact, only revealed decades later, was that de Gaulle, terrified of the mutinous mob gathering outside his presidential palace, had fled the country.

The French President and his family, in a top-secret military operation not even revealed to government ministers, had been flown by jet to an undisclosed location in Germany. De Gaulle was convinced a second French Revolution was imminent, this time inspired not by Voltaire and Rousseau but by Sartre and Foucault.

De Gaulle did return less than twenty-four hours later, after receiving advice that the wildly oscillating tide of public opinion seemed to be swinging back in his favour. It was as if his brief and mysterious disappearance had rattled France enough for it to reconsider its options.

Many of France's citizens were also becoming increasingly disturbed by interviews with the protest movement's leaders they saw on television. Unkempt, wild-eyed spokesmen babbled about capitalism, anarchism, revolution, and apocalypse in a way that frightened many who had been initially sympathetic. The broadcast, night after night, of demonstrators shouting incomprehensible ideological gibberish about the need to occupy the nation's institutions was, for many, starting to wear thin.

This helps to explain why, when de Gaulle called snap elections in June to resolve the impasse, he was, somewhat surprisingly, returned to power. From that time on, the protest activity that had taken France to the brink rapidly tapered off, before eventually stopping completely.

De Gaulle and his ministers had, though, been irrevocably chastened by the May 1968 events, and were terrified at the prospect of it happening again. To help ensure against such a possibility, they came up with a post-election initiative that left many of their traditional supporters dumbfounded.

The government announced it would establish an experimental university in which the radical ideologies of structuralism, post-structuralism, Maoism, and other -isms that had almost caused the collapse of the country could be studied, explored, and perhaps even put into practice in useful ways. There was, along with this announcement, a promise that the proposed new university would be totally independent and free of any government interference. Hopeful of appeasing and neutralising his enemies, de Gaulle made this one of his first announcements after re-election.

He also announced the somewhat unusual location of this new university, out on the outskirts of Paris, in a place called Vincennes. It would appear the government wanted to ensure that, if further disturbances broke out, they wouldn't disrupt the critical inner-city areas of Paris in the way that the May 1968 uprisings had done.

Soon after de Gaulle's announcement, Foucault received an invitation. He was asked if he would like to head up the philosophy department of the new university at Vincennes.

Vincennes

Eager to return to France in the wake of May 1968, Foucault accepted the position at Vincennes University without delay. Defert was able to secure a position at Vincennes, too, as a lecturer in sociology.

Although Foucault and Defert were excited to be part of this bold new experiment, some of the other appointees at Vincennes were not so excited to see them. News of Foucault's appointment was, in fact, viewed with suspicion by some members of staff. There were whispers that he was a 'Gaullist', planted there as a stooge to advance the government's revisionist agenda. After all, as his critics pointed out, he wasn't even in Paris during the momentous events of May 1968.

Within days of arriving, however, Foucault managed to assuage the concerns of his new colleagues and gain their respect.

The first thing that helped in this regard was his striking new appearance. In Tunisia, Foucault had started a ritual of having Defert shave his head every morning, a ritual he continued on his return to Paris. The enigmatic philosopher had always projected a towering presence, but he seemed even taller now with his shiny, tight-skinned dome and new wire-rimmed glasses, these features brought into even greater prominence by his oversized teeth that flashed shards of gold whenever he spoke. All who encountered him could see that an inner, as well as outer, transformation had taken place in the years he had been away. Foucault was more than happy to have others think that. As he confided to one of his friends, he wanted to say to those who were critical of his appointment:

> While you were having fun on your Latin Quarter barricades, I was working on serious things in Tunisia.[15]

The other way in which Foucault quickly reassured his critics was by appointing academics to his department who were not only intellectually gifted, but who had impeccable credentials as radicals. The appointees included Jean-François Lyotard, first to use the term 'postmodernism', and the militantly subversive *philosophes* Alain Badiou and Gilles Deleuze.

Of all the staff that Foucault employed, however, the most extreme *provocateur* was Judith Miller, daughter of Jacques Lacan. Some of Miller's actions would later almost lead to the fledging university being shut down.

With recruitment of its staff completed, Vincennes became a hotbed of not only structuralists, post-structuralists, deconstructionists, and postmodernists, it also welcomed into its embrace Maoists, Trotskyists, and other ultraleft neo-Marxists. The new university overflowed with all the '-isms' that pervaded radical student politics in France, and beyond, in the 1960s.

In January 1969 Vincennes University officially opened its doors for enrolments, offering courses such as 'Marxism-Leninism', 'Cultural Revolutions', and 'Class Struggle'. An article in *Le Monde* on 15 January reported:

> The atmosphere at Vincennes is like that of a noisy beehive, each one seeking his place.[16]

On 23 January, only a few days after the university opened, all hell broke loose.

The problems began when Vincennes students started a protest in response to reports that police had again visited the campus of Sorbonne University. Within hours, students stormed the new administration buildings at Vincennes, barricading themselves in with desks, chairs, and shelves. To their surprise and delight, however, the protesting students soon found themselves joined by their teacher Foucault and his partner Defert. Along with five hundred other bodies, the two lovers bunkered down in the administration offices overnight.

In the early hours of 24 January police stormed the one-week-old university with batons and tear gas. Some students escaped onto the roof of the building, where they found, again to their delight, that their professor Foucault had joined them. From the roof, he joined his much younger accomplices in throwing debris onto the police below. It was at this moment – captured by television cameras and broadcast live into France's living rooms – that Foucault's notoriety truly began. The philosopher was no longer describing history; he was creating it.

The next morning, people throughout France were greeted by a striking photograph on the front page of their newspapers: a mob of long-haired, bearded protesting youths in jeans with a man in an immaculately tailored suit at their centre – the completely bald, towering figure of Michel Foucault. One imagines this image would have delighted Defert, who for some time had been trying to educate his partner about the theatrics of staging an effective protest.

Compared to the frightening and brutally repressed demonstrations he had witnessed in Tunisia, the protest at Vincennes was for Foucault just a light-hearted game. The students and staff of Vincennes, however, took the bold actions of their new leader very seriously. As did the authorities. The government's strategy of employing

Foucault and other radical thinkers at the new university to calm students tensions appeared, already, to be badly misfiring.

After this initial spectacle, protests at the university continued almost daily. During these actions, and the subsequent inevitable clashes with police, Foucault showed his peers and the authorities that, unlike many other intellectuals and writers, he was willing to get physical, to put his body on the line in dangerous and unpredictable situations.

For Foucault, this was the first time he had associated political freedom with the freedom to do with his body as he wished, something he would explore in even more dramatic and transgressive ways in years to come. In an interview at around this time, he declared:

> We must free ourselves from this cultural conservatism, as well as from political conservatism. We must uncover our rituals for what they are: completely arbitrary things, tied to our bourgeois way of life; it is good – and that is the real theater – to transcend them in the manner of play, by means of games and irony; it is good to be dirty and bearded, to have long hair, to look like a girl when one is a boy (and vice versa); one must put 'in play', show up, transform, and reverse the systems which quietly order us about. As far as I am concerned, that is what I try to do in my work.[17]

As the government watched on helplessly, occupation of buildings and pitched battles with police became the norm at Vincennes for the next few months. On one occasion, in response to rumours that police had bugged the university, students ripped open all the ceilings to look for the imagined devices. Lecturers became increasingly brazen in their radical gestures, refusing to give out marks, and declaring that examinations and other assessments were forms of capitalist oppression. Lectures became more like political speeches than exercises in education.

There was no united front, however, amongst the various radical groups gathered at Vincennes. There was a lot of splintering, splitting, name-calling, and mutual denunciation between the competing Marxist and neo-Marxist groups. Opposing militants would frequently disrupt lectures attended by their rivals and enemies, chanting slogans and shouting abuse to drown out the class.

The final straw for the government came when Lacan's daughter, Judith Miller, started handing out credit for courses to strangers on a public bus. This came after she proclaimed that the collective she had formed with students had decided 'to give a diploma to anyone who thinks they deserve one'.[18] Miller explained to journalists at the weekly news magazine *L'Express* that 'the university is a figment of capitalist society'.[19]

The government moved quickly and decisively after hearing Miller's provocation, announcing that no graduate of Vincennes would be allowed to teach in France's secondary schools. In fact, from here their qualifications would not be recognised. This didn't, however, deter or slow down the protests at Vincennes in any way; the daily menu of radical actions and happenings continued unabated.

After several months, however, the forty-three-year-old Foucault started to tire of this unrelenting radicalism. The novelty of protesting students barging into and interrupting his lectures was wearing thin; their daily chants and slogans were becoming for him increasingly mindless and irritating. One of the first signs Foucault was losing his patience came early one evening after one of his lectures. One of his students approached to ask if he would visit their study group to give a talk about Marx. To the shock of this student, and others gathered within earshot, Foucault shot back:

> Don't talk to me about Marx any more! I never want to hear anything about that man again. Ask someone whose job it is. Someone paid to do it. Ask the Marxist functionaries. Me, I've had enough of Marx.[20]

Foucault would later admit that, despite his initial enthusiasm for the goings-on at Vincennes:

> The eruption of theories, of political discussions, of anathemas, of exclusions, of sectarianism, scarcely interested and completely frustrated me.[21]

Although Defert would stay on at Vincennes for another twenty years, Foucault would leave after only two. He had, by then, become well and truly disillusioned with the intellectual limitations of the Left.

Something else had, however, caught his attention – a brand new political movement, of great interest and relevance to him personally. This movement had only just started to stir on the other side of the Atlantic.

Gay Liberation

Foucault first heard about the Stonewall riots in late June 1969. Like many others, he read with interest the newspaper reports of violent clashes between protesting homosexuals and police in Greenwich Village, New York City.

The riots erupted on 27 June after police conducted a raid on the Stonewall Inn, a bar in Greenwich Village frequented by homosexual patrons. At that time, in New York City, as in Paris and everywhere else in the western world, homosexuality was illegal, and raids of such venues and harassment of their clientele by police were commonplace. But on this occasion – for the first time in history – gay and lesbian people fought back against such persecution. Customers at the Stonewall that day vigorously resisted police attempts to arrest them and close down their venue. As word of the standoff spread into neighbouring bars, a large crowd gathered in the street to express their solidarity with the Stonewall's patrons. Some in the crowd then started abusing and throwing bricks at the police. The situation rapidly escalated into a fully blown street battle that raged on through the night.

These events were considered extraordinary at the time, as homosexuality was not only still illegal, it remained a highly shameful and taboo topic even amongst the more liberal and progressive sectors of society. Foucault wasn't only interested in the Stonewall riots because of his sexuality – which he had largely kept private up to this time – but because the rights and freedoms of homosexuals had never before been broached this way in the public domain. Although one of the rallying cries of those involved in May 1968 had been a call for greater sexual freedom, there had been little specific mention of homosexuality. Similarly, at Vincennes, when Foucault and his lover Defert fought side-by-side with their comrades demanding greater political freedoms, there had been no mention of gay rights. In fact, at that point in time, the term 'gay rights' had not yet been invented.

All that, however, was about to change.

As the sun rose over Greenwich Village on the morning after the riots, local residents were shocked at the scene that greeted them – a deserted wasteland of damaged property, smashed windows, damaged vehicles, and smouldering bins. The Stonewall Inn had been burnt to the ground. Many protesters had been arrested, and many others were seriously injured in the previous night's mêlée.

Over the next few days, however, two words never seen before started to appear, graffitied on walls and shopfronts all throughout the village. Those two words were 'Gay Power'.

A few weeks later an organisation calling itself the Gay Liberation Front was founded; it inundated shops, cafés, and bars around Greenwich Village with leaflets and posters that declared:

We are a revolutionary homosexual group of men and women formed with the realization that complete sexual liberation of all people cannot come about unless existing social institutions are abolished. We reject society's attempt to impose sexual roles and definitions of our nature.[22]

One of the Front's first targets was the same institution that Foucault had targeted several years earlier – psychiatry. In 1969 the American Psychiatric Association still classified homosexuality as a psychiatric disorder, a mental illness requiring treatment to 'reverse' it.

At the APA's annual conference in San Francisco in May 1970, psychiatrists found themselves accosted and heckled by gay rights activists as they walked into their conference. Protesters shouted at them to reverse their position on homosexuality being a mental illness. These demands, however, fell largely on deaf ears, as at the time it was an unquestioned assumption amongst psychiatrists, and in the wider community for that matter, that homosexuality was a pathological deviation from the norm.

At the psychiatrists' subsequent annual congress in 1971, however, the Gay Liberation Front upped the ante, arriving in greater numbers and engaging in much more aggressive tactics. This time they made their way into the conference hall and interrupted speakers who viewed homosexuality as a mental disorder with shouts and ridicule from the floor. At one point gay activist Frank Kameny stormed the podium, snatched the microphone off a psychiatrist, and shouted to the stunned audience:

> Psychiatry is the enemy incarnate. Psychiatry has waged a relentless war of extermination against us. You may take this as a declaration of war against you.[23]

Leaders of the gay liberation movement saw Foucault as a natural ally in their cause. After all, his first major work, *Madness and Civilisation*, had argued that society, through psychiatry, had constructed the idea

259

of mental illness to keep silent those it felt the need to oppress. However, most people in the movement didn't yet know that Foucault was gay. In keeping with the mores of the day, Foucault had not made any public declarations about his sexuality – it was something only known to his closest friends.

The two separate worlds of Foucault's philosophical work in Paris and the gay liberation movement in America were, however, just about to collide.

In 1970 an opportunity arose for the forty-four-year-old Foucault to make his first visit to the United States. Buffalo University had invited him to give a series of lectures. His first lecture was in the same state in which the Stonewall riots had taken place a few years earlier, but he made no reference to them or, for that matter, the gay liberation movement, in his academic presentations. Buffalo University invited him back in 1972. By this time an increasing number of academics had read *Madness and Civilisation*, *Birth of the Clinic*, *The Order of Things*, and Foucault's most recent book *The Archaeology of Knowledge*, and like his readers in France, were entranced by the philosopher's masterful erudition and bold new ideas. In his works, they found valuable tools and new methodologies for analysing and critiquing the structures of power.

Just before Foucault left France for his second American visit, the gay liberation movement had begun to establish itself in his home country. The newly formed *Front Homosexual d'Action Révolutionnaire* commemorated the anniversary of the Stonewall riots with France's first ever gay pride march through the streets of Paris.

Discipline and Punish

After two exhausting years of daily interruptions to his lectures by rowdy activists, Foucault leapt at an offer of a post at France's most prestigious academic institution, the *Collège de France*. In an acknowl-edgement of the fact he had almost single-handedly developed a new way of looking at society and culture, Foucault was invited to suggest a title for his position. He thereby became the Collège de France's first Professor of The History of Systems of Thought.

At his inaugural address to the Collège, Foucault faced a packed auditorium. The audience included many students and academics who had participated in the May 1968 events, as well as more traditional members of faculty who had not read his work, but were curious to learn what all the fuss was about. A journalist from *Le Monde*, one of Paris's leading newspapers, would report the next day that:

> [Before an audience] waiting to be enchanted, [there appeared] a hairless personage, of ivory tint, Buddhist in demeanour, Mephis-tophelean in his gaze, undeterred by the gravity of the occasion from expressing an irrepressible irony.[24]

A year after his appointment to the Collège, Foucault turned his at-tention to another group of individuals lacking a voice in society. Pris-oners. He was inspired to move in this direction by Defert, who had many Maoist comrades who were imprisoned during and after the May 1968 uprisings. Visiting them in prison with Defert, Foucault became aware of the unspeakable conditions in France's correctional facilities. He was determined to start a conversation that had not yet taken place in French society – a conversation about the rights of pris-oners.

Foucault kicked off this conversation in dramatic fashion. On 8 February 1971 the smooth-headed, suit-jacketed Foucault and his younger, more casually dressed collaborator Defert stood before mi-crophones and cameras at the Montparnasse train station to announce their launch of the *Group d'Information sur les Prisons* (Prisons

Information Group). The location chosen for this launch was significant. As those in the press and public attending the event knew, only two weeks earlier a group of Maoists had staged a hunger strike at the same train station in protest against the unacceptable conditions of their comrades in prison. The formation of the Prisons Information Group was Defert's idea, but he was more than happy for his charismatic and authoritative partner to take the lead and be the movement's public figurehead.

Foucault announced he would lead a self-styled commission of investigation into the conditions inside France's prisons. Keeping true to his word, a few weeks later he secured funding for a psychiatrist to visit the prisons and report on what she found. The report shocked the public with its accounts of inmates being shackled, dehumanised, and abused, and attempting suicide at alarmingly high rates. The findings of this report stimulated Foucault to commence a historiographic analysis of the criminal justice system.

The resulting book, *Surveiller et Punir* (*Discipline and Punish*), traced how, in modern times, the methods of punishment used by those in power has become more sophisticated, but no less harmful and horrific. The shift from brute violence to more scientific, effective, and 'humane' methods of managing prisoners, Foucault argued, represented a sinister turn towards near-total control over detainees' minds and bodies.

Foucault opens *Discipline and Punish* with a quote from an eighteenth-century decree describing the punishment of Damiens, convicted of attempted regicide, and the last man in France to be drawn and quartered. According to this document, Damiens was sentenced to be:

> brought on a cart, naked but for shirt, holding a torch of burning wax weighing two pounds; [then,] in said cart taken to the place

de Grève, where, on a scaffold that will be erected there, the flesh will be torn from his breasts, arms, thighs, and calves with red-hot pincers, his right hand, holding the knife with which he committed the said [crime], burned with sulphur, and on those places where the flesh will be torn away, poured molten lead, boiling oil, burning resin, wax and sulphur melted together, and then his body drawn and quartered by four horses and his limbs and body consumed by fire, reduced to ashes and his ashes thrown to the wind.[25]

Foucault followed this with a quote from the French prison reformer Leon Faucher eight decades later in 1838, in which he proudly describes his modern and more humane regimen for prisoners:

At the first drum-roll, the prisoners must rise and dress in silence, as the supervisor opens the cell doors. At the second drum-roll, they must be dressed and make their beds. At the third they must line up and proceed to the chapel for morning prayer. There is a five-minute interval between each drum-roll.

Later, Faucher continues:

At half-past-seven in summer, half-past eight in winter, the prisoners must be back in their cells after the washing of hands and the inspection of clothes in the courtyard; at the first drum-roll, they must undress, and at the second get into bed. The cell doors are closed and the supervisors go to the rounds in the corridors, to ensure order and silence.[26]

In *Discipline and Punish*, Foucault argued that this more civilised approach to regulating prisoners' behaviour is perhaps a worse evil than the gruesome public executions that preceded it. For Foucault, this modern, precise, systematic approach has an even more devastating effect, crushing any vestiges of dignity, independence, or individuality. Foucault then demonstrates how these techniques have been adapted for use in schools, hospitals, and other institutions to control the bodies and minds of large sections of the populace.

When Foucault later described *Discipline and Punish* as his attempt to 'produce a genealogy of modern morals through a political history of bodies', he was again acknowledging his debt to Nietzsche, the author of *A Genealogy of Morals* almost a century earlier.[27] Foucault's view of the Enlightenment, a view that marked him as one of the first postmodernists, was that the advance of reason and science had not necessarily been as positive a development as had been portrayed by society's leaders. In *Surveiller et Punir*, judged by some to be his finest work, Foucault warned that 'the human body was entering a machinery of power that digs into it, breaks it down and rearranges it'.[28] Foucault saw this 'machinery of power' everywhere he looked – in psychiatry, medicine, the prison system, and science in general. He also saw it, as he would articulate in his next work, in the flowering of freedoms that had come to be known as the sexual revolution.

Folsom Street

Immediately after writing *Discipline and Punish*, Foucault started on his next work, *The History of Sexuality*. As Defert recalls:

On the same day he finishes one, he starts the other, that was very surprising.[29]

The idea of writing a historiography of sexuality had been on Foucault's mind for some time – ever since, as a young man, he had painfully experienced his own sexuality being invalidated as a mental illness. He would later explain:

I had this idea from the moment I began writing the 'History of Madness'. They were twin projects. Even then, I wanted to see

264

how the normal and the pathological are divided in the case of sex as well.[30]

Foucault took a similar approach to researching the history of sexuality that he had with all his previous histories – of madness, medicine, and the prison system. He not only sought out texts that chronicled society's changing views about sexuality over time, he tried to identify how those views, in particular views as to what was 'normal', had been constructed by those in power to suit their own vested interests.

Foucault, of course, had his own vested interests in writing this work. His experience, in his younger days, of being driven to suicidal despair by a society that stigmatised his sexuality, had spurred him on to critique the societal institutions – psychiatry, medicine, and the legal system – that had labelled him as abnormal, unhealthy, and criminal. *The History of Sexuality* would be his most personal work, the work for which all his other books had, in effect, been a preparation. Foucault would later declare that everything he had written was, in essence, an autobiography. His life's work had come about in response to a society that had tried, unsuccessfully, to invalidate his sexuality and individuality, and repress his true self.

Foucault had a rather grandiose vision for this work. He planned to write an encyclopaedic six-volume analysis of the ways sexuality had been constructed in Western history from ancient times to the current day. Before he finished his first draft, however, he had a series of explosive personal experiences that would challenge everything he thought he knew about sex, and force him to reconsider his whole approach.

The experiences that transformed Foucault came about after he accepted an invitation from the University of California to spend the spring of 1975 teaching at its Berkeley campus in San Francisco. As

Foucault would discover, San Francisco's gay scene was flourishing like never before. In fact, the city was now home to one of the most sexually liberated communities on the planet.

It didn't take long after Foucault settled into Berkeley for him to become aware that, across the bay, a whole world of previously forbidden pleasures awaited him.

A few days after arriving, Foucault moved from his campus accommodation in Berkeley to a room near Folsom Street, where San Francisco's sadomasochistic scene was in full swing. Here, fetish bars such as the *The Boot Camp*, *The Brig*, and *The Barracks* flaunted their business with an openness that Foucault found hard to believe. In these colourful, throbbing, strobe-lit venues opportunities for group sadomasochistic sex were available every night of the week.

Defert didn't accompany Foucault on his visit to America, but later comments he made suggest he had no problem with Foucault sampling what was on offer. Although Foucault had been to countries such as Sweden where there was considerable tolerance in matters of sexuality, Defert would later note that his partner had never been to a place where transgressive sexual acts were organised on such a mass scale:

> In America he had the possibility of different experiences that were organised socially…What Foucault appreciated, I think, in the Californian culture was that those experiences were experiences of [a] community [rather than a] psychological drama for individuals.[31]

Soon after arriving, Foucault came across a copy of *The Leatherman's Handbook*. This recently published, underground treatise functioned as a guide for newcomers to Folsom's leather district. In its opening pages, it helpfully defines its central topic, sadomasochistic sex, as involving:

a dominant-submissive relationship; giving and receiving of pain that is pleasurable to both parties; fantasy and/or role playing on the part of one or both partners; a conscious humbling of one partner by the other (humiliation); some form of fetish involvement; [and] the acting out of one or more ritualised interactions (bondage, flagellation, etc.).[32]

Foucault found a like-minded colleague amongst the staff at Berkeley who took him shopping for accessories that he could wear in the leather bars. The philosopher's shopping list included a leather jacket, a black leather cap and visor, handcuffs, nipple clamps, hoods, gags, blindfolds, and a riding crop.

It took Foucault only a few nights of frequenting Folsom Street's S&M bars to learn the unwritten codes of the scene – a handkerchief in the left pocket indicated a 'sadist' who liked to be on top, the right pocket a 'masochist' who preferred to be underneath. A blue kerchief indicated its owner preferred old-fashioned sex; a black one that he was into more extreme S&M practices. Foucault spent many long, glorious evenings in Folsom Street's varied venues, exploring dungeons with chains, whips, and cells, and dimly lit mazes where anonymous bodies lay in wait to be joined in dark private cubicles. Foucault regularly surrendered himself to the seemingly endless opportunities for group sex in Folsom Street's saunas, which stayed open all through the night.

A State of Passion

After a few weeks of such indulgences, Foucault took up an invitation to speak in Irvine, near Los Angeles. After his talk he was approached by Simeon Wade, an assistant professor from the nearby Claremont Graduate School. Dressed in T-shirt, headband, jeans, and sneakers, Wade certainly didn't come across as a conventional academic. In fact,

267

he soon made it clear to Foucault that he was an avowed hedonist, forever on the lookout for new and pleasurable experiences. Wade invited Foucault to join him and his boyfriend Michael on a trip to Death Valley.

Several weeks later, Wade and his partner took Foucault on a drive that seemed to go on forever in the warm Californian countryside. Eventually they arrived at Death Valley, where, unknown to Foucault, Wade had prepared a new experience for the French visitor.

Wade found a secluded spot just a few yards from the edge of a cliff overlooking the desert and laid out some blankets. A cool chill hit the air as the late afternoon sun dipped below the horizon. Wade popped a cassette into the portable music machine he had brought with him, and the three shivering men huddled under a blanket as the eerie notes of an unnatural ambient music wafted out over them and into the valley beyond. It was then that Wade produced the new experience he wanted Foucault to partake – a small tablet of LSD.

Foucault's first response was to decline, but, on giving it some thought, decided to surrender to what was being offered, just as he had a few weeks earlier on Folsom Street. The next few hours passed deliciously slowly as the three men watched the ascent of a fat ivory moon from behind the canyon. When Simeon and his partner turned to check on their guest, they found him smiling beatifically, with tears streaming down his face.

What is it, Michel?' Simeon gently inquired of his guest.

After a long pause, Foucault replied:

The only thing I can compare this experience to in my life is sex with a stranger. Contact with a strange body affords an experience of the truth similar to what I am experiencing now.

His face soaked in tears, the Professor of History of Systems of Thought whispered: 'I now understand my sexuality.'[33]

Foucault would later describe what happened that evening as the most moving experience of his life.

The following morning, the trio drove back in blissful near-silence, enjoying the Californian sunshine as it filtered through the windows of Wade's automobile, soothing their still-buzzing, drug-affected bodies.

Later that night, back in the city, they went to a party. A handsome young man came up to Foucault, recognising him as the illustrious professor from France, and asked: 'What do you think of Gay Lib?'

Foucault's reply showed that, after fighting a society hell-bent on labelling his sexuality, he wasn't going to let the gay liberation movement do the same thing:

> Our pursuit of pleasure has been limited in a large part by a vocabulary foisted upon us. People are neither this nor that, gay nor straight. There is an infinite range of what we call sexual behavior...[34]

Foucault's response, which no doubt disappointed some who overheard it, would later be repeated and expanded upon by the philosopher when he was interviewed by a gay activist magazine. In this interview, Foucault questioned the whole concept of gay identity:

> The relationships we have to have with ourselves are not ones of identity, rather they must be relationships of differentiation, of creation, of innovation. To be the same is really boring.[35]

Foucault was as wary of the recent construction of 'gay' as an identity as he was of the earlier psychiatric concept of homosexuality as a disease. This was one of the main reasons he resisted the pressure from many in the gay community to 'come out'. For Foucault, sexuality was a fluid thing that one should feel free to explore, construct, and create, rather than a box to be pushed into by the expectations of society, or, for that matter, a newly formed subculture.

As mentioned, Foucault's experiences in San Francisco led him to completely rethink the book he was working on. He had experienced a revelation, and now saw excruciatingly pleasurable experiences of consensual sadomasochistic play as a way to deconstruct the body, to break it down using pain, pleasure, and where necessary, bondage and humiliation. Exposure to these practices had revolutionised Foucault's thinking about the possibilities associated with sex and other 'limit-experiences', as he called them. He saw how such experiences could be used to liberate oneself from the programming and power of the dominant culture.

Foucault shared these insights in an interview with the gay press a few years after his return to Paris. He explained to his interviewer that as far as he was concerned, S&M practices allowed for 'the real creation of new possibilities of pleasure'.[36]

Foucault believed that even something as private as sexual pleasure was constructed by the norms and rules of the historical circumstances in which one finds oneself. Foucault outlined in detail in his final work how constructions of sexuality had changed over the course of history. In this book, he asserted that we should try to strip away the identities that society has foisted upon us, so that we can discover and create who we truly are and what we can be. Foucault explained in the interview:

It's a question of escaping from all that: it is necessary to invent with the body, with its elements, its surfaces, its volumes, its depths, a nondisciplinary eroticism: that of the body plunged into a volatile and different state through chance encounters and incalculable pleasures.[37]

In 1976 Foucault published the first volume of his long-awaited *History of Sexuality*.

Soon afterwards, the philosopher, who up until now had been very guarded about his personal life, revealed something about his sexuality, albeit in an oblique, rather opaque fashion. He announced in a public interview that he had 'lived for eighteen years in a state of passion towards someone'.[38]

That someone was, of course, Daniel Defert. Foucault's partner had remained steadfast and loyal during these years despite the philosopher's frequent flights across the Atlantic to revisit San Francisco's bathhouses. In the public interview, Foucault somewhat awkwardly tried to describe the nature of his attachment to Defert:

> At some moments, this passion has taken the form of love. But in truth, it is a matter of a state of passion between the two of us.[39]

Les Fleurs du Mal

In the same year that fifty-one-year-old Foucault publicly referred to his longstanding state of passion with Daniel Defert, a rather inconspicuous article appeared in the *New York Native*, a biweekly news magazine for the city's gay community. Beneath a headline that read 'Disease Rumours Largely Unfounded', the article reported on rumours that a number of homosexual men were being treated for a rare strain of pneumonia in intensive care units throughout New York City.[40] The journalist writing the story, Lawrence Mass, quoted public health officials' reassurances that fears about a disease sweeping through the gay community were totally unfounded.

A few weeks later, however, on 5 June 1981, the US Centre for Disease Control reported on a cluster of Pneumocystis pneumonia in five homosexual men on the other side of the country in Los Angeles.

On 3 July *The New York Times*, under the headline 'Rare Cancer Seen in 41 Homosexuals', reported on forty-one men in New York City and San Francisco who had suddenly developed a rare skin cancer known as Kaposi's sarcoma.[41]

By the end of 1981, 121 people had died from a syndrome the general press now referred to as GRID (Gay-related Immune Deficiency). Later, when it became clear the disease was not limited to homosexuals, the term AIDS (Acquired Immune Deficiency Syndrome) was coined by medical authorities to describe this frightening and highly infectious affliction that seemed to have come out of nowhere.

AIDS swept through San Francisco, decimating and crippling its once flourishing and buoyant gay and S&M community. Wave after wave of previously fit and healthy men succumbed to the deadly syndrome. Epidemiologists were eventually able to trace many of the cases to a single French–Canadian flight attendant called Gaëten Dugas, who had paid his first visit to a New York City bathhouse on 31 October 1980. After hundreds of anonymous and fleeting sexual contacts in bars and bathhouses throughout the country, Dugas died of kidney failure caused by AIDS-related infections three and a half years later.

As panic – and despair – set in amongst homosexual communities around the world, Michel Foucault's initial reaction, like that of many others, was one of denial. He was highly sceptical of the way the medical profession was presenting this new illness. His whole philosophical career had been based on demonstrating how authorities had used their knowledge and power to subjugate the voiceless, and marginalise those who deviated from the mainstream. To him, AIDS sounded like a perfect medical construction for oppressing and stigmatising gay people just as they were gaining some respect and legitimacy in society.

Edmund White, American author and a friend of Foucault's, remembers having a conversation with the philosopher in late 1981, just after the first reports appeared of a deadly disease that seemed to be targeting homosexual people. White recalls:

> Living in San Francisco in the seventies [Foucault] had been promiscuous. He loved the bathhouses and all that...Around this time I was warning Foucault about AIDS. When I first told him about the disease he said: 'Oh that's perfect Edmund: you American puritans, you're always inventing diseases. And one that singles out blacks, drug users and gays – how perfect!'.

In looking back on his conversation with Foucault, White explains:

> Gay rights had been so hard to fight for that AIDS felt like a real reversal. It just seemed to be too perfect for him to believe it. I tried to insist it was real despite its ideological aspects.[42]

In the summer of 1983, Foucault returned from one of his visits to San Francisco looking very unwell. His friends in Paris couldn't help noticing his hacking dry cough and the fact he had lost a lot of weight. Defert recalls that at that time 'everybody in the [US] was talking about AIDS'. Foucault dismissed his lover's concerns, insisting it 'was a simple pulmonary infection'.[43]

In September, Foucault told Defert he wanted to return to California in the fall. When concerns were again expressed about his welfare, Foucault reiterated he simply had a chest infection, nothing to worry about, and was sure he would feel better as soon as he was back in sunny California.

When Foucault returned from this trip, however, Defert was devastated at the sight that he beheld at the airport. His partner had been reduced to not much more than skin and bone. Several months later, in early June 1984, Foucault collapsed in his apartment and was rushed to the Hôpital de la Salpêtrière. This was, ironically, the same hospital Foucault had written about in *Madness and Civilisation*, where Paris's destitute, lepers, mentally ill, and other outcasts had been rounded up centuries earlier to be classified and stripped of their dignity in the name of a newly arrived Age of Reason.

The last cogent conversation Defert had with Foucault took place two weeks into his stay at the hospital. Sitting at Foucault's bedside, Defert cradled his lover's wasted hand and said:

If it turns out to be AIDS, your last books are just like *Les Fleurs du Mal*.[44]

Foucault recognised immediately what Defert was referring to. The second and third volumes of Foucault's *History of Sexuality* had gone to press only a few days before he had been rushed to hospital. *Les Fleurs du Mal* had been the last work of Charles Baudelaire, the nineteenth-century French poet much-loved by Foucault and Defert. Translating as *The Flowers of Evil*, this notorious work had described in detail the poet's sexual life, as well as his final suffering as he approached – without any regrets – a death due to syphilis.

At the mention of this reference, the bed-bound Foucault looked up at Defert with a laugh and said: 'Why not?'[45]

On 25 June 1984 France's three major newspapers – *Le Monde*, *Le Figaro*, and *Libération* – greeted their morning readers with headlines announcing that philosopher Michel Foucault had died the day before in Paris's Hôpital de la Salpêtrière. All three broadsheets were circumspect about the cause of death. *Le Monde* quoted a medical report that had been approved for release by Foucault's family:

Michel Foucault entered the clinic for diseases of the nervous system at the Hôpital de la Salpêtrière on 9 June, 1984, in order to allow complementary investigation of neurological symptoms complicated by septicemia. These examinations revealed the existence of cerebral suppuration. Antibiotic treatment at first had a favourable effect: a remission allowed Michel Foucault in the last week to take notice of the initial reactions to the appearance of his latest books.[46]

These 'latest books' were the second and third volumes of *The History of Sexuality*.

Volumes Four, Five, and Six would never be written.

On the morning of 29 June, four days after Foucault's death, several hundred mourners gathered in the cramped courtyard of the Hôpital de la Salpêtrière for the ceremony of *la levée du corps* (raising of the body), a traditional French ritual performed at the time a body is removed from the morgue. Defert had only expected a small gathering, but the courtyard was packed to standing room only.

Already, by the time of his passing, Foucault had become France's most esteemed public intellectual, his works published in more than fifteen languages. In the years following his death, his works would become even more widely read. In fact, his name would soon become the most frequently cited name in the humanities. He had, it seems, finally achieved his goal of replacing Sartre as Europe's most celebrated philosopher.

As with the funeral of his predecessor, this occasion in the Hôpital de la Salpêtrière brought together some of country's finest minds. Amongst those gathered to pay their respects was the man soon to be known as the father of deconstruction, Jacques Derrida, his frightening shock of white hair standing out amongst the mourners.

Also in the audience was Gilles Deleuze, co-author of the 1972 work *Capitalism and Schizophrenia: Anti-Oedipus*. He had been a close friend of Foucault's ever since their heady days together at Vincennes, and it was Deleuze, who, on receiving a nod from the presiding minister, shuffled through the crowd, mounted a small box, and proceeded to read to those gathered in the small hospital courtyard.

He read from the preface of Volume Three of *The History of Sexuality*:

> As for the motive that compelled me, it was very simple. In the eyes of some, I hope it will suffice by itself. It was curiosity – the only kind of curiosity, in any case, that merits being practised with a little obstinacy: not the kind that searches out in order to digest whatever is agreeable to know, but rather the kind that permits one to get free of oneself...what is philosophy today – philosophical activity, I mean – if not the critical labour of thought upon itself?[47]

After the reading was over, Foucault's coffin was raised and carried to the waiting hearse, where it would begin its long journey back to the philosopher's birthplace in Poitiers.

It would take some time after Foucault's death before his family, and even Defert, could acknowledge that the philosopher had died from AIDS. His death had come at a time when there was still much shame and controversy surrounding the condition.

Eventually the cause of Foucault's death was revealed in print by Defert himself. By that time, Defert the activist had already set up *AIDES*, France's first organisation dedicated to supporting and defending the rights of people infected with HIV.

Defert would devote the rest of his years to combating the stigma associated with both homosexuality and HIV, remaining the president of *AIDES* until 1991.

Chapter 7

Derrida's Desires

A Fractured Identity

Jacques Derrida was born in 1930 in El Biar, a small village outside Algiers. At the time Algeria was a French colony, but a terrible and violent war of independence was looming.

Derrida was conceived in the midst of his mother's grief, only three months after she lost a baby boy. Derrida was born one day short of a year after that tragic event. Throughout his childhood and beyond, Derrida would never be able to shake the feeling that he was an inadequate replacement for this loss, a shadow in his brother's wake.

This ill-begotten start to life laid the foundation for a shaky and fragile sense of identity in the young philosopher-to-be that would only be exacerbated by other aspects of the shifting world into which he was thrown. His family were Jewish but couldn't speak Hebrew. He was raised in Algeria but couldn't speak Arabic. His family, who only spoke French, had lost touch with their Gallic roots but not yet assimilated into their country of residence. As Derrida would later observe:

I have only one language and it is not mine.[1]

The streets of El Biar immersed Derrida from a young age into a melting pot of cultures. His family were descendants of Sephardic Jews who had fled Spain during the Inquisition. When the French invaded

Algeria in the 1800s, all Sephardic Jews were made French citizens, as opposed to the local Muslims and indigenous Berbers with whom the Derridas lived side by side. The noisy alleyways of El Biar, with their bustling markets and mosques, hid behind their doorways longstanding tensions between French nationals and the local indigent population. The Jewish quarter of town, where Derrida and his family lived, was viewed with envy and resentment by the Muslims, and with an ancient suspicion by the French Christians.

The sense of not belonging that Derrida experienced from his earliest days was brought home in a devastating way on his first day of high school in 1942. This was the day the French Vichy government, in collaboration with the Nazi authorities, started implementing anti-Semitic quotas in Algeria. On arriving at the school gates, the twelve-year-old Derrida's excitement turned to confusion and shame when he was told he could no longer attend classes because he was Jewish. As Derrida's teacher explained to him before sending him home: 'French culture is not made for little Jews.'

Derrida recalls:

[A]nti-Semitism became the official doctrine of the French government. They expelled from school all the Jewish children, all the Jewish professors, and all the Jewish administrators, with just a few exceptions…I was thrown out of school…My brother and sister as well. No one told us why…The principal just said, 'Go home and your parents will explain.' But what was most painful wasn't simply the administrative decision to expel us from school. It was what took place in the streets, the insults, the children calling us 'dirty Jews'.[2]

Within a few weeks the local Sephardic community had organised a makeshift school for Derrida and other Jewish children, but nothing could undo the fact that Europe's Holocaust had now arrived on Africa's shores.

Derrida's early sense of displacement and confused identity wasn't helped by the fact that even his first name was fluid, constructed, and lacking in permanence and substantiality. In a curious and unusual move, Derrida's parents named their baby boy 'Jackie', an Americanism they found modern and forward-looking, but that for him became another burden, a millstone around his neck that made him feel separate from the Noahs and the Isaacs – not to mention the Mohammeds – in his local playground. For young 'Jackie', his parents' ill-conceived attempt at moving with the times only further fractured his identity into splinters of American, Jew, Algerian, and Frenchman.

In giving their son an American moniker, Derrida's parents had, however, anticipated his future, for it would be in the United States that the philosopher's work would be first appreciated, and on American campuses that his ideas would first take root and flourish. Many years later, when asked to explain what deconstruction was, Derrida would quip:

America is deconstruction.[3]

During his teenage years, however, Derrida showed no such affinity for the New World. In fact, when he moved from Algeria to Paris in 1949, the bloody war for independence erupting behind him, the nineteen-year-old Jackie changed his first name to *Jacques* to align with the only language he spoke. After arriving in France, he felt a greater sense of belonging than he had ever known in his home town. In particular, he immediately identified with the French tradition of the public intellectual. Paris's streets brought back memories of his years as a teenager, when, in El Biar, he had read Sartre's *Nausea*, and when he had gone to see, on his own, the same writer's play *No Exit* when it came to Algiers. By the age of nineteen, Derrida had decided he was

French. He had also learned – in a foreshadowing of the philosophical ideas he was to develop in years to come – that identity was a fluid thing that could be changed as easily as changing a name.

An Algerian in Paris

Derrida was bedazzled by the wealth of culture and learning that greeted him in France's capital. He enrolled in the Lycée Louis-le-Grand, a public secondary school in Paris's Latin Quarter renowned for its rigor in preparing students for the entrance exams to France's elite *Grandes Écoles*. Derrida, like Foucault before him, struggled to fit in, though for different reasons to his predecessor. As 'a little black and very Arab Jew' (words he would later use to describe how others saw him), he was highly aware of his outsider status in relation to his urbane Parisian classmates.[4]

It took Derrida three attempts to pass his entrance exams. His written answers baffled his markers, just as his philosophical works would later perplex many who encountered them. As one examiner observed, his 'answers are brilliant in the very same way they are obscure'.[5] This same examiner failed Derrida's efforts with the following advice:

> An exercise in virtuosity, with undeniable intelligence, but with no particular relation to the history of philosophy…Can come back when he is prepared to accept the rules and not *invent* where he needs to be better *informed*.[6]

Another examiner couldn't hide his irritation at Derrida's attempt to analyse Diderot's *Encyclopédie:*

> Look, this text is quite simple; you've simply made it more complicated and laden with meaning by adding ideas of your own.[7]

At twenty-two, Derrida eventually muscled his way into the École Normale Supérieure, joining the ranks of his idol Sartre and fellow outsider Foucault. In fact, Foucault, who was only four years older than Derrida, taught one of the courses the Algerian newcomer enrolled in. The course was called experimental psychology, but functioned more like a free-flowing forum for Foucault to think aloud as he developed his latest theories. Derrida would later recall that Foucault's 'eloquence, authority and brilliance were impressive'.[8]

Derrida felt more at home in the heady and iconoclastic ENS than he had at the rather stuffy and conventional Lycée Louis-le-Grand. He spent hundreds of hours in the École's high-ceilinged libraries, familiarising himself with the Ancient Greeks, with Nietzsche, and with the writings of Heidegger, Marx, and Freud. Unlike most other students in his philosophy class, he also read voraciously in linguistics and literature.

Derrida met some important mentors – and made some lifelong friends – at the ENS. His teachers included Foucault's former adviser Jean Hyppolite, who introduced him to the works of Hegel and Husserl. Derrida's first published paper, written while he was still at the École, provided a taste of things to come. In this work, an incredibly self-assured young Derrida boldly dismissed Husserl's attempts to catalogue the different aspects of consciousness, arguing that such attempts are doomed to fail due to the inherently elusive nature of language. Another important mentor was Roland Barthes, whose idea – articulated in his essay *Death of the Author* – that words themselves have more substance and autonomy than the person who writes them, left a lasting impression on Derrida.

On his very first day at the École Normale Supérieure, Derrida also met and befriended the brilliant, ill-fated Louis Althusser. Althusser belonged to an influential group of neo-Marxist, neo-Freudian thinkers that included Herbert Marcuse, Jürgen Habermas, and Jacques Lacan. All these writers were interested in reviving Marx and Freud's ideas in a world in which Soviet communism had clearly failed. For these thinkers, a consumer-driven capitalist society propelled by nothing other than a soulless search for profits was a prospect almost as chilling as the totalitarian excesses of Russia's failed experiment in Marxism.

Although Althusser became a good friend and valued source of inspiration for Derrida, his legacy would later be overshadowed by an unspeakably horrific turn of events. More than two decades after he met Derrida, the sixty-two-year-old Althusser would stagger out of his apartment at the École Normale Supérieure, screaming that he had just murdered his wife. The disgraced elder statesman of neo-Marxist philosophy would subsequently be declared unfit for trial due to insanity, and committed to spend his last years in the Sainte-Anne psychiatric facility.

One wonders if Derrida was drawn, even back then, to some disturbance in Althusser that was stirring within himself, for the young Algerian suffered terribly during his early years at the École – as Foucault had before him – from repeated bouts of anxiety, depression, hypochondriasis, and suicidal ideation.

Derrida also continued to be nagged by a sense of rootlessness, of not really belonging anywhere. This sense of ethereal non-substantiality would continue to characterise not only the philosopher's sense of his own life, but his near-incomprehensible philosophical writings in the years that followed. Although Derrida, at the École, had already started to develop his revolutionary new method for interrogating texts that came to be known as deconstruction, he was also becoming increasingly afflicted by fits of inexplicable despair. As he lamented in a letter to a friend around this time:

I'm no good for anything except taking the world apart and putting it together again.[9]

Marguerite

Another fateful friendship that Derrida made at the École Normale Supérieure was with Czechoslovakian student Michel Aucouturier. In 1953 Aucouturier was given a car by his father for passing his entrance exam to the ENS, and to celebrate he drove the twenty-three-year-old Derrida and a couple of other classmates to the Carroz-d'Arâches ski resort in Haute-Savoie, where they joined Aucouturier's family for their annual winter vacation.

Derrida was not an accomplished skier. He hadn't the opportunity to learn in Algeria, unlike his French and Czechoslovakian classmates, but he did manage to catch the eye of an admirer while he was there. Aucouturier's sister Marguerite would always remember the first time she saw Derrida, from a distance, unsteadily making his way down the beginners' slope.

When, later that day, Marguerite and Derrida met for the first time in the resort's noisy bar, one of the first things that struck her was his jet-black hair (it wouldn't turn into the shock of white for which he became famous until he turned forty). Derrida, for his part, would only find out later that Marguerite's fragile appearance was due to the fact she was recovering from a long and debilitating bout of tuberculosis. Despite her poor health, Aucouturier's tenacious twenty-year-old sister had already started training to become a psychoanalyst. We don't know whether the topic arose at their first meeting, but the theories of Freud and his followers would certainly be a common topic of conversation between the two in the years that ensued.

Although both would later admit to feelings of attraction at that first encounter in Haute-Savoie, it wouldn't be until eighteen months later, when Marguerite moved from Prague to Paris, that she and Derrida started their relationship.

In 1956 Derrida received a grant to visit Harvard. He invited Marguerite to join him, an offer she enthusiastically accepted. Derrida spent much of the next year in the reading room of Harvard's Widener Library, reading and studying James Joyce's *Ulysses*. The influence of Joyce would later be detectable in Derrida's works, many of which would read more like avant-garde literature than philosophy.

In 1957 Derrida and Marguerite were married in Boston in a perfunctory ceremony attended by one witness, their friend Margot. Soon afterwards, Derrida was required to return to Algeria for military service. The couple moved to Algiers, where Derrida was assigned duties appropriate to his literary skills, teaching English and French in a socioeconomically deprived school. During their time there, Marguerite gained a better sense of the exotic and complex world in which her husband had spent his early years.

After Derrida completed his posting, they returned to Paris. In 1960 they drove their old and battered Citroën all the way from Paris to a conference in Prague, where Derrida delivered a paper on Husserl. Afterwards, they spent some time in the capital with Marguerite's family. By this time Marguerite had started a private psychoanalytic practice in Paris, a fact which no doubt made her family, of humble origins, very proud. What her family didn't know, however, was that Marguerite was having to draw considerably on her newly acquired skills to help their new son-in-law, who was suffering from severe bouts of anxiety and depression. In fact, later that year, at the age of thirty, Derrida suffered a complete 'nervous collapse', and sank into a deep depression.[10]

Derrida had found, in Marguerite, a source of much-needed security, acceptance, and forbearance that was helping him to cope, day by day, with the feelings of anxious groundlessness that had plagued him ever since his fractured and confusing childhood. With her solid and consistent presence at his side, he would soon feel safe and anchored enough to give full rein to his freakish intellectual and creative potential, and to be brave, playful, and exploratory in his work. Unfortunately for Marguerite, he would also feel a restless need to be just as playful and exploratory in his love life, a need which he would express itself in the form of multiple extramarital liaisons and affairs.

At this point, though, their marriage had not yet been sullied by any such behaviours. In 1963 Marguerite gave birth to their first son, Pierre. Their second son, Jean, arrived in 1967, just after a major event took place in Derrida's career, an event that would launch his reputation as one of Europe's most original thinkers.

Structure, Sign, and Play

In 1966 Derrida was invited to present a paper at America's first ever conference on structuralism. The conference, rather grandly titled *The International Colloquium on Critical Languages and the Sciences of Man*, was held at Johns Hopkins University in Baltimore, about four hundred miles south of where Derrida had immersed himself in the works of Joyce only a few years earlier.

The university was hosting the conference to introduce American audiences to the new, exciting, but somewhat mystifying movement of structuralism which, in Europe at least, was having a revolutionary effect not just on philosophical discourse, but on the humanities in general.

Derrida was part of a small invited French delegation that included two of his teachers from the ENS – Jean Hyppolite and Roland Barthes – as well as his controversial contemporary, the psychoanalyst Jacques Lacan. Derrida was invited as an afterthought after another speaker had pulled out, so he only had a few days to prepare his paper. However, from the time he arose to speak until his closing words fifty minutes later, this previously unheard of Algerian–French philosopher electrified his audience with a distillation of the ideas that had been simmering in his mind for some time. The highly provocative pronouncements in his paper ignited a discourse that overhauled continental philosophy from that day onwards, giving it a new lease of life that has continued up to the present day.

The thoughts articulated in Derrida's watershed paper – *Structure, Sign, and Play in the Discourse of the Human Sciences* – would be expanded upon in three books he wrote and published the following year. These books, which would cement his position as continental philosophy's boldest and most influential thinker for decades to come, were *Writing and Difference*, *Speech and Phenomena*, and *On Grammatology*.

Oranges

One of the key ideas in Derrida's works – an idea that would generate a massive number of papers in the years that followed – was the simple but unsettling suggestion that _words are more real_ than the world we _think of them as representing_. This idea arose as part of a broader movement known as the *linguistic turn*, in which many thinkers – including 'non-continental' philosophers such as Bertrand Russell and Ludwig Wittgenstein – were trying to unravel and better understand the complex relationship between language, truth, and reality.

Derrida's take on this relationship can be illustrated by way of the following example.

If one takes the word *orange*, referring to the colour, Derrida would note that this word (like all words) has three different aspects to it. First, it can be seen simply as referring to the arrangement of the letters 'O-R-A-N-G-E' in print (or the sound made when this combination of letters is uttered in speech). Secondly, it refers to the colour we see in our mind's eye when we come across the word – for example, if we read or hear the phrase: 'I bought an orange shirt.' Thirdly, it can refer to the colour when we actually see it in real life; for example, if we see someone wearing an orange shirt.

According to the early twentieth-century linguist Ferdinand de Saussure, whose work greatly influenced Derrida's thinking, the word 'orange' is an example of a *sign* that has two aspects to it – the word itself, which Saussure termed the *signifier*, and the picture of the colour orange we get in our mind's eye, which he called the *signified*. A third term, the *referent*, describes the colour orange when we see it in real life. These distinctions highlight the fact that a lot of the time when we are using words in conversation or writing, we are using them to refer to things that we have a shared imagining of in our minds (that is, as signifiers), rather than using the word to refer to actual objects we can point to in a particular time in the real world (referents).

Derrida argued that the history of philosophy had been a circular, never-ending argument about which was more real, or if you like, which came first – the idea of 'orange' in the mind or the actual colour orange we see in an object in the real world.

According to Derrida, this central problem of philosophy – of mind versus matter, of idea versus object – has been unresolvable because the whole time we have been looking in the wrong place for where ultimate reality resides. He contended that our most primary reality is to be found neither in the idea nor in the object, but in a third place – in the domain of language, in *words*. He believed the word 'orange' was, in fact, more substantial – more real, if you like – than either the colour we imagine in our mind's eye or the colour we see in the world.

Derrida's radical assertion was that words, rather than referring to objects or ideas, actually construct reality, or at least our experience of

287

it (which, as Kant had demonstrated, is as close to reality as we'll ever get). Although such a notion, at first glance, might seem implausible and even outrageous, an examination of the history of the word 'orange' reveals how much our knowledge and experience of that colour, which seems so self-evident and unchanging to us, has been shaped by the arrival and presence of the word itself.

It is a quaint and not well-known fact that 'orange' only became a word *and a recognised colour* in England after oranges began to be imported from the Mediterranean during the Renaissance. After the importation of this new exotic fruit, a new colour – *orange* – came into existence, a colour that occupied a space between red and yellow, a 'space' that until then no one had recognised as existing. This seems to indicate, strangely, that the colour orange did not exist in England until the word that referred to it had entered the language.

Another key idea in Derrida's work is that the meaning of each word is inherently unstable, destined to be altered *in an unpredictable way* by future developments and events. In our example the colours red and yellow seemed stable and definite to all in England before the Renaissance, but in fact a lot of what was seen as red and yellow would later become orange. Derrida pointed out the only access we have into what we call reality – and into our mental concepts – is through language, through words. Derrida believed an unavoidable consequence of the fact that the meaning of words is inherently fluid is that the same must be said of reality.

Derrida went on to argue that philosophy – in fact the whole Western metaphysical tradition including religion, science, politics, psychology, and other disciplines of thought – has always wrongly assumed there is something beyond words. Over history this belief in an unchanging and solid presence that transcends language has been conceptualised in many different ways – as God, Spirit, Mind, Truth,

Being, Freedom, Justice, Beauty, Existence, Reality, and so on. Derrida coined a term for this belief in a presence beyond words – he called it *logocentrism*. Derrida asserted that there is no underlying or actual reality that words refer to – he believed that words *are* reality, or are at least the closest we can ever get to it.

Derrida summarised this controversial conclusion with his notorious and much-quoted phrase:

There is nothing outside of the text.[11]

Deconstruction

Derrida did not deny the existence of a reality beyond words, but he believed there is no way to know this reality without the mediating effect of words or other signs.

In *Of Grammatology*, he explained:

From the moment there is meaning there is nothing but signs. We think only in signs.[12]

This realisation led Derrida to two conclusions. The first, as we have heard, was his belief that all philosophical (and other) texts to date have been *logocentric* – that is, they all contain within them an implicit, and, in his view untenable, assumption that there is some fundamental imagined reality beyond words. Derrida coined the term *deconstruction* to refer to his method of reading texts to identify and expose these hidden logocentric beliefs.

The other conclusion Derrida reached was that, rather than becoming depressed by the realisation there is no transcendent truth beyond words, we should embrace the opportunity provided by such a realisation, and actively engage in creating new meanings and realities through a playful and liberated use of language. From here onwards, Derrida took his own advice to heart, creating works abounding with neologisms that he had invented, and prose so playful that most readers, in truth, struggled to understand it.

A Multitude of Followers

It is interesting to consider how much Derrida's childhood might have influenced the direction of his thinking about language and reality. Growing up with the unspoken but ever-present feeling he was an inadequate 'replacement' for his dead brother may well have instilled in him, from an early age, a sense of not being real, substantial, or solid, a sense he may have correspondingly projected on to the world around him. Even the country in which he grew up, French-colonised Algeria, was a reality that would disappear in his lifetime. From his earliest years, as we have heard, he experienced how words can bestow on one different realities and identities. He had lived the different realities associated with being labelled variously as Jew, Algerian, French, or American. His whole childhood had been spent juggling different names, labels, and identities. Perhaps it's no wonder that he came to see words as more powerful and real than the worlds they described.

Whatever the origins of Derrida's philosophical worldview, his suggestion that we could create new truths and realities by being fluid and playful with language would influence not only philosophers, but writers, artists, critics, and many others working in the humanities. His ideas would inspire minority groups and activists to construct positive new identities through the creative use of language and other signs. Urban African Americans would develop the languages of rap and hip-hop, with bands such as Niggers With Attitude showing how those oppressed by even the most hurtful and offensive words could rise up and brazenly reclaim those words to expose and disarm their oppressors. Similarly pejorative words such as 'queer' and 'gay' would be reclaimed and repackaged to be used as emblems of pride amongst those with different gender and sexual identities.

Derrida's notion that all texts could, and should, be deconstructed spread like wildfire. Not only did the philosopher himself churn out a huge number of works based on this idea – almost one every year for the next thirty years – he also inspired a multitude of followers, just as Sartre a generation earlier had inspired an army of existentialists. Almost overnight, in universities around the world, academics and their students were deconstructing anything they could get their hands on, from philosophical and literary texts to cultural products such as movies, TV shows, and popular songs. Soon everything – even so-called low-brow culture – was seen as 'text' to be deconstructed. Many would blame Derrida for collapsing the distinction between high and low culture, although in truth the responsibility for this lay more with the mimicking – and often less discerning – 'deconstructionists' who followed him.

Derrida's insinuation that all classical texts contained something false within them that needed to be exposed infuriated many establishment thinkers. Many saw the increasingly popular philosopher as an irresponsible charlatan whose work was eroding respect for truth, tradition, authority, and morality. Derrida became a highly polarising figure, a target of both admiration and intense loathing for his role in leading the philosophical movement of deconstruction and its ambivalently regarded bedfellow, postmodernism.

A Multitude of Lovers

Derrida's playful and creative approach to philosophy would be mirrored, as we have heard, in his personal life. As a lover, Derrida was similar to how he was as a philosopher – productive, fecund, hyperactive even, and paying little respect to the usual boundaries or

291

traditions. As his fame increased, so did his extramarital affairs. As one of his biographers put it, he was 'a grand seducer…capable of numerous fidelities'.[13] Although he went to great extremes to keep this aspect of his life discreet, he did let slip in one interview that he thought himself ill-suited to monogamy, an institution he described as being 'imposed upon Jews by Europeans'.[14]

Derrida's need for secrecy did not just extend to his affairs. For the first two decades of his career, Derrida had an extreme aversion to any image of his face being shown in public. He repeatedly refused media requests for photographs, and was meticulous in asking those in the media not to publish his picture if they took it without his permission. To the frustration of publishers, he wouldn't even allow a photograph of himself as author to grace the covers of his books. He would later reveal that during these years he found any image of himself disturbing, for reasons he could not explain. One wonders whether this peculiarity was somehow related to the extremely unsettled and fractured sense of identity he experienced in his younger years.

Marguerite, whose psychoanalytic practice was now well established, was highly tolerant and forgiving of her husband's seemingly ever-growing list of quirks and idiosyncrasies. This tolerance and forbearance extended to his frequent extra-conjugal wanderings.

She would, however, draw the line at one particular affair that seemed to her not just a playful distraction like the others, but a serious entanglement that could bring harm and pain to a lot of people. She could see that her beloved husband was in too deep in this liaison and was losing his perspective. As it turned out, he would lose a lot more than this. He would, as Marguerite feared, lose the love and respect of his children. And he would also lose, in excruciating circumstances that he would find unbearable, his precious and much-cherished privacy and anonymity.

Sylviane

Derrida first noticed the 'breathtakingly beautiful' Sylviane Agacinski in 1970, when she was attending his seminars at the École Normale Supérieure. Their affair didn't begin, however, until two years later, when they were both attending a philosophical conference in northern France in the city of Lille. Twenty-seven-year-old Sylviane brought her boyfriend, the writer Jean-Noël Vuarnet, with her to the conference, but he would no longer be her partner by the time the conference ended.

Derrida was now forty-two, and married for fifteen years; his boys Pierre and Jean nine and five years old. By this time he had developed a reputation as a ladies' man. According to reports from his associates, he had a knack of seducing women simply by the way he listened to them. Derrida would later admit that during the height of his career only attractive women were capable of holding his attention. Although his ideas about language and power had actually done much to advance feminist thinking, a sensitivity to feminist principles wasn't evident in the way he related to women. He once described himself to a friend as 'a horrible Mediterranean macho man'.[15]

Of all the lovers Derrida had outside his marriage, none would affect him like the elegant, confident, and fiercely intelligent Sylviane Agacinski. Derrida couldn't resist approaching this strikingly beautiful, dark-haired philosophy graduate at the conference and introducing himself. Sylviane, one imagines, would have felt flattered to be singled out by the brilliant and controversial philosopher, who, with his dapper suit and trademark snow-white hair, cut quite a compelling figure at an event populated by the usual uninspiring offerings of conservative, grey-haired academics.

Sylviane and Derrida soon became not only passionate lovers, but close friends and associates. He helped edit her first book, and she

293

subsequently worked as programme director for the *Collège International de Philosophie*, a non-institutional centre for philosophical research that Derrida had recently established.

Sylviane, who hailed from a family of immigrant Poles, would go on to become a professor at Paris's School for Advanced Studies in the Social Sciences, and have a stellar career as philosopher, feminist thinker, and author. She would also become a leading figure in a branch of French feminism known as differentialism. This strand of feminism thought, which was partly inspired by Derrida's theories, contended that the human condition could not be understood without reference to both sexes. Sylviane would later declare in her book *Sexual Politics*:

> We want to keep the freedom to seduce and be seduced. There will never be a war of the sexes in France.[16]

Sylviane couldn't have been more wrong, however, when it came to the case of her own affair with Derrida. Six years into their relationship, she, at thirty-two, fell pregnant to her married and much-esteemed lover. His response to this news set in train a series of conflicts and recriminations that would reverberate for decades to come.

Throughout 1978, after Sylviane fell pregnant, she and Derrida argued almost constantly. Sylviane wanted to continue the pregnancy. Derrida did not. He insisted she have a termination. Sylviane eventually gave in to his demands, having an abortion towards the end of 1978.

In 1980 Derrida did something most unusual, even by his standards. He published a work called *The Postcard* that was written in the form of a letter to an unnamed lover. For the small handful of people in the know about Derrida's private affairs, it was clear this work was addressed to Sylviane. One particularly unpleasant and insensitive line said:

To the devil with the child, the only thing we ever will have discussed, the child, the child, the child.[17]

For many of Derrida's critics, this strange work that intertwined personal catharsis with indecipherable prose only confirmed their views as to why he should not be taken seriously as a philosopher. Derrida's admirers, on the other hand, praised *The Postcard* as another example of the maestro boldly exploring new literary and philosophical ground.

One person who did take note of Derrida's latest work, and not because he appreciated its brilliance, was his eldest son, Pierre, now aged seventeen. Pierre was so disgusted at Derrida's allusions to adultery and his disputes with his mistress over their pregnancy in *The Postcard*, that he disowned his father there and then.

Love Child

To make it even clearer to his father that he wanted nothing to do with him, Pierre Derrida changed his last name after he left home. As he would later explain: 'The name Derrida wasn't really mine.'[18] Pierre, it seems, was doomed to experience the same struggles and confusion with name and identity that had afflicted his father a generation earlier.

Derrida's marriage, on the other hand, did survive the dramas of Agacinski's pregnancy and termination. Even more surprisingly, Derrida's relationship with Sylviane survived these tribulations.

In fact, Sylviane became pregnant to Derrida again in early 1984. Once again, Derrida insisted she have a termination, but on this occasion, with her fortieth birthday approaching, Sylviane made it very clear she would be continuing with the pregnancy.

Later that year, Sylviane Agacinski – now a renowned feminist philosopher – gave birth to a baby boy, Daniel. Derrida refused, at first, to acknowledge the existence of the child, let alone the fact that he was the father. It was at this point that Marguerite intervened, insisting her husband take some responsibility for his actions. As a result, Derrida acknowledged to Sylviane, in 1986, that Daniel was his, though he still refused to have anything to do with him.

Derrida and Sylviane's twelve-year affair didn't survive these events, and from that time on their only communication with each other was a vicious to and fro of increasingly bitter recriminations. Although Sylviane would move on with her life, she would never forget Derrida's disgraceful behaviour. Indeed, she would take every opportunity in the coming years to ensure he got his comeuppance.

In 1983, just before she became pregnant to Derrida for the second time, Agacinski had met Lionel Jospin, the future prime minister of France. Jospin was a guest at the wedding of Sylviane's sister Sophie, at the time one of France's most celebrated actresses. Sylviane found the good-humoured and respectful attentions of this charming and magisterial forty-six-year-old a welcome respite from the treatment she had been receiving from Derrida in recent years. Although he was, like Derrida, confident, ambitious, and destined for fame, he differed greatly from his predecessor in that he treated Sylviane with kindness, thoughtfulness, and respect from the day of their first meeting.

It's unclear when Sylviane and Jospin's relationship began, but they would marry in 1994, ten years after this first encounter. Their high-society wedding was attended by many of France's leading intellectuals, artists, celebrities, and politicians. Needless to say, Derrida wasn't on the guest list.

'Obscurantisme Terroriste'

It wasn't just Derrida's personal life that was under strain during these years. His professional life had become exceedingly busy, with his philosophical works generating an increasing amount of criticism and, at times, outright hostility.

Throughout the 1980s Derrida worked non-stop, compulsively and frenetically, lurching from one project to another. In addition to publishing seven books in less than ten years, he was in high demand as a speaker, giving talks across the globe in North and South America, Europe, Israel, and Japan. During these years he became the world's most widely translated French philosopher.

But as Derrida's fame and popularity increased, so did the vehemence of public attacks on his works, and indeed, on him as a person. Most of these attacks came from analytic philosophers in Britain and America, who were not only outraged that his turgid, flowery prose was being accepted as philosophy, but that it was receiving so much praise and adulation. In the eyes of his fiercest critics, Derrida was a fraud, a nihilistic and destructive pretender whose works didn't deserve to belong to the hallowed and noble tradition of philosophy.

Derrida's works – more than any other philosopher's – cracked open a fault line that had been building for some time between the analytic and continental traditions in philosophy. In the early part of the twentieth century, analytic philosophers such as G.E. Moore, Gottlob Frege, and Bertrand Russell rejected the obscurity of Hegel and other continental philosophers in favour of a stripped-down, concise, logical approach that aligned philosophy with the aims and methods of science. The neologistic, playful, literary, and creative approaches taken by European philosophers such as Nietzsche and Heidegger were like a red rag to a bull for the analytic philosophers, who were trying to streamline and pin down meaning rather than complicate or 'construct' it. The analytic philosophers saw Derrida as the worst offender in derailing philosophy from the conceptual clarity they were striving to achieve. The fact that Derrida's approach to texts had become fashionable and even *de rigueur* in some quarters only increased the irritation of his Anglophone critics.

Those sympathetic to the continental tradition, on the other hand, saw the analytic philosophers as unnecessarily narrow in their focus. For the continentals, science represented only one world view among many, a world view that had become so dominant and unquestioned it warranted even closer critical scrutiny. Continental philosophers were just as interested, if not more so, in the truths of 'non-scientific' disciplines such as literature, history, politics, and the arts.

In the 1980s and 90s, Derrida came to represent all that was bad – or good – about continental philosophy, depending on which side one took in this increasingly hostile battle of ideas that came to be known as the culture wars. One of the most damaging salvos against Derrida in this battle would be fired not by his British or American critics, but by a fellow countryman. Michel Foucault, a couple of years before his death, let slip – in a private conversation with the analytic philosopher John Searle – his views about Derrida and his work. Searle revealed the content of this damning conversation in an essay he wrote for the *New York Review of Books* in 1983:

> Michel Foucault once characterised Derrida's prose style to me as *'obscurantisme terroriste'*. The text is written so obscurely that you can't figure out exactly what the thesis is (hence *'obscurantisme'*) and then when one criticises this, the author says, '*Vous m'avez mal compris, vous êtes idiot* [you have misunderstood me, you are an idiot]' (hence *'terroriste'*).[19]

For Derrida to be accused of what his enemies long believed to be true by 'one of his own' was a particularly damaging blow. It didn't, however, stop Derrida's postmodernist disciples from continuing to

find gems of genius and meaning in his increasingly oblique and eso-
teric texts.

In 1992 the culture wars reached a new pitch when news got out
that Cambridge University planned to award an honorary doctorate
to Derrida for his contribution to philosophy.

Amidst the subsequent howls of protest from scholars around the
globe, one offered his opinion that awarding Derrida an honorary doctorate was 'like appointing a pyromaniac to the post of chief fireman'.
The *Observer* chimed in with an editorial that likened Derrida's work
to a computer virus. A group of concerned academics from the US,
UK, Australia, and other countries published an open letter to Cambridge University protesting that Derrida's work did 'not meet accepted standards of clarity and rigour.'[20] The letter concluded with a
warning that:

> Academic status based on what seems to us to be little more than
> semi-intelligible attacks upon the values of reason, truth, and
> scholarship is not, we submit, sufficient grounds for the awarding
> of an honorary degree in a distinguished university.[21]

There, were, however, academics who felt otherwise, who believed
that Derrida's original, groundbreaking work did merit such acknowledgement. As one defender pointed out, 'a litany of charges' had been
brought against the philosopher 'without citing a single supporting
quote or reference to his work'.[22] This same commentator wondered
how many opposed to Derrida's honorary degree had actually read his
work.

In the end, Cambridge University held a ballot to determine
whether the degree should be awarded, the first time in thirty years
that such an extraordinary measure had been taken. Derrida's supporters prevailed by a vote of 336 to 204, and the doctorate was awarded.

Not in the Mood

In 1995 Lionel Jospin declared he would run as the Socialist Party candidate for the French presidency. There was a buoyant and optimistic mood amongst those on the Left; many believed the time was ripe for them to gain power after decades in the wilderness. Derrida even got involved in the campaign, though as might be expected, this newfound collegiality between him and his ex-lover's husband's team did not last very long.

Jospin was not successful, but he was appointed Prime Minister from 1997 to 2002.

In 2001 Jospin announced he would be running for the presidency again. On this occasion, Sylviane took a much more active and public role in his campaign.

Towards the end of 2001, as public interest in the campaign intensified, two biographies of Lionel Jospin were published. Both revealed something that the French public had been unaware of up unto this point – that Sylviane's seventeen-year-old son Daniel, adopted by Jospin, was actually the child of France's most notorious intellectual.

Derrida was enraged that this closely guarded secret had been disclosed to Jospin's biographers.

As reports of his love child dominated the news, a downcast Derrida admitted in an interview with a journalist that he hadn't even bothered to vote in the first round of presidential elections, because he was not 'in the mood'.

Sylviane Agacinski-Jospin pounced on her ex-lover's comments, responding in a column she was commissioned to write for one of Paris's broadsheets:

> So it's a question of *mood*, yet again! ...Let's hope at least that the philosopher will be in a better mood for the second round.[23]

Jospin went on to lose the presidential race again, this time to his right-wing Gaullist rival, Jacques Chirac.

Derrida's personal fortunes had hit an all-time low. He had been exposed and humiliated, and estranged from two of his three sons. It was now more evident than ever that there wouldn't be any love lost in future between him and Sylviane Agacinski-Jospin.

Throughout these ordeals, the faithful and patient Marguerite remained loyal. Her forbearance, tolerance, and understanding were in some ways reminiscent of Simone de Beauvoir, who more than a generation earlier had played a similar supportive role in the life of the equally restless and priapic Jean-Paul Sartre.

It was just as well for Derrida that he had the steady and comforting presence of Marguerite in his life, for an even greater adversity would soon present itself, one from which he would never recover.

Before this final catastrophe descended on Derrida, however, the mercurial philosopher surprised all who knew him by discarding his longstanding demands for privacy and anonymity, and agreeing to be filmed for a very personal documentary about his life and work.

Derrida on Display

In October 2002, just after Derrida's seventy-second birthday, a premiere of the documentary film *Derrida* was shown to an audience of his fans and followers at the Film Forum in Greenwich Village, New York City. The film opens with a scene of Derrida ambling through unidentified Paris streets. The camera pans to capture Derrida's iconic profile, in a stylish black raincoat, his collar up high around his neck. His shock of white-grey hair, serious black eyebrows, a perfectly formed straight nose, and dark olive skin complete the picture of the charismatic philosopher. To top off this sublime silhouette, a mahogany pipe extends out of Derrida's brooding mouth. As we walk with the philosopher, one of the film's co-directors, Amy Ziering Kofman, narrates some random facts about his life:

[Derrida's] older brother lives only seven days, dying just a year before he is born.[24]

As a child, 'he cries out: "Mommy I'm scared" every night until she let him sleep on a sofa near them'.[25]

Also, as a child, 'he was given a secret name Eli, after the Jewish prophet Elija that isn't on his birth certificate'.[26]

The narrator tells us that Derrida, as an adolescent, dreamed of being a champion soccer player. And that as an adult he was tortured for many years by chronic sleeplessness, eventually suffering a nervous collapse from the overuse of sleeping medications and amphetamines.

The film then cuts to a domestic scene, with Derrida and Marguerite being interviewed in their home. This middle-aged couple are clearly very comfortable together. The interviewer asks how they met. Derrida looks at the camera and then to his wife.

'Should we tell or no?'

Marguerite encourages her husband:

'Go ahead tell. Tell.'

Derrida says: 'I'm not going to tell you everything. No. I'm just going to tell you superficial things. I was a student with Marguerite's brother at the same school, the École Normale Supérieure, in 1952.'

Marguerite adds: 'So there was a pretty strong probability that we'd meet.'

Derrida continues: 'Then one winter, the first year we were to-gether at this school, we went skiing together, her brother, me and some friends. And that's when I met Marguerite. I'm not going into more detail, but it was in '53. And then we didn't see each other for a while, then she invited me to have lunch with her family, and it started like that.'

The interviewer turns to Derrida's wife:

'Marguerite, do you remember the first time you saw Jacques?'

Marguerite: 'Yes. yes. In the snow.'

Derrida, referring to the interviewer, observes: 'She seems to be surprised that we actually remember...'

Marguerite: 'He came to the village in the mountains where I was staying.'

At this point, Derrida moves to close things down:

'You've hit an area where you're not going to get much information from us. It's very difficult to speak of these things in front of a camera. I can give you the facts, the dates...We were married in the States in 1957. These are facts. Raw facts.'

Interviewer: 'Yes. It seems you have rules – you've already decided to only tell me facts. Why have you imposed this decision to not disclose anything?'

Marguerite comes to her husband's defence: 'It's just not that easy...'[27]

In another part of the film, Derrida is asked a question about his work. He explains, in mellifluous French, translated at the bottom of the screen, his experience of the writing process. He comes across as warm, engaging, naturally charismatic, and – perhaps surprisingly – easy to understand, even when he discusses his ideas. One can't help notice at this point, however, that the woman interviewing Derrida – the young, dark-haired Californian Amy Kofman – is extraordinarily attractive. Derrida is sporting crisp burgundy shirtsleeves, behind him against his office bookshelves is a blur of books. Derrida is giving a surprisingly personal account of what writing is like for him:

Each time that I write something and it feels like I'm advancing into new territory, something I haven't seen before, this type of advance often requires certain gestures that can be taken as aggressive with regard to other thinkers or colleagues.

His eyes widen a little as he turns towards his interlocutor, elaborating:

I'm not someone who is by nature polemical but it's true that deconstructive gestures appear to destabilise or cause anxiety and even hurt others.[28]

At this point it's hard to tell if the philosopher is performing for the camera or is genuinely and painfully aware – apologetic would be too strong a word – of the effect his work has on others. He goes on to explain that he often experiences attacks of fear – usually just as he is falling asleep after a writing session – that he is doing something terrible and unforgivable in deconstructing others' works, but he feels that he must write what he writes, that it comes from something beyond him. On watching the film, one senses that, for the interviewer, Derrida's very presence requires an intimate response. He is clearly a difficult man to ignore or dismiss when encountered in the flesh.

A week before the film's first screening, Derrida granted an interview with another female journalist – Kristine McKenna of *LA Weekly*. In her article, McKenna admits that, having no particular expertise in philosophy, she felt somewhat apprehensive about meeting her subject. She wondered how she was going to be able to make this mysterious philosopher and his subject matter comprehensible for a general audience. But, to her relief, she found Derrida 'surprisingly approachable in person', with his 'ideas seeming considerably less daunting in conversation than on the page'. McKenna, who had been given an opportunity to preview the film before it screened publicly, described the

Derrida she interviewed as 'very charming', with a 'charisma that comes across clearly in [the film]'.[29]

When McKenna asks the seventy-two-year-old, in what would be one of the last interviews of his life:

'What is the most widely held misconception about you and your work?', he replies:

> That I'm a skeptical nihilist who doesn't believe in anything, who thinks nothing has meaning, and text has no meaning...It's a misreading of my work that began 35 years ago, and it's difficult to destroy. I never said everything is linguistic and we're enclosed in language. In fact, I say the opposite, and the deconstruction of logocentrism was concerned to dismantle precisely this philosophy for which everything is language. Anyone who reads my work with attention understands that I insist on affirmation and faith, and that I'm full of respect for the texts I read.[30]

Although Derrida's reply appears heartfelt and genuine in this interview, one is still left with the sense of not quite grasping what his work is all about. In fact, one suspects the slippery, endlessly creative, and playful deferment of meaning in his work will always leave one feeling uncertain, dissatisfied, and frustrated, never able to finally capture exactly what he means. This experience of Derrida's work reflects a central idea in his philosophy – that meaning isn't permanently housed somewhere out beyond language, but is endlessly suspended, recreated, and altered by language itself.

On the Wednesday evening *Derrida* is first screened in New York, the audience at the Film Forum are in for a special treat. Immediately after the screening, co-directors Amy Ziering Kofman and Kirby Dick are joined on stage by the subject of the film, Derrida himself, to talk about the creation of the documentary. The auditorium is packed with young people, amongst them many starry-eyed students of film, literature, art, and philosophy. This session has been recorded for posterity, and, on viewing it, one is struck again by how personable – and understandable – the philosopher seems when speaking to an audience.

Derrida on stage, dressed in a blue shirt, dark jacket, crumpled grey tie, and ill-fitting rectangular glasses, does look considerably less commanding in real life, however, than he did in the film that has just been shown. He looks older, wrinkled, somewhat shrunken. Even his signature mane of white hair looks flat and subdued. But when he starts to speak to the audience in a perfect, near-accentless English, he seems to enlarge, immediately captivating his audience with his humour, humility, and candour.

The first question from a member of the audience:

'Why did you agree to make the film?'

With a response that could only come from the father of deconstruction, Derrida explains:

At first I was very reluctant. I kept saying 'No, No,' but there was a misunderstanding and they thought that 'No' meant 'Yes'.[31]

At this point the philosopher pretends to look genuinely puzzled, but the good-humoured, mischievous look in his eye lets the audience know he is joking, and the whole auditorium erupts into laughter. He then adds, in a more serious tone, that he was very anxious and self-conscious throughout the making of the film, but there were times he forgot he was being filmed and that was okay.

He is asked by another member of the audience if he interfered with the editing process in any way. He replies there was only one piece of feedback he gave after viewing the initial unedited footage, which the filmmakers took heed of:

Marguerite, my wife, was shown in the kitchen too often. She is a psychoanalyst and I am at home more than she. So that representation of her would have been untrue, unfair and misleading.[32]

One gets a sense, on hearing Derrida defend Marguerite in this way, that the seventy-two-year old's relationship with his lifelong partner has grown, over the years, into something solid and enduring. It would appear that the thinker whose life's work was devoted to declaring there is nothing transcendent in the world, has nevertheless found something of such a nature in his bond with Marguerite.

Towards the end of Kristine McKenna's interview with Derrida, she asks him: 'What is important to you today?'

He replies:

How can I answer such a question? Many things private, public and political are important to me, but I think of all these things is a constant awareness that I'm ageing, I'm going to die, and life is short. I'm constantly attentive to the time left to me, and although I've been inclined this way since I was young, it becomes more serious when you reach seventy-two. So far I haven't made my peace with the inevitability of death, and I doubt I ever will, and this awareness permeates everything I think. It's terrible what's going on in the world, and all these things are on my mind, but they exist alongside this terror of my own death.[33]

The following year Derrida was diagnosed with pancreatic cancer, an aggressive neoplasm that kills most of its victims within a year. The ever-anxious Derrida, who still felt he had plenty of work left in him, plaintively admitted on hearing of his grim prognosis that 'unlike...Socrates, he was not ready to die'.[34] But on 9 October 2004, two years after sitting on a stage and answering questions about himself at the Film Forum in New York, Derrida died in a Paris hospital bed with his loving wife by his side.

In *Derrida*, continental philosophy's last great philosopher was also asked another question: 'If you were to watch a documentary about a philosopher – Heidegger, Kant or Hegel, what would you like to see in it?'

His reply was unexpected, clearly taking his young interviewer, Amy Kofman, by surprise:

> Their sex lives. If you want a quick answer. I would like to hear them speak about their sexual lives. I would like to hear them speak about it. What is the sexual life of Hegel or Heidegger?

When the interviewer asks him 'Why?', Derrida expands:

> …Because it's something they don't talk about. I'd love to hear about something they refuse to talk about. Why do philosophers present themselves asexually in their work? Why have they erased their private lives from their work? Or never talk about anything personal? There is nothing more important in their private life than love. I'm not talking about making a porno film about Hegel or Heidegger. I want them to speak about the part that love plays in their lives. So you could take a microphone up to Hegel…One knows some things about Hegel or Heidegger already. But not from things they've said. I'd like to hear them speak on this.[35]

Epilogue

It was only in the last few days of my research for this book that I came across the comment by Derrida that he would like to hear philosophers 'speak about the part that love plays in their lives'.

I felt a strange thrill, after many years of exploring the love lives of these seven philosophers, to find that the seventh had the same idea as me. Derrida's comment, his rationale for it, and the fact that he mentioned Hegel and Heidegger – two of the philosophers whose amorous lives I had been researching – was a coincidence so striking I allowed myself the indulgence of seeing it as a sign this book should be written. It was a discovery that gave me a neat and satisfying sense of closure.

Almost.

There was one other thing I felt needed to be done. I felt a strong need to visit the place that had inspired me to write this book. The place where Beauvoir first met Sartre, before she started writing novels that portrayed him as a lover as well as a thinker. Novels that had got me wondering about the lovers of other philosophers.

And so, with my thirteen-year-old daughter in tow, I took a twenty-seven-hour flight from Brisbane to Paris to pay a visit to the École Normale Supérieure, the place where Beauvoir and Sartre's paths first crossed.

It is a beautiful, crisp, sunny autumn afternoon when I first stand, with my daughter at my side, outside the gates of the school in which Sartre, Foucault, and Derrida all studied philosophy. I am surprised, and even a little disappointed, at how nondescript and unassuming this building is, hidden away in the back streets of one of Paris's leafy inner-city suburbs. Only a small sign over the building's front entrance confirms that this is, indeed, the École Normale Supérieure.

As I watch students strolling to and from their classes in the gentle autumn sunshine, I wonder how many of them know, or even care, about the lives of the famous students who walked these grounds before them: Sartre, Beauvoir, Foucault, Derrida, and their esteemed teachers Bergson, Hyppolite, Althusser, and Merleau-Ponty. I wonder, too, how much they know about the great German thinkers – Kant, Hegel, Nietzsche, Heidegger, and Arendt – who established the continental tradition well before the French school started to bloom.

It takes a while to convince the security guard, a young North African man, to let us in at the front gate. I try to explain, in my mangled French, that I am researching a book on Jean-Paul Sartre and other philosophers. He doesn't understand a word I say, but after a few minutes of looking through the university directory for the name Jean-Paul Sartre, he shrugs his shoulders and lets us in.

We climb the seven stairs that lead to the École's main building, and proceed through a long dark corridor that eventually opens up into a sunny open-air courtyard.

Almost twelve years to the day after Derrida drew his last breath, I feel exhilarated to be standing in this grassy open space inside the École Normale Supérieure. Some students are taking advantage of the good weather to read or socialise at outdoor tables scattered throughout the square. Birds flitter and insects hover in the warm air above the courtyard's lush gardens. I sit with my daughter in a cool stone recess in one of the four walls that border the courtyard. We do our best to look inconspicuous as we survey the scene before us.

It occurs to me that I might be sitting in the exact location where Beauvoir first laid eyes on Sartre almost ninety years ago. I look up and see a half-opened window on the second storey that looks down over the courtyard. Was this, I wonder, the window a young, mischievous Sartre looked out of before he poured a bucket of water on to his unsuspecting colleagues and shouted 'Thus Pissed Zarathustra!'?

We sit for about half an hour in the courtyard, watching its giant plane trees swaying gently in the afternoon breeze. Did Beauvoir and Sartre sit under these very same trees? Lean, young students in jeans and pullovers, books under their arms, saunter in and out of this pleasant, dappled outdoor space. At one table a middle-aged male lecturer sits close to a much younger female student, looking through her manuscript. I try not to let my imagination run away from me at what might be happening there.

We wander out the far door of the courtyard to arrive in a cool, tiled foyer. On its walls noticeboards promote lectures about Derrida, Pascal, and other great European thinkers. Beside one of the noticeboards is a memorial honouring ENS alumni who fell in World War II. I scroll down until I come to the name Paul Nizan, who was with Sartre on the day Beauvoir first met him. The memorial tells me Nizan enrolled at the ENS in 1924. In 1940 he would be killed in the Battle of Dunkirk, aged thirty-five.

We return to the courtyard, and the sun has gone behind a cloud; everything has gone cold and grey in this previously sunny space. I indicate to my daughter it's time to leave. We walk back along the corridor we came from, down the stairs and out the front gate.

Our pilgrimage is over.

Outside on the street I turn around for one last look at the building I travelled 26,000 kilometres to visit. And then I see it. What I had been looking for all along, but didn't really expect to find.

A young man and woman are standing, facing each other, just outside the large doorway of the university's main building. The long shadows of their figures betray a body language that is unmistakable –

the language of tentative desire. She, blonde-brown hair falling over her shoulders, her mouth half-open and smiling, is locked in a steady gaze with the man with black, ruffled hair, a book in his hand. It is the end of the university day and groups of other students are streaming past them. But these two keep nodding and smiling, oblivious to the movement and noise. It is as if a silent and invisible tunnel connects them as they talk, privileging them with its perfect stillness as the world bustles on.

There's also an awkward shyness in their posture that tells me they are not yet lovers.

'C'mon, Dad, let's go.'

My daughter has been very patient.

We turn around and walk into the streets beyond in search of a café or park to rest in, but I keep in mind – for as long as I can – a cherished image of these two future lovers of philosophy.

Bibliography

General

- Bakewell, Sarah, *At the Existentialist Café: Freedom, Being and Apricot Cocktails* (2016), Chatto & Windus
- Bowie, Andrew, *German Philosophy: A Very Short Introduction* (2010), Oxford University Press
- Bunnin, Nicholas & Tsui-James, Eric, *The Blackwell Companion to Philosophy* (1995), Wiley-Blackwell
- Collinson, Diané, *Fifty Major Philosophers* (1987), Routledge
- Craig, Edward, *Philosophy: A Very Short Introduction* (2002), Oxford University Press
- Botton, Alain de, *The Consolations of Philosophy* (2008), Penguin
- Dufourmantelle, Anne, *Blind Date: Sex and Philosophy* (2007, translated by Catherine Porter), University of Illinois Press
- Gaarder, Jostein, *Sophie's World* (1996), Phoenix
- Grayling, A.C., *The History of Philosophy* (2019), Viking
- Honderich, Ted (Ed.), *The Oxford Companion to Philosophy* (1995), Oxford University Press
- Judt, Tony, *Postwar* (2005), William Heinemann
- Kul-Want, Christopher & Piero, *Introducing Continental Philosophy: A Graphic Guide* (2013), Icon
- Mitchell Stephen A. & Black, Margaret J., *Freud and Beyond* (1995), Basic Books
- Murdoch, Iris, *Metaphysics as a Guide to Morals* (1993), Penguin

- Popkin, Richard H. (ed.), *The Philosophy of the 16th and 17th Centuries* (1966), The Free Press
- Russell, Bertrand, *History of Western Philosophy* (2004), Routledge
- Stokes, Philip, *Philosophy: The Great Thinkers* (2010), Arcturus
- Watson, Peter, *A Terrible Beauty* (2000), Weidenfeld & Nicolson
- Watson, Peter, *Ideas* (2006), Phoenix
- Wilson, Colin, *The Outsider* (1978), Picador

Kant

- Gulyga, Arsenij, *Immanual Kant: His Life and Thought* (2012), Springer
- Kant, Immanuel, *Correspondence* (1999, translated and edited by Arnulf Zweig), Cambridge University Press
- Kant, Immanuel, *Critique of Pure Reason* (1781/2008), Penguin ClassicsKant, Immanuel, *Practical Philosophy* (1996, translated by M. J. Gregor), Cambridge University Press
- Kant, Immanuel, *Prolegomena to Any Future Metaphysics* (1783/2004, translated by G. C. Hatfield), Cambridge University Press
- Kant, Immanuel, *The Critique of Judgement* (1790/1952), Oxford University Press
- Körner, S., *Kant* (1955), Penguin
- Kuehn, Manfred, *Kant: A Biography* (2001), Cambridge University Press
- Kul-Want, Christopher & Klimowski, Andrzej, *Introducing Kant: A Graphic Guide* (2011), Icon
- Scruton, Roger, *Kant: A Very Short Introduction* (2001), Oxford University Press

- Wood, Allen W. (ed.), *Basic Writings of Kant* (2001), Modern Library
- Zammito, John H., *Kant, Herder, and the Birth of Anthropology* (2002). Chicago University Press

Hegel

- Gibbon, Edward, *The History of the Decline and Fall of the Roman Empire: Abridged Edition* (1788/2000), Penguin
- Hegel, G.W.F., *Phenomenology of Spirit* (1807/1996, translated by A.V. Miller), Oxford University Press
- Hegel, G.W.F., *Philosophy of Right* (1821/2005, translated by S. W. Dyde), Dover
- Hegel, G.W.F., *The Science of Logic* (1816/2015, translated by G. D. Giovanni), Cambridge University Press
- Isnaemi, Hendri F., *Hegel's Son of War in Java* (2010, my translation), https://historia.id/militer/articles/anak-hegel-perang-di-tanah-jawa-vVGlP
- Loomis, Joshua S., *Epidemics: The Impact of Germs and Their Power Over Humanity* (2018), ABC-CLIO
- Marx, Karl & Engels, Friedrich, *The Communist Manifesto* (1848/2010), Vintage
- Pinkard, Terry, *Hegel: A Biography* (2000), Cambridge University Press
- Singer, Peter, *Hegel: A Very Short Introduction* (1983), Oxford University Press
- Thomson, David, *Europe Since Napoleon* (1966), Pelican Books

Nietzsche

- Allison, David B., *Reading the New Nietzsche* (2001), Rowman & Littlefield
- Andreas-Salomé, Lou, *Looking Back: Memoirs* (1991, translated by Breon Mitchell), Paragon House
- Armstrong, John, *Life Lessons from Nietzsche* (2013), Macmillan
- Brown, Malcolm, *Nietzsche Chronicle* (2011), https://www.dartmouth.edu/~fnchron/
- Cate, Curtis, *Nietzsche: A Biography* (2005), Abrams
- Corbett, Rachel, *You Must Change Your Life: The Story of Rainer Maria Rilke and Auguste Rodin* (2016), WW Norton & Co
- Diethe, Carol, *Nietzsche's Women: Beyond the Whip* (2013), De Gruyter
- Douglas, Burnham & Jesinghausen, Martin, *Nietzsche's Thus Spoke Zarathustra* (2010), Edinburgh University Press
- Gane, Laurence & Piero, *Introducing Nietzsche: A Graphic Guide* (2013), Icon
- Hollingdale, R.J., *Nietzsche: The Man and His Philosophy* (1999), Cambridge University Press
- Jensen, A.K. & Heit, H., *Nietzsche as a Scholar of Antiquity* (2014), Bloomsbury
- Joachim Köhler, *Zarathustra's Secret: The Interior Life of Friedrich Nietzsche* (2015, translated by Ronald Taylor), Yale University Press
- Kaufman, Walter (ed.), *The Portable Nietzsche* (1976), Penguin
- Kaufman, Walter, *Nietzsche: Philosopher, Psychologist, Antichrist* (1974), Princeton University Press

- Knell, David Farrell & Bates, Donald, *The Good European: Nietzsche's Work Sites in Word and Image* (1997), University of Chicago Press
- Köhler, Joachim & Taylor, Ronald, *Nietzsche and Wagner: A Lesson in Subjugation* (1998), Yale University Press
- Köhler, Joachim, *Richard Wagner: The Last of the Titans* (2004), Yale University PressLeiter, Brian, *Nietzsche on Morality* (2014), Routledge
- Nietzsche, Friedrich, *Beyond Good and Evil* (1886/1990, translated by R.J. Hollingdale), Penguin
- Nietzsche, Friedrich, *Ecce Homo* (1888/1992, translated by R.J. Hollingdale), Penguin
- Nietzsche, Friedrich, *Nietzsche's Writings as a Student* (2012), The Nietzsche Channel
- Nietzsche, Friedrich, *Selected Letters of Friedrich Nietzsche* (1996, translated by Christopher Middleton), Hackett
- Nietzsche, Friedrich, *The Birth of Tragedy* (1872/1993, translated by S Whiteside), Penguin
- Nietzsche, Friedrich, *The Will to Power* (1968, translated by W Kaufmann & R. J. Hollingdale), Vintage, 1968
- Nietzsche, Friedrich, *Why I Am So Wise* (2004), Penguin
- Peters, H.F., *My Sister, My Spouse: A Biography of Lou Andreas-Salomé* (1962), Norton
- Prose, Francine, *The Lives of the Muses* (2013), Union Books
- Rose, Jonathan, *The Holocaust and the Book: Destruction and Preservation* (2001), University of Massachusetts Press
- Safranski, Rüdiger, *Nietzsche: A Philosophical Biography* (2002, translated by Shelley Frisch), Granta
- Salomé, Lou, *Nietzsche [Friedrich Nietzsche in seinen Werken]* (1894/2001, translated by S Mandel), University of Illinois Press

- Tanner, Michael, *Nietzsche: A Very Short Introduction* (1994), Oxford University Press
- Thomas, R.H., *Nietzsche in German Politics and Society* (1983), Manchester University Press
- Vickers, Julia, *Lou von Salome: A Biography of the Woman Who Inspired Freud, Nietzsche and Rilke* (2014), McFarland
- Wagner, Cosima, *Cosima Wagner's Diaries* (1978, translated by Geoffrey Skelton, Harcourt Brace Jovanovich
- Young, Julian, *Friedrich Nietzsche: A Philosophical Biography* (2010), Cambridge University Press

Heidegger

- Arendt, Hannah & Heidegger, Martin, *Letters, 1925-1975* (2003, edited by Ursula Ludz and translated by Andrew Shields), Harcourt
- Arendt, Hannah, 'Thinking and moral considerations: A lecture', *Social Research*, 38(3), 417–446 (1971)
- Arendt, Hannah, *Eichmann in Jerusalem: A Report on the Banality of Evil* (2007), Penguin Classics
- Arendt, Hannah, *Martin Heidegger at Eighty* (1971), New York Review of Books
- Arendt, Hannah, *The Origins of Totalitarianism* (2017), Penguin
- Babka, S.P., *Through the Dark Field* (2017), Liturgical Press
- Ettinger, Elżbieta, *Hannah Arendt/Martin Heidegger* (1995), Yale University Press
- Heidegger, Martin, 'Letter on Humanism', *Basic Writings* (1977, edited and translated by David Farrell Krell), Harper & Row

- Heidegger, Martin, *Basic Concepts of Aristotelian Philosophy* (2009. translated by R.D. Metcalf & M.B. Tanzer), Indiana University Press

- Heidegger, Martin, *Being and Time* (1926/1962, translated by J Macquarie & E Robinson), Blackwell

- Heidegger, Martin, *Contributions to Philosophy* (1999, translated by P Emad & K Maly), Indiana University Press

- Heidegger, Martin, *Letters to His Wife 1915-1970* (2010), Polity

- Inwood, Michael, *Heidegger: A Very Short Introduction* (1997), Oxford University Press

- Maier-Katkin D. & Maier-Katkin B., *Heidegger: Calumny and the Politics of Reconciliation* in Human Rights Quarterly Vol.28, No. 1 (Feb., 2006), Johns Hopkins University Press

- Maier-Katkin, Daniel, *Stranger from Abroad: Hannah Arendt, Martin Heidegger, Friendship and Forgiveness* (2010), W.W. Norton

- Nixon, Jon, *Hannah Arendt and the Politics of Friendship* (2015), Bloomsbury

- Petzet. Heinrich Wiegand. *Encounters and Dialogues with Martin Heidegger, 1929–1976* (1983), University of Chicago Press

- Philipse, Herman, *Heidegger's Philosophy of Being: A Critical Interpretation*

- Rorty, Richard, *Essays on Heidegger and Others* (1991), Cambridge University Press

- Safranski, Rüdiger, *Martin Heidegger: Between Good and Evil* (1999), Harvard University Press

- Sheehan, Thomas (ed.), *Heidegger: The Man and The Thinker* (2017), Routledge

- Smith, Gregory B., *Martin Heidegger: Paths Taken, Paths Opened* (2007), Rowman & Littlefield

- Wrathall, Mark, *How to Read Heidegger* (2006), WW Norton & Co

- Young-Bruehl, Elisabeth, *Hannah Arendt: For Love of the World* (2004), Yale University Press

Sartre

- Appignanesi, Lisa, *Simone de Beauvoir* (2005), Haus
- Åsbrink, Elisabeth, *1947: Where Now Begins* (2018), Other Press
- Bair, Dierdre, *Simone de Beauvoir: A Biography* (1991), Touchstone
- Beauvoir, Simone de, *Adieux: A Farewell to Sartre* (1986), Penguin
- Beauvoir, Simone de, *Memoirs of a Dutiful Daughter* (1958), Penguin
- Beauvoir, Simone de, *She Came to Stay* (1966), Penguin
- Beauvoir, Simone de, *The Mandarins* (1957), Fontana
- Beauvoir, Simone de, *The Prime of Life* (1920, translated by Peter Green), Andre Deutsch and Weidenfeld & Nicolson
- Beauvoir, Simone de, *The Second Sex* (1952), Random House
- Elpidorou, Andreas, *Propelled: How Boredom, Frustration, and Anticipation Lead Us to the Good Life* (2020), Oxford University Press
- Kaufman, Walter (ed.), *Existentialism From Dostoyevsky to Sartre* (1956), Meridian
- Kaye, Sharon M. (ed.), *What Philosophy Can Tell You About Your Lover* (2012), Open Court
- Kirkpatrick, Kate, *Becoming Beauvoir: A Life* (2019), Bloomsbury
- Lamblin, Bianca, *A Disgraceful Affair* (1996), Northeastern University Press

- O'Donohoe, Benedict, 'Living with Mother: Sartre and the problem of Maternity', *Sens public* (2006), http://sens-public.org/articles/300/

- Poirier, Agnès, *Left Bank* (2018), Bloomsbury

- Rowley, Hazel, *Tête-à-Tête: The Lives and Loves of Simone de Beauvoir & Jean-Paul Sartre* (2007), Vintage

- Sartre, Jean-Paul, *Iron in the Soul* (2002), Penguin

- Sartre, Jean-Paul, *Nausea* (1938/1965), Penguin

- Sartre, Jean-Paul, *The Age of Reason* (2017), Penguin

- Sartre, Jean-Paul, *The Reprieve* (2001), Penguin

- Sartre, Jean-Paul, *The Words* (1964/1981, translated by Bernard Frechtman), Vintage

- Sartre, Jean-Paul, *War Diaries: Notebooks from a Phoney War 1939–40* (2012), Verso

- Seymour-Jones, Carole, *A Dangerous Liaison* (2011), Random House

- Thody, Paul & Read, Howard, *Introducing Sartre: A Graphic Guide* (2011), Icon

Foucault

- Bayer, Ronald, *Homosexuality and American Psychiatry: The Politics of Diagnosis* (1987), Princeton University Press

- Dosse, François, *Gilles Deleuze and Félix Guattari: Intersecting Lives* (2010), Columbia University Press

- Eribon, Didier, *Michel Foucault* (1991, translated by Betsy Wing), Faber & Faber

- Foucault, Michel, *Discipline and Punish: The Birth of the Prison* (1977, translated by Alan Sheridan), Vintage

- Foucault, Michel, *History of Madness* (2006), Taylor & Francis

- Foucault, Michel, *The Birth of the Clinic* (2003), Routledge
- Foucault, Michel, *The History of Sexuality: Volume 1; The Will to Knowledge* (2008), Penguin
- Foucault, Michel, *The History of Sexuality: Volume 2; The Use of Pleasure* (1992), Penguin
- Foucault, Michel, *The Order of Things* (1966/2002), Routledge
- Gutting, Garry, *Foucault, A Very Short Introduction* (2005), Oxford University Press
- Horrocks, Chris & Jevtic, Zoran, *Introducing Foucault: A Graphic Guide* (2009), Icon
- Miller, James, *The Passion of Michel Foucault* (1993), Doubleday
- Rabinow, Paul (ed.), *The Foucault Reader* (1986), Penguin
- Sheridan, Alan, *Michel Foucault: The Will to Truth* (1980), Tavistock
- Sherman, D.J., Dijk R. van & Alinder J, *The Long 1968: Revisions & New Perspectives* (2013), Indiana University Press
- Simon, John K., 'A Conversation with Michel Foucault', *Partisan Review* 38: 2 (1971), 196, 201.
- Stein, Marc, *The Stonewall Riots: A Documentary History* (2019), NYU Press

Derrida

- Bennington, Geoffrey & Derrida, Jacques, *Jacques Derrida* (1993), University of Chicago Press
- Derrida, Jacques, *Memories for Paul de Man* (1986), Columbia University Press
- Derrida, Jacques, *Monolingualism of the Other, Or, The Prosthesis of Origin* (1998, translated by P Mensah), Stanford University Press

- Derrida, Jacques, *Of Grammatology* (1967/1997, translated by G. C. Spivak), Johns Hopkins University Press
- Derrida, Jacques, *The Post Card: From Socrates to Freud and Beyond* (2020), University of Chicago Press
- Derrida, Jacques, *Writing and Difference* (2001), Routledge
- Deutscher, Penelope, *How to Read Derrida* (2006), WW Norton & Co
- Dick, Kirby, Ziering Kofman, Amy, and Derrida, Jacques, *Derrida: Screenplay and Essays on the Film* (2005), Manchester University Press
- Glendinning, Simon, *Derrida: A Very Short Introduction* (2011), Oxford University Press
- Leitch, Vincent B., *Literary Criticism in the 21ˢᵗ Century: Theory Renaissance* (2014), Bloomsbury
- Mimics, David, *Who was Jacques Derrida?: An Intellectual Biography* (2009), Yale University Press
- Peeters, Benoît, *Derrida: A Biography* (2013, translated by Andrew Brown), Polity
- Powell, Jason, *Jacques Derrida: A Biography* (2006), Continuum
- Reynolds, Jack & Roffe, Jonathan, *Understanding Derrida* (2004), Continuum
- Salmon, Peter, *An Event, Perhaps: A Biography of Jacques Derrida* (2020), Verso
- Searle, John, 'The Word Turned Upside Down', *NYRB*, Oct 21–Nov 3, 1982
- Shatz, Adam, 'Not in the Mood', *The London Review of Books* (22 Nov 2012), 34:22

Notes and References

Kant

[1] Zammito, *Kant, Herder, and the Birth of Anthropology*, 121

[2] Gulyga, *Immanual Kant: His Life and Thought*, 14

[3] Kuehn, *Kant: A Biography*, 97

[4] Kuehn, *Kant: A Biography*, 335

[5] Kuehn, *Kant: A Biography*, 116

[6] Kuehn, *Kant: A Biography*, xii

[7] Kuehn, *Kant: A Biography*, xii

[8] Kuehn, *Kant: A Biography*, 117

[9] Kuehn, *Kant: A Biography*, 117

[10] Kuehn, *Kant: A Biography*, 117

[11] Kuehn, *Kant: A Biography*, 116

[12] Kuehn, *Kant: A Biography*, 116

[13] Zammito, *Kant, Herder, and the Birth of Anthropology*, 123

[14] Kuehn, *Kant: A Biography*, 165

[15] Kuehn, *Kant: A Biography*, 165

[16] Kuehn, *Kant: A Biography*, 117

[17] Kuehn, *Kant: A Biography*, 154

[18] Kuehn, *Kant: A Biography*, 241

[19] Kant, *Prolegomena to Any Future Metaphysics*, 4:260

[20] Kul-Want & Klimowski, *Introducing Kant: A Graphic Guide*, 81

[21] Kuehn, *Kant: A Biography*, 218

[22] Kuehn, *Kant: A Biography*, 240

[23] Kuehn, *Kant: A Biography*, 272

[24] Kuehn, *Kant: A Biography*, 322

[25] Kuehn, *Kant: A Biography*, 322

[26] Wikipedia, *Caroline von Keyserling*, retrieved 29 Jan 2021, https://de.wikipedia.org/wiki/Caroline_von_Keyserling

[27] Kulturstiftung der deutschen Vertriebenen, retrieved 29 Jan 2021, https://kulturportal-west-ost.eu/biographien/keyserlingk-charlotte-caroline-amalie-grafin-von-2

[28] Kulturstiftung der deutschen Vertriebenen, retrieved 29 Jan 2021, https://kulturstiftung.org/biographien/keyserlingk-charlotte-caroline-amalie-grafin-von-2

[29] Kuehn, *Kant: A Biography*, 386

[30] Kuehn, *Kant: A Biography*, 386, 390

[31] Kuehn, *Kant: A Biography*, 422

[32] Kant, *Practical Philosophy*, 257

Hegel

[1] Pinkard, *Hegel: A Biography*, 3

[2] Pinkard, *Hegel: A Biography*, 29

[3] Pinkard, *Hegel: A Biography*, 26

[4] Pinkard, *Hegel: A Biography*, 70

[5] Pinkard, *Hegel: A* Biography, 71

[6] Pinkard, *Hegel: A Biography*, 71

[7] Pinkard, *Hegel: A Biography*, 191

[8] Pinkard, *Hegel: A Biography*, 191

[9] Pinkard, *Hegel: A Biography*, 228

[10] Pinkard, *Hegel: A Biography*, 230

[11] Pinkard, *Hegel: A Biography*, 228

[12] Pinkard, *Hegel: A Biography*, 256

[13] Pinkard, *Hegel: A Biography*, 257

[14] Pinkard, *Hegel: A Biography*, 611

[15] Pinkard, *Hegel: A Biography*, 611

[16] Pinkard, *Hegel: A Biography*, 295

[17] Pinkard, *Hegel: A Biography*, 237

[18] Pinkard, *Hegel: A Biography*, 295

[19] Pinkard, *Hegel: A Biography*, 295

[20] Pinkard, *Hegel: A Biography*, 296

[21] Pinkard, *Hegel: A Biography*, 297

[22] Pinkard, *Hegel: A Biography*, 298

[23] Pinkard, *Hegel: A Biography*, 298

[24] Pinkard, *Hegel: A Biography*, 301

[25] Pinkard, *Hegel: A Biography*, 301

[26] Pinkard, *Hegel: A Biography*, 317

[27] Pinkard, *Hegel: A Biography*, 317

[28] Pinkard, *Hegel: A Biography*, 354

[29] Pinkard, *Hegel: A Biography*, 356

[30] Pinkard, *Hegel: A Biography*, 299

[31] Pinkard, *Hegel: A Biography*, 430

[32] Pinkard, *Hegel: A Biography*, 432

[33] Pinkard, *Hegel: A Biography*, 434

[34] Isnaemi, *Hegel's Son of War in Java*

[35] Isnaemi, *Hegel's Son of War in Java*

[36] Isnaemi, *Hegel's Son of War in Java*

[37] Loomis, *Epidemics*, 153

[38] Pinkard, *Hegel: A Biography*, 653

[39] Pinkard, *Hegel: A Biography*, 655

Nietzsche

[1] Nietzsche, *Nietzsche's Writings as a Student*, 15
[2] Young, *Friedrich Nietzsche: A Philosophical Biography*, 13
[3] Young, *Friedrich Nietzsche: A Philosophical Biography*, 14
[4] Young, *Friedrich Nietzsche: A Philosophical Biography*, 17
[5] Young, *Friedrich Nietzsche: A Philosophical Biography*, 17
[6] Young, *Friedrich Nietzsche: A Philosophical Biography*, 21
[7] The Nietzsche Channel (1999–2021), retrieved 6 Feb 2021, http://www.thenietzschechannel.com/bio/bio.htm
[8] The Nietzsche Channel (1999–2021), retrieved 6 Feb 2021, http://www.thenietzschechannel.com/bio/bio.htm
[9] The Nietzsche Channel (1999–2021), retrieved 6 Feb 2021, http://www.thenietzschechannel.com/bio/bio.htm
[10] Brown, *Nietzsche Chronicle*, '1864-68', retrieved 31 Jan 2021
[11] Brown, *Nietzsche Chronicle*, '1864-68', retrieved 31 Jan 2021
[12] Jensen & Heit, *Nietzsche as a Scholar of Antiquity*, 94
[13] Allison, *Reading the New Nietzsche*, 8
[14] Kaufman, *The Portable Nietzsche*, 7-8
[15] Kaufman, *Nietzsche: Philosopher, Psychologist, Antichrist*, 23
[16] Cosima Wagner, *Cosima Wagner's Diaries*, Vol 1, 186
[17] Cosima Wagner, *Cosima Wagner's Diaries*, Vol 1, 138
[18] Cosima Wagner, *Cosima Wagner's Diaries*, Vol 1, 303
[19] Cosima Wagner, *Cosima Wagner's Diaries*, Vol 1, 164
[20] Cosima Wagner, *Cosima Wagner's Diaries*, Vol 1, 184

[21] Wikipedia, *The Birth of Tragedy*, retrieved 31 Jan 2021, https://en.wikipedia.org/wiki/The_Birth_of_Tragedy

[22] Brown, *Nietzsche Chronicle*, '1872', retrieved 31 Jan 2021

[23] Cosima Wagner, *Cosima Wagner's Diaries*, Vol 1, 445

[24] Cosima Wagner, *Cosima Wagner's Diaries*, Vol 1, 446

[25] Cosima Wagner, *Cosima Wagner's Diaries*, Vol 1, 555

[26] Cosima Wagner, *Cosima Wagner's Diaries*, Vol 1, 148

[27] Cosima Wagner, *Cosima Wagner's Diaries*, Vol 1, 399

[28] Young, *Friedrich Nietzsche: A Philosophical Biography*, 234

[29] Köhler, *Richard Wagner: The Last of the Titans*, 523

[30] Cosima Wagner, *Cosima Wagner's Diaries*, Vol 1, 931

[31] Brown, *Nietzsche Chronicle*, '1878', retrieved 31 Jan 2021

[32] Köhler, *Richard Wagner: The Last of the Titans*, 523

[33] Brown, *Nietzsche Chronicle*, '1876', retrieved 1 Feb 2021

[34] Young, *Friedrich Nietzsche: A Philosophical Biography*, 216

[35] Young, *Friedrich Nietzsche: A Philosophical Biography*, 216

[36] Young, *Friedrich Nietzsche: A Philosophical Biography*, 216

[37] Cate, *Nietzsche: A Biography*, 219

[38] Cate, *Nietzsche: A Biography*, 220

[39] Young, *Friedrich Nietzsche: A Philosophical Biography*, 217

[40] Köhler, *Zarathustra's Secret*, 100

[41] Safranski, *Nietzsche: A Philosophical Biography*, 249

[42] Nietzsche, *Selected Letters of Friedrich Nietzsche*, 186

[43] Nietzsche, *Selected Letters of Friedrich Nietzsche*, 186

[44] Vickers, *Lou von Salome: A Biography of the Woman Who Inspired Freud, Nietzsche and Rilke*, 11

[45] Vickers, *Lou von Salome: A Biography of the Woman Who Inspired Freud, Nietzsche and Rilke*, 18

[46] Vickers, *Lou von Salome: A Biography of the Woman Who Inspired Freud, Nietzsche and Rilke*, 20

[47] Vickers, *Lou von Salome: A Biography of the Woman Who Inspired Freud, Nietzsche and Rilke*, 20

[48] Flutante, *Nietzsche, Rée, Salomé: a relationship triangle through letters*, retrieved 4 Feb 2021, https://flutuante.wordpress.com/2013/05/10/nietzsche-ree-salome-a-relationship-triangle-through-letters/

[49] Flutante, *Nietzsche, Rée, Salomé: a relationship triangle through letters*, retrieved 4 Feb 2021, https://flutuante.wordpress.com/2013/05/10/nietzsche-ree-salome-a-relationship-triangle-through-letters/

[50] Andreas-Salomé, *Looking Back: Memoirs*, 167

[51] Peters, *My Sister, My Spouse: A Biography of Lou Andreas-Salomé*, 100

[52] Peters, *My Sister, My Spouse: A Biography of Lou Andreas-Salomé*, 100

[53] Young, *Friedrich Nietzsche: A Philosophical Biography*, 344

[54] Young, *Friedrich Nietzsche: A Philosophical Biography*, 344

[55] Kaufman, *Nietzsche: Philosopher, Psychologist, Antichrist*, 61

[56] Helmut Walther, *Lou von Salomé, Paul Rée and Friedrich Nietzsche*, retrieved 5 Feb 2021, http://www.f-nietzsche.de/lou2_e.htm

[57] Helmut Walther, *Lou von Salomé, Paul Rée and Friedrich Nietzsche*, retrieved 5 Feb 2021, http://www.f-nietzsche.de/lou2_e.htm

[58] Dufourmantelle, *Blind Date: Sex and Philosophy*, 90

[59] Knell & Bates, *The Good European*, 131

[60] Nietzsche, *Selected Letters of Friedrich Nietzsche*, 188

[61] Cate, *Nietzsche: A Biography*, 350

[62] Peters, *My Sister, My Spouse: A Biography of Lou Andreas-Salomé*, 118

[63] Young, *Friedrich Nietzsche: A Philosophical Biography*, 346

[64] Young, *Friedrich Nietzsche: A Philosophical Biography*, 346

[65] Peters, *My Sister, My Spouse: A Biography of Lou Andreas-Salomé*, 121

[66] Young, *Friedrich Nietzsche: A Philosophical Biography*, 349

[67] Genderi.org (2019), retrieved 5 Feb 2021, http://genderi.org/friedrich-nietzsche.html?page=171

[68] Flutante, *Nietzsche, Rée, Salomé: a relationship triangle through letters*, retrieved 5 Feb 2021, https://flutuante.wordpress.com/2013/05/10/nietzsche-ree-salome-a-relationship-triangle-through-letters/

[69] Peters, *My Sister, My Spouse: A Biography of Lou Andreas-Salomé*, 118

[70] Peters, *My Sister, My Spouse: A Biography of Lou Andreas-Salomé*, 118

[71] Peters, *My Sister, My Spouse: A Biography of Lou Andreas-Salomé*, 118

[72] Brown, *Nietzsche Chronicle*, '1882'. Retrieved 5 Feb 2021

[73] Helmut Walther, *Lou von Salomé, Paul Rée and Friedrich Nietzsche*, retrieved 5 Feb 2021, http://www.f-nietzsche.de/lou2_e.htm

[74] Vickers, *Lou von Salome: A Biography of the Woman Who Inspired Freud, Nietzsche and Rilke*, 57

[75] Nietzsche, *Ecce Homo*, 70

[76] Kaufmann, *The Portable Nietzsche*, 124

[77] Ian Johnston, *On the Genealogy of Morals by Friedrich Nietzsche*, retrieved 5 Feb 2001, http://fs2.american.edu/dfagel/www/Class%20Readings/Nietzsche/genealogy3.htm

[78] Wikipedia, *Bernhard Förster*, retrieved 5 Feb 2021, https://en.wikipedia.org/wiki/Bernhard_Förster

[79] Wikipedia, *Elisabeth Förster*-Nietzsche, retrieved 5 Feb 2021, https://en.wikipedia.org/wiki/Elisabeth_Förster-Nietzsche

[80] Nietzsche, *The Will to Power*, 460

[81] The Nietzsche Channel (1999–2021), retrieved 5 Feb 2021, http://www.thenietzschechannel.com/correspondence/eng/nlett-1889.htm

[82] The Nietzsche Channel (1999–2021), retrieved 5 Feb 2021, http://www.thenietzschechannel.com/correspondence/eng/nlett-1889.htm

[83] The Nietzsche Channel (1999–2021), retrieved 5 Feb 2021, http://www.thenietzschechannel.com/correspondence/eng/nlett-1889.htm

[84] The Nietzsche Channel (1999–2021), retrieved 5 Feb 2021, http://www.thenietzschechannel.com/correspondence/eng/nlett-1889.htm

[85] Kaufman, *Nietzsche: Philosopher, Psychologist, Antichrist*, 32

[86] Hollingdale, *Nietzsche: The Man and His Philosophy*, 253

[87] Hollingdale, *Nietzsche: The Man and His Philosophy*, 253

[88] Nietzsche, Why I Am So Wise, 59

[89] Trove, retrieved 6 Feb 2021, https://trove.nla.gov.au/work/12535797

Heidegger

[1] I have indulged in some poetic license here to recreate the essence of Heidegger's famous Marburg lectures of summer, 1924

[2] Arendt, *Martin Heidegger at Eighty*, 1

[3] Arendt & Heidegger, *Letters, 1925-1975*, 10 Feb 1925

[4] Arendt & Heidegger, *Letters, 1925-1975*, 21 Feb 1925

[5] Nixon, *Hannah Arendt and the Politics of Friendship*, 65

[6] Arendt & Heidegger, *Letters, 1925-1975*, 6

[7] Safranski, *Martin Heidegger: Between Good and Evil*, 85

[8] Smith, *Martin Heidegger:Paths Taken, Paths Opened*, 21

[9] Heidegger, *Contributions to Philosophy*, 307

[10] Interview I conducted with Hermann Heidegger, Freiburg, April 2013

[11] Interview I conducted with Hermann Heidegger, Freiburg, April 2013

[12] Interview I conducted with Hermann Heidegger, Freiburg, April 2013

[13] Interview I conducted with Hermann Heidegger, Freiburg, April 2013

[14] Babka, *Through the Dark Field*, 30

[15] Letter read to me by Hermann Heidegger, Interview, Freiburg, April 2013

[16] Interview I conducted with Hermann Heidegger, Freiburg, April 2013

[17] Interview I conducted with Hermann Heidegger, Freiburg, April 2013

[18] Arendt & Heidegger, *Letters, 1925-1975* [1929]

[19] Maier-Katkin, *Heidegger: Calumny and the Politics of Reconciliation*, 100

[20] Young-Bruehl, *Hannah Arendt: For Love of the World*, 155

[21] Ettinger, *Hannah Arendt/Martin Heidegger*, 69

[22] Ettinger, *Hannah Arendt/Martin Heidegger*, 70

[23] Ettinger, *Hannah Arendt/Martin Heidegger*, 70

[24] Ettinger, *Hannah Arendt/Martin Heidegger*, 71–72

[25] Ettinger, *Hannah Arendt/Martin Heidegger*, 81

[26] Ettinger, *Hannah Arendt/Martin Heidegger*, 84

[27] Arendt, *The Origins of Totalitarianism*, xi

[28] Arendt, *Eichmann in Jerusalem: A Report on the Banality of Evil*, 276

[29] Arendt, Thinking and moral considerations: A lecture. *Social Research*. 438

[30] Petzet, *Encounters and Dialogues with Martin Heidegger, 1929–1976*, 13

[31] Ettinger, *Hannah Arendt/Martin Heidegger*, 121

[32] Maier-Katkin, *Stranger from Abroad*, 13

[33] Ettinger, *Hannah Arendt/Martin Heidegger*, 122

[34] Ettinger, *Hannah Arendt/Martin Heidegger*, 84

[35] Ettinger, *Hannah Arendt/Martin Heidegger*, 131

[36] Sheehan (ed.), *Heidegger: The Man and The Thinker*, 73

Sartre

[1] Heidegger, 'Letter on Humanism' in *Basic Writings* (Ed. Krell), 208

[2] Sartre, *The Words*, 40

[3] Sartre, *The Words*, 15

[4] Sartre, *The Words*, 19

[5] Sartre, *The Words*, 18

[6] Sartre, *The Words*, 22

[7] Sartre, *The Words*, 21

[8] Sartre, *The Words*, 141

[9] Rowley, *Tête-à-Tête*, 18

[10] Rowley, *Tête-à-Tête*, 18

[11] Rowley, *Tête-à-Tête*, 18

[12] Rowley, *Tête-à-Tête*, 19

[13] Rowley, *Tête-à-Tête*, 19

[14] Rowley, *Tête-à-Tête*, 18

[15] Kirkpatrick, *Becoming Beauvoir*, 89

[16] Bair, *Simone de Beauvoir: A Biography*, 127

[17] Beauvoir, *Memoirs of a Dutiful Daughter*, 309

[18] Beauvoir, *Memoirs of a Dutiful Daughter*, 309

[19] Beauvoir, *Memoirs of a Dutiful Daughter*, 310

[20] Bair, *Simone de Beauvoir: A Biography*, 142

[21] Beauvoir, *Memoirs of a Dutiful Daughter*, 334

[22] Bair, *Simone de Beauvoir: A Biography*, 143

[23] Appignanesi, *Simone de Beauvoir*, 30

[24] Rowley, *Tête-à-Tête*, 14

[25] Rowley, *Tête-à-Tête*, 14

[26] Rowley, *Tête-à-Tête*, 14

[27] Bair, *Simone de Beauvoir: A Biography*, 60

[28] Rowley, *Tête-à-Tête*, 15

[29] Rowley, *Tête-à-Tête*, 26

[30] Rowley, *Tête-à-Tête*, 27

[31] Bair, *Simone de Beauvoir: A Biography*, 157

[32] I have used poetic license here to imagine this line of dialogue

[33] Imagined dialogue continues in this paragraph and the one preceding it

[34] Dialogue in this paragraph also reconstructed/amended. Aron actually said, 'you can talk about this cocktail and make philosophy out of it!' according to Bakewell, *At the Existentialist Café*, 3

[35] Sartre, War Diaries, 284–285

[36] Beauvoir, *The Prime of Life*, 149

[37] Rowley, *Tête-à-Tête*, 54

[38] Rowley, *Tête-à-Tête*, 54

[39] Rowley, *Tête-à-Tête*, 66

[40] Rowley, *Tête-à-Tête*, 60

[41] Rowley, *Tête-à-Tête*, 58

[42] Bair, *Simone de Beauvoir: A Biography*, 195

[43] Lamblin, *A Disgraceful Affair*, 25

[44] Lamblin, *A Disgraceful Affair*, 31

[45] Rowley, *Tête-à-Tête*, 88

[46] Kirkpatrick, *Becoming Beauvoir*, 170

[47] Elizabeth C. Bachner, *Lying and Nothingness* (2008), retrieved 7 Aug 2021, https://medium.com/@elizabethc.bachner/lying-and-nothingness-struggling-with-simone-de-beauvoirs-wartime-diary-1939-1941-d6f1ea5e55c9

[48] Rowley, *Tête-à-Tête*, 76–77

[49] Rowley, *Tête-à-Tête*, 77

[50] Rowley, *Tête-à-Tête*, 157

[51] Rowley, *Tête-à-Tête*, 59

[52] Rowley, *Tête-à-Tête*, 137–138

[53] Sartre, *Nausea*, 182–186

[54] Kaufman (Ed.), *Existentialism From Dostoyevsky to Sartre*, 295

[55] Kaufman (Ed.), *Existentialism From Dostoyevsky to Sartre*, 291

[56] Kaufman (Ed.), *Existentialism From Dostoyevsky to Sartre*, 295

[57] Elpidorou, *Propelled*, 128

[58] Rowley, *Tête-à-Tête*, 141

[59] Wikipedia, *The Roads to Freedom*, retrieved 7 Aug 2021, https://en.wikipedia.org/wiki/The_Roads_to_Freedom

[60] O'Donohoe, *Living with Mother: Sartre and the problem of Maternity*

[61] Rowley, *Tête-à-Tête*, 128

[62] Beauvoir, *The Mandarins*, 423

[63] Åsbrink, *1947: Where Now Begins*, 98

[64] Rowley, *Tête-à-Tête*, 193

[65] Seymour-Jones, *A Dangerous Liaison*, 460

[66] Beauvoir, *The Second Sex*, 758

[67] Rowley, *Tête-à-Tête*, 211

[68] Rowley, *Tête-à-Tête*, 211

[69] Vulliamy, 'Claude Lanzmann: the man who stood witness for the world' in *The Observer*, 4 March 2012.

[70] Vulliamy, 'Claude Lanzmann: the man who stood witness for the world'

[71] Vulliamy, 'Claude Lanzmann: the man who stood witness for the world'

[72] Vulliamy, 'Claude Lanzmann: the man who stood witness for the world'

[73] Vulliamy, 'Claude Lanzmann: the man who stood witness for the world'

[74] Rowley, *Tête-à-Tête*, 224

[75] Rowley, *Tête-à-Tête*, 228

[76] Rowley, *Tête-à-Tête*, 229

[77] Rowley, *Tête-à-Tête*, 265

[78] Rowley, *Tête-à-Tête*, 309

[79] Rowley, *Tête-à-Tête*, 293

[80] Rowley, *Tête-à-Tête*, 339

[81] Rowley, *Tête-à-Tête*, 332

[82] Kaye, *What Philosophy Can Tell You About Your Lover*, 158

[83] Toledo Blade, *Sartre's Funeral Attracts 50,000* (20 Apr 1980), https://news.google.com/newspapers?nid=1350&dat=19800420&id=Yh1PAAAAIBAJ&sjid=jwIEAAAAIBAJ&pg=7231,50057&hl=en retrieved 9 Feb 2021

[84] "Femmes, vous lui devez tout!" *Le nouvel observateur* 39 (April 1986): 18–24

Foucault

[1] Eribon, *Michel Foucault,* 280

[2] Eribon, *Michel Foucault,* 16

[3] Eribon, *Michel Foucault,* 17

[4] Eribon, *Michel Foucault,* 102

[5] Eribon, *Michel Foucault,* 110

[6] Eribon, *Michel Foucault,* 110

[7] Eribon, *Michel Foucault,* 111

[8] Eribon, *Michel Foucault,* 108

[9] Eribon, *Michel Foucault,* 113

[10] Eribon, *Michel Foucault,* 113–115

[11] Eribon, *Michel Foucault,* 142

[12] Miller, *The Passion of Michel Foucault*, 185–186

[13] Wikipedia, *May 68*, retrieved 12 Feb 2021, https://en.wikipedia.org/wiki/May_68,

[14] Wikipedia, *May 68*, retrieved 12 Feb 2021, https://en.wikipedia.org/wiki/May_68

[15] Sherman et al, *The Long 1968: Revisions & New Perspectives*, 25

[16] Eribon, *Michel Foucault*, 205

[17] Simon, "A Conversation with Michel Foucault", *Partisan Review*, 38: 2, 201

[18] Dosse, *Gilles Dekeuze and Félix Guattari: Intersecting Lives*, 346

[19] Miller, *The Passion of Michel Foucault*, 180

[20] Eribon, *Michel Foucault*, 266

[21] Miller, *The Passion of Michel Foucault*, 177

[22] Stein, *The Stonewall Riots: A Documentary History*, 188

[23] Bayer, *Homosexuality & American Psychiatry: The Politics of Diagnosis*, 105

[24] Miller, *The Passion of Michel Foucault*, 183

[25] Miller, *The Passion of Michel Foucault*, 208

[26] Foucault, *Discipline and Punish*, 7

[27] Miller, *The Passion of Michel Foucault*, 432

[28] Miller, *The Passion of Michel Foucault*, 241

[29] Miller, *The Passion of Michel Foucault*, 240

[30] Miller, *The Passion of Michel Foucault*, 251

[31] Miller, *The Passion of Michel Foucault*, 253

[32] Miller, *The Passion of Michel Foucault*, 264

[33] Miller, *The Passion of Michel Foucault*, 251

[34] Miller, *The Passion of Michel Foucault*, 254

[35] Miller, *The Passion of Michel Foucault*, 256

[36] Miller, *The Passion of Michel Foucault*, 263

[37] Miller, *The Passion of Michel Foucault*, 278

[38] Miller, *The Passion of Michel Foucault*, 186

[39] Miller, *The Passion of Michel Foucault*, 186

[40] James Thomas, *The Dawn of a Plague* (2 Apr 2019), retrieved 12 Feb 2021, https://mcdreeamie.medium.com/the-dawn-of-a-plague-the-first-publications-of-hiv-aids-469a0ee682cc

[41] Lawrence K. Altman, 'Rare Cancer Seen in 41 Homosexuals' in *The New York Times*, (3 Jul 1981), retrieved 12 Feb 2021, https://www.nytimes.com/1981/07/03/us/rare-cancer-seen-in-41-homosexuals.html

[42] Edmund White and Sameer Rahim, 'Edmund White recalls a night at the opera with Michel Foucault in 1981' in *The Telegraph* (28 Feb 2014), retrieved 12 Feb 2021, https://www.telegraph.co.uk/culture/books/authorinterviews/10663337/Edmund-White-recalls-a-night-at-the-opera-with-Michel-Foucault-in-1981.html?fb

[43] Miller, *The Passion of Michel Foucault*, 26

[44] Miller, *The Passion of Michel Foucault*, 34

[45] Miller, *The Passion of Michel Foucault*, 34

[46] Miller, *The Passion of Michel Foucault*, 21

[47] Miller, *The Passion of Michel Foucault*, 35–36

Derrida

[1] *Monolingualism of the Other, Or, The Prosthesis of Origin*, 25

[2] Dick et al, *Derrida: Screenplay and Essays on the Film*, 86:87

[3] Derrida, *Memories for Paul de Man*, 8

[4] Bennington & Derrida, *Jacques Derrida*, 58

[5] Salmon, *An Event, Perhaps*, 37

[6] Peeters, *Derrida: A Biography*, chapter 3, p. 5 [e-book]

[7] Peeters, *Derrida: A Biography*, 54

[8] Peeters, *Derrida: A Biography*, chapter 2, p. 7 [e-book]

[9] Peeters, *Derrida: A Biography*, chapter 7, p. 7 [e-book]

[10] Powell: Jacques *Derrida: A Biography*, 22

[11] Derrida, *Of Grammatology*, 158

[12] Derrida, *Of Grammatology*, 50

[13] Leitch, *Literary Criticism in the 21ˢᵗ Century: Theory Renaissance*, 116

[14] Mikics, *Who Was Jacques Derrida?*, 25

[15] Peeters, *Derrida: A Biography*, chapter 4, p. 3 [e-book]

[16] Wikipedia, *Sylciane Agacinski*, retrieved 13 Feb 2021, https://en.wikipedia.org/wiki/Sylviane_Agacinski

[17] Derrida, *The Post Card*, 2020

[18] Shatz, 'Not in the Mood' in *The London Review of Books*, 34:22

[19] Searle, 'The Word Turned Upside Down', *NYRB*, Oct 21–Nov 3, 1982, p. 26

[20] From Professor Barry Smith & others, *The Times* (London). Saturday, May 9, 1992, retrieved 13 Feb 2021, https://philarchive.org/archive/SMIDDA-6

[21] Reynolds & Roffe, *Understanding Derrida*, 1

[22] Glendenning, *Derrida: A Very Short Introduction*, 12

[23] Shatz, "Not in the Mood" in *The London Review of Books*, 34:22

[24] Dick et al, *Derrida: Screenplay and Essays on the Film*, 60:61

[25] Dick et al, *Derrida: Screenplay and Essays on the Film*, 60:61

[26] Dick et al, *Derrida: Screenplay and Essays on the Film*, 60:61

[27] Dick et al, *Derrida: Screenplay and Essays on the Film*, 74:75

[28] Derrida, *Fear of Writing*, retrieved 13 Feb 2021, https://www.youtube.com/watch?v=qoKnzsiR6Ss&feature=emb_logo

[29] Kristine McKenna, 'The Three Ages of Jacques Derrida' in *LA Weekly* (6 Nov 2002), retrieved 13 Feb 2021, https://www.laweekly.com/the-three-ages-of-jacques-derrida/

[30] Kristine McKenna, 'The Three Ages of Jacques Derrida' in *LA Weekly* (6 Nov 2002), retrieved 13 Feb 2021, https://www.laweekly.com/the-three-ages-of-jacques-derrida/,

[31] Joel Stein, 'Life with the Father of Deconstructionism' in *Time* (18 Nov 2002), retrieved 13 Feb 2021, http://content.time.com/time/nation/article/0,8599,391685,00.html

[32] Dick et al, *Derrida: Screenplay and Essays on the Film*, 110–117

[33] Kristine McKenna, 'The Three Ages of Jacques Derrida' in *LA Weekly* (6 Nov 2002), retrieved 13 Feb 2021, https://www.laweekly.com/the-three-ages-of-jacques-derrida/

[34] Powell: Jacques *Derrida: A Biography*, 227

[35] Dick et al, *Derrida: Screenplay and Essays on the Film*

CPSIA information can be obtained
at www.ICGtesting.com
Printed in the USA
BVHW031415170322
631771BV00006B/455

9 781839 191527